CAXTON: England's First Publisher

nobles and vyllaynes cam to his scole for to lerne .
n these dayes y⁹ Saturne began thus to floure ꝯ was
xx. yere of age and his broder .xl. Wranus their fader
by a sekenes that he had dyed and deptid out of this
world leupng his wyf Vesca endowed largely of
possessions. his deth was noyous and sorowfull to
Vesca his wife. whyche causid her to wepe out of
mesur and his sones and doughtirs also they dide his
obsequye reuerently in habondyng of grete and bittir
sorow. the obsequye don ther wepyng and sorow
yet during vesca saw that Tytan her eldest sone pre
tnded to haue and eniope the success[i]on of his ffader
she on a day callid her der sone Saturne wyth Ty
tan and other of the Contre and there reherced ꝯ said
vnto them that her yong sone Saturne shold succede
and hiue the herytages of her husbond Tytan heryng
the wyll of hys moder redoublid hys sorow and cau
sid hym to wepe grete plente of teeris and knelyd to
fore his moder humbly and sayd in thys wyse Moder
y am ryght infortunate whan ye wyll that my right
patrymonye be put from me And that naturelli me
ought to haue by ryght shold be gyuen fro me and
yat because y⁹ y am not so well formed of membres
as my broder satorne ye whiche sorow is to me pas
syng noyous ye wil putte from me my ffortune and
burthe whiche ye may not do by lawfull reson y am
your first sone ye haue norysshid me wyth y⁹ substāce
of your blood as your chyld born in your bely .ix. mo
nethes Also y am he that first dwellid and enhabited
your femynyn chambres None to fore me toke there
ony seasyng whan y toke that tho ye gaf me your due

CAXTON: *England's First Publisher*

N. F. Blake

BARNES & NOBLE
BOOKS
10 East 53d St., New York 10022
(a division of Harper & Row Publishers, Inc.)

Published in the U.S.A. 1976 by
Harper & Row Publishers, Inc.

Barnes & Noble Import Division

ISBN 0-06-490450-4

Printed in Great Britain

For DORINDA JANE

CONTENTS

ILLUSTRATIONS

PREFACE

This book has been written to mark the quincentenary of the beginning of printing in England. In my earlier book, Caxton and his World, *I tried to cover the literary aspects of Caxton's work. In this book I have attempted to consider some of the technical aspects of his book production, for it is not possible to come to a full understanding of his press without them. The two books are meant to complement each other.*

I wish to acknowledge the following for providing me with, and giving me permission to reproduce, the photographs as listed: John Rylands Library, University of Manchester: frontispiece and plates 29, 33–4, 43, 46, 48, 55; Radio Times Hulton Picture Library: plates 11, 18, 21, 23–5, 61–2; National Portrait Gallery: plates 9, 16–17, 26, 60; British Library Board: plates 38, 40, 49; the Master and Fellows of Magdalene College, Cambridge: plate 27; Public Record Office: plate 14; Victoria and Albert Museum: plate 44; Huntington Library, San Marino: plate 47. I particularly wish to thank the St Bride Printing Library for help and advice with research, and for providing me with and giving me permission to reproduce plates 2–8, 10, 12–13, 15, 19, 20, 22, 30–32, 35–7, 39, 41–2, 45, 50–54, 56–9, 63.

Finally, I would like to thank my secretary, Miss Janice Ironmonger, for her help with the typescript.

I
GUTENBERG AND THE
BEGINNINGS OF PRINTING

Reading and writing are the hallmarks of human culture and have existed for so long that most people think of them as natural to man. Without them European civilisation could hardly have developed as it did. But printing is a relatively modern invention, whose late appearance in Europe may in part be ascribed to the nature of the alphabet in use there. The Chinese used printing before Europeans because their written language consists of characters representing individual words or syllables which recur only infrequently. It is thus possible to carve such characters in wood on a reasonably large scale. European writing systems which are based on the Roman alphabet can be printed only by using the individual letters as the basis for the type. This means in effect that a small number of letters are used again and again. As the basic symbols are letters they must be small enough so that a sufficient amount of material can be reproduced on one page and strong enough so that they can withstand constant use. Only metal can be used in the production of type like this. At the same time in order to make a page of printing aesthetically satisfying the individual letters have to be of the same width and length so that they lie evenly in the forme and produce a straight regular line of print. It is these difficulties which impeded the technical realisation of printing by movable type until relatively late in Western European history.

More primitive forms of printing were practised before printing with movable type was invented. Woodcuts were made from which prints could be mechanically reproduced, and stamps for printing letters on leather or other materials were familiar enough. Large initial letters found in some vellum manuscripts are printed from blocks. But blocks for these purposes could be large and were used infrequently so that wood was a suitable medium. This type of printing was known in Europe from the end of the fourteenth century and it may have been inspired by Eastern models. The main centres of production were in the Burgundian lands along the Rhine and in Flanders, where the method was used particularly for the multiplication of religious figures and emblems. Representations of saints are especially common and may have been made for the convents and monasteries dedicated to the saint in question so that they could resell them to their visitors. It was a short step from the portrayal of the saint to the inclusion of a few words with the image. The saint's name or a prayer or some other short inscription was carved with the picture and reproduced with it.

From pictures with words the next stage was to gather individual pages into a book, and 'blockbooks', as they are called, were made from the early fifteenth century. Most are relatively coarse artistically, and simple in their message. They are usually short and typically have a picture with a short text on each page. They are more in the nature of picture books with text than of books as we understand them. They deal with popular religious subjects such as the Bible stories (in books called significantly *Biblia pauperum*), the passion of Christ, the history of the Virgin, and the lives of saints. Books of this type could never replace manuscripts and they were never produced for the more educated and aristocratic end of the book market. The disadvantages of this type of production were that the cutting of the letters in the wood was a laborious process and there was no means of correcting what had been written once it was carved. While it is therefore possible that the appearance of these books may have given a new impulse to the search for a form of printing with movable type, the two processes are so different that the block-book can have made no significant contribution to the discovery of printing. Indeed the production of these books continued after the invention of printing, for the two methods were not in direct competition.

The discovery of printing is now attributed to Johan Gens-fleisch zum Gutenberg, or more simply Johan Gutenberg, who was a goldsmith of patrician family at Mainz, the city standing at the confluence of the Rhine and the Main. Of particular importance is his profession of goldsmith, since of the three discoveries which were essential for the new process—the press itself, a thick enough ink, and the type—the last is undoubtedly the most important. As a goldsmith Gutenberg was used to working in metal, particularly in the fabrication of small letters on medallions or other precious objects, and he would be familiar with the techniques of working in relief which had been known to gold-smiths for some time. These skills were essential for the delicate work needed to make type. At the basis of the discovery was the creation of a mould which allowed the manufacture of any quantity of type uniform in all respects. Gutenberg solved the problem in this way. He first made a letter in relief in a very hard metal which he then used to punch the letter in reverse in a matrix made of a somewhat softer metal, often brass. This matrix was a thin strip of metal with the punched letter in reverse at its head. The matrix was then put into the mould, in which there was a four-sided cavity with one side that was hinged. When the matrix was at the bottom of this cavity with the punched letter facing upwards, the hinged side was closed and molten lead or some other soft metal was poured in from the top. When this metal hardened the letter would be in relief at the top of a thin shank which could be easily removed by opening the hinged side of the mould. Since all letters were made in the same mould they would all have a shank of the same dimensions. Different letters were obtained simply by changing the matrix in the mould. The manufacturing process was simple enough and could be performed by one man, who would melt the metal in a crucible and make the necessary type by hand. This way of making type remained substantially unchanged for centuries.

It is not possible to date this invention exactly, partly because as there was no patent law then the inventors wanted to keep the details of the process a secret. Most of our evidence comes from legal documents associated with lawsuits in which Gutenberg figured. The first of these is dated 12 December 1439 in Strasburg when the court issued its verdict. Gutenberg left Mainz about 1428 as a result of political manœuvres in the city. He went to Strasburg, where he cannot have been too poor since several annuities were paid to him there. Even when an amnesty was declared in Mainz in 1430 he preferred to stay on in Strasburg. It may be that he had already begun his experiments in printing. Gutenberg taught several Strasburg citizens various skills of the goldsmith's trade. Then in 1438 he signed a contract with an Andreas Dritzehn and two other people to instruct them in some secret skills. An interesting clause in this contract was that if one of the partners died his heirs were not to be admitted in his place. Instead they would be financially compensated while the equipment and other business stock would remain the sole property of the remaining three partners. When Dritzehn died a year later his brothers took Gutenberg to court because he would not admit them in Andreas's place. Gutenberg won the suit in the verdict given on 12 December 1439. In view of his later discovery of the printing process it is very probable that the four partners under Gutenberg's leadership were trying to perfect a form of printing with type, though as the parties in the suit wished to disclose as little as possible of the technicalities involved we cannot be certain of this. What is clear is that the experiments were expensive, for considerable sums had been spent. However, the contract expired in 1443 and was apparently not renewed, though Gutenberg was still in Strasburg in 1444. If he did manage to print anything in Strasburg it has not yet been located or identified, and so we may assume that it was only after his return to Mainz that he succeeded with his invention.

The date of his return is uncertain. He was certainly there by October 1448, though no doubt he had gone back to his native city somewhat before then. Our next piece of evidence is an abstract of an oath made by a certain Johan Fust in front of a notary concerning a lawsuit between himself and Gutenberg. This document is dated 6 November 1455, and as it is brief and couched in legal language it is difficult to interpret what it says with confidence. The story behind it may be something like this. About 1450 a Mainz lawyer named Fust had lent Gutenberg 800 guilders on condition that he was taken into partnership with him for his work on books (*Werk der Bücher*). Gutenberg continued with this work till about 1455 when Fust foreclosed on him for the two loans and accumulated interest, a sum which amounted to over 2,000 guilders. As Gutenberg was unable to repay the money the court judged that Fust should take sole charge of the equipment. Fust then proceeded to run the press on his own, though he acted as financier and publisher and he kept on Gutenberg's chief helper, Peter Schoeffer, as his pressman. Schoeffer was no doubt quite familiar with all the technical details.

It is easy to take sides in this matter and to think that one or other of the partners was the injured party. That Fust foreclosed on Gutenberg in 1455 is almost certainly accounted for by the completion of the so-called 42-line Bible about then. The copy of this Bible now in the Bibliothèque Nationale at Paris has a note that the vicar of St Stephen's at Mainz finished rubricating and binding it on 24 August 1456. As the book is lengthy this work could well have taken him several months, so the 42-line Bible may be dated to late 1455 or early 1456. It need not have been the first thing printed in Mainz, but it was almost certainly the first extensive work to be completed. Its sale could well bring the publishers considerable profits. It has no printer's name or place and date of publication, but there can be little doubt that it was substantially the work of Gutenberg. But Fust's action stopped him from profiting financially. Was Fust so tired of Gutenberg's endless procrastination and incompetence in money matters that he decided he could run the business more efficiently alone, simply employing Schoeffer as a master printer? Or was Fust afraid that when Gutenberg started to get the money from the sale of the Bible he would pay him off, so that Fust would have nothing to show for his financial support over so many years? Unfortunately the reasons behind the suit cannot be decided on the present evidence, but the later history of printing suggests that the former solution is more likely to be nearer the truth. Of Gutenberg's later life little is known, though no other book can with certainty be attributed to his workmanship. Fust and Schoeffer went on to print the Mainz Psalter on 14 August 1457. This is the earliest book to contain details of its printing. Its workmanship is sufficiently accomplished to make it likely that Gutenberg may have had a hand in its production before he was ousted from the business; it certainly has none of the characteristics of a first attempt.

Several works were printed in the early days at Mainz, though few can be dated closely. They include grammar books or Donatuses, almanacks, letters of indulgence, the 36-line Bible and the *Catholicon* of Giovanni Balbi. Possibly some of the minor pieces may have been printed by Gutenberg before he started on the 42-line Bible; but most were the work of his former assistants. The 42-line Bible is a book of considerable size and it has been estimated that eight presses were used to print it. If we assume there were two workmen to every press, the number of people who knew the secret of printing was too large for the invention to remain private. Indeed after Fust foreclosed on Gutenberg some of these workmen may have lost their jobs and they would naturally start printing on their own account. The way was open for the spread of printing. But the works printed in Mainz are almost all anonymous and can be grouped only in accordance with their type.

While it is now generally accepted that Gutenberg invented printing in Europe, some remarks attributed to Ulrich Zell, the first printer of Cologne, have led some scholars to think that it may have originated in Holland. The inventor in this case is said to be a certain Coster of Harlem. Though there is extant some prototypographic material from the Low Countries, none

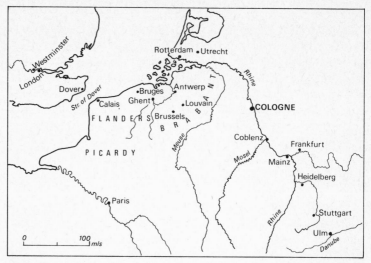

1. *North-west Europe in the fifteenth century*

of it can be dated before 1455. Possibly Zell had blockbooks in mind as the precursors of printing, and as we have seen they were produced frequently in the Low Countries. It was in Mainz that printing started and from there that it spread to the rest

2. *Death and the printers*

of Europe. Indeed in its early years it was almost exclusively a skill associated with Germans. Some wandered far. Johan Neumeister, for example, was printing in Foligno in 1470. But after serving a term in prison for debt, he returned to Mainz, which he left later for Albi in Southern France where he was established by 1480. He then made his way to Lyons, where he died early in the sixteenth century still a poor man.

The printers went where there were patrons to assist them. Each of Neumeister's moves appears to have been at the instigation of a patron. Unfortunately patrons could not guarantee sufficient sales to keep the printers solvent and many incurred heavy debts. Among the more important patrons were universities and religious houses, and the educated classes remained important customers of the printers, which is why so many books in Latin were printed. Printing at Paris was sponsored by the Sorbonne, and at Cologne both the university and religious leaders played an important part in establishing the press. But the success of the press was guaranteed more effectively by the existence of a substantial reading public or by the siting of a town on an

3. *A German printing press*

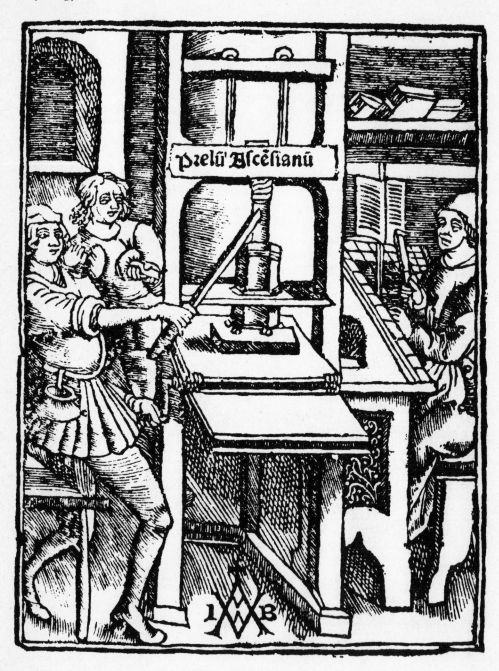

prelū Ascēsianū

I B

important trading route so that the books could be distributed along normal channels of trade.

It is difficult to be sure exactly when printing was established in the different towns, but the following outline will help to provide a general picture of its spread. By 1460 the new art was well established in Mainz and probably also in Strasburg where Johan Mentelin had a workshop at an early date. He produced bibles in German and Latin as well as vernacular texts. In the decade following 1460 the assistants of Gutenberg and Schoeffer took printing to many German cities. Ulrich Zell of Hanau started in Cologne about 1464, Berthold Ruppel in Basle about 1466, Günther Zainer in Augsburg in 1468, and Heinrich Kepfer and Johan Sensenschmidt in Nuremberg in 1470. In Italy Sweynheim and Pannartz, two more Mainz workmen, went to the monastery of Subiaco outside Rome about 1465 and Neumeister was in Foligno by 1470. In the same decade printing had been established at Venice and Paris, and it may have reached the Low Countries since some of the proto-typographic material has been dated about 1470, possibly in Utrecht. The following decade saw the spread of printing to a whole host of further German and Italian cities and to most

5. *Dürer's printers*

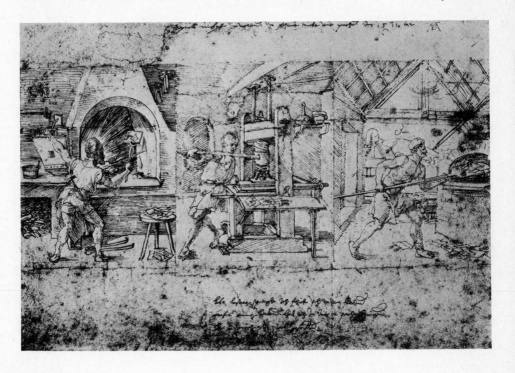

countries in Europe from Spain in the West to Poland in the East. Its arrival in England in 1476 was relatively late by European standards. But the man who brought this new art to Westminster, William Caxton, was different from many of the early practitioners of printing and it is time now to consider what is known of his life and how he came to be England's first printer.

7. *A spurious Caxton portrait*

II
THE LONDON MERCHANT

Little is known of Caxton's early life. He refers to his parents once and says that they sent him to school. But we do not know what they were called, what occupation they followed, or where they lived. That they were comfortably off is probable and that his father was some kind of merchant is possible. Caxton's own place of birth is indicated in that famous reference to his early life he made in his prologue to the *History of Troy*, which he printed in 1473:

. . . for in France was I never, and was born and lerned myn Englissh in Kente in the Weeld, where I doubte not is spoken as brode and rude Englissh as is in ony place of Englond.

This reference tells us only that he was born in Kent, and the rest of what it says may well be a little exaggerated. We must bear in mind that though most of our information about Caxton's early life comes from his own writings, information of this sort was included for particular literary reasons. It was customary then for an author to claim that he had suffered many disadvantages so that a reader would make all possible allowances for his work, which must have been written under great difficulties. Thus Caxton, who wrote for an aristocratic and fashionable audience, stresses his own unfamiliarity with good breeding. He was born in the Weald in Kent, he says, because it was a place that was then considered backward, wild, and uncivilised. It may be that though he was born in Kent he was not born in the area of the Weald in a strict geographical sense, for its boundaries were in any case somewhat uncertain. He may have stretched the facts a little by including the Weald as his birthplace in order to emphasise the point of his lowly origins.

Various attempts have been made to localise his birthplace within Kent. Two principal methods have been followed: to link him with places named Caxton or with places where a Caxton family has been traced. Such places are numerous. At the time of the Festival of Britain in 1951 it was Tenterden which claimed him as one of her sons, though few now accept this claim. These attempts were pure guesswork because there is nothing to prove that the printer had a connexion with any of the places adduced. More recently some charters mentioning a William Caxton of Little Wratting in Suffolk have been discovered. Since they refer to various people who played some part in Caxton's life, it has been suggested that this Caxton of the charters and the printer are the same man and that consequently we could learn a lot from them about his early life. But once again we are forced to accept that the identification is dubious. The weakness of all these theories has been the absence of any definite link between the place or person suggested and the printer. The one theory which has tried to overcome this difficulty is that linking Caxton with Strood in Kent. Caxton added bits of information to some of the texts he printed and this information is often of a personal nature. In his edition of the *Golden Legend* there is a story about St Augustine of Canterbury. According to it, when he was preaching in Dorset Augustine was pelted with fishtails by the locals. They were suitably punished when their children were born with fishtails. The usual version of the story ends with this detail, but Caxton's edition adds, 'It is sayd comynly that thys fyl at Strode in Kente, but blessyd be God at this day is no suche deformyte.' All available evidence indicates that Caxton added this sentence himself, and the way it is phrased suggests that the writer felt a personal association with Strood. It may well be that either he was brought up in Strood or that he was born there. This theory is also hypothetical, but it has the merit that it is the only one so far which has definitely linked Caxton with a place in Kent, and the *Golden Legend* is the work which contains the greatest number of his personal reminiscences. Strood is situated on the Medway in close proximity to Rochester. Its position ensured that by the fifteenth century it had become a prosperous community. It would be quite reasonable to imagine that Caxton's father was a merchant either in Strood itself or even in near-by Rochester.

Caxton's date of birth is as uncertain as his place of birth. The earliest known reference to Caxton is the entry in the Wardens' Account Book of the Mercers' Company, which records that the fee for his enrolment as an apprentice was paid in 1438. Unfortunately one cannot assume that he started as an apprentice in that year since the fees were often paid several years late. All we can say is that he had been enrolled by 1438. We know he was still an apprentice in 1441, for in that year his master,

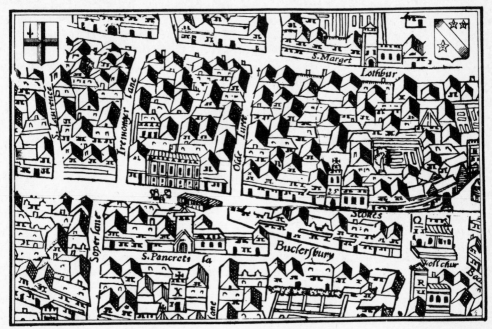

Robert Large, died and he refers to his apprentice Caxton in his will. As the normal practice seems to have been that boys started as apprentices about the age of fourteen, and had usually completed their term by the age of twenty-six, the limits of his date of birth are between 1415 and 1424. It is not possible to get any closer than that.

8. Mercers' Hall, City of London

Robert Large, to whom Caxton was apprenticed, was an important member of the Mercers' Company, who became Lord Mayor of the City of London in 1439. Large's position makes it likely that Caxton's parents were comfortably off and sufficiently influential to get their son placed so advantageously. For Large had a flourishing business and employed several apprentices, many of whom became important men in their own time. By joining this circle Caxton gained valuable business experience and contacts which were to prove useful to him in later life.

Each London guild was based round a particular commodity and the mercers dealt originally in 'mercery', such things as haberdashery, cloth, and silk. These were the goods they sold retail in England. But there were no restrictions on the wholesale trade, which consisted to a large extent of the import and export of goods to and from the Low Countries. Here the mercers had built up a commanding position and many individual mercers had made their fortunes. By the time Caxton became a mercer, this guild formed the nucleus of the Merchant Adventurers' Company, the association of English merchants holding a monopoly of the trade between England and the Low Countries. In fact there was often little to distinguish the Mercers' Company from the Merchant Adventurers' Company. The records of the Mercers are full of details of the cross-Channel trade, and it would not be unfair to say that the records of the Mercers' Company are those of the Merchant Adventurers'. So by becoming a mercer Caxton not only became a member of one of the oldest and most influential guilds, but he also became a member of the guild most closely associated with the trade to Belgium and Holland. It would be a matter of course that he should become involved in this trade.

When this happened we cannot tell. As an apprentice with Large he would have gained an insight into this trade and he may even have travelled abroad. But Large died in 1441 while Caxton was still an apprentice. We do not know what became of him at this stage. But it was common for the widow or a son to take over the business when the husband or father died, and we may imagine that something like this happened with Large's business. A document from 1450 shows that Caxton was in Bruges then and its wording implies that he may have been trading on his own by this time, even though the date of his first livery payment to make him a full member of the company was 1453. Once again this probably records a payment which was overdue and too much significance should not be given it. We can assume that sometime in the 1440s Caxton became a trader on his own and started to engage in the trade with Belgium and Holland. There is nothing to indicate whether his independence came early or late in that decade.

Because of his statement in the prologue to the *History of Troy* that he had spent thirty years abroad, many scholars assumed that he had gone to Bruges soon after Large's death and stayed there without a break. This is improbable. Such a statement is another example of his exaggeration for a particular literary effect. It was unusual for merchants to spend long periods abroad, and at the beginning of his career as a merchant we may accept that he spent a lot of his time going backwards and forwards across the Channel. His home was probably in England, where he disposed of the goods he acquired abroad. As a mercer he took part in the wool and cloth trade, though we also find him handling such materials as pewter. Mercers were also active in the luxury trade. Flanders was then the greatest centre of manuscript production in Northern Europe, and the books produced in the Flemish workshops were treasured for their craftsmanship and fine miniatures. We know that at a later date Caxton participated in the book trade across the Channel, and it is more than likely that he started in this business as a young man. It was here that he made his first acquaintance with books as merchandise. Otherwise the records from this period show that he behaved like any other merchant adventurer. He spent some time in Bruges which was then the headquarters of the Merchant Adventurers' Company abroad. But he also visited other important trading centres like Ghent and Antwerp. We see him standing surety for fellow merchants and engaging in negotiations with local officials. At this stage in his career there is nothing to set him apart from his fellow merchants.

By the 1460s he was clearly an influential and possibly a wealthy merchant. The respect with which he was considered is suggested by his election to the governorship of the English nation at Bruges. The nationals of each trading community were grouped in nations or associations to safeguard their interests and discipline their own members. The governor was thus the chief disciplinary officer and the spokesman of the English community in Flanders. Caxton may have been elected to this position about 1462, and from then on he may well have spent much more of his time in Bruges, since his services would be in frequent demand. It was not an easy job. There was the constant temptation of bribery by individual Flemish towns for favourable treatment (a fault which had caused the downfall of his predecessor), and there was the unending round of negotiations either to get better terms for the English merchants or to smooth out the difficulties which arose at a national level between England and the Duchy of Burgundy. For Flanders at this time was linked through marriage to the Dukes of Burgundy, who maintained the richest and most lavish court in Northern Europe. Ostensibly vassals of the French king, the dukes tried to maintain an independent political position and in doing so made use of the English. Flanders was essential for England because it was the main recipient of English wool, which provided the crown with its most regular source of income. It was part of England's attempt to achieve stability in its relations with Burgundy which led Edward IV to marry his sister Margaret to the then Duke of Burgundy, Charles the Bold, in 1468. The ceremony was accompanied by magnificent pageants and displays. As governor, Caxton may have had a hand both in arranging the marriage and in

9. *Edward IV*

escorting the bride, for as a seasoned negotiator he was used by Edward IV in many of the negotiations with Burgundy. He was gradually rising in the world.

Although we do not know a great deal about this first period of Caxton's life, it is wrong to think of it as unimportant. There was no sudden break in his career as many in the past have thought. The importance of his time as a merchant is that he learned the art of financing projects, he knew how to raise capital and float loans, he made important contacts with influential men of affairs, and he knew the trade between England and the Low Countries. All these accomplishments were to prove useful to him in later life. For when he learned the art of printing he became a publisher rather than a simple printer. He chose the texts to print and he was responsible for the financial viability of the project. England is different from most countries in that a merchant was her first printer. Other European countries acquired printing through the efforts of an artisan printer who knew the trade of printing but had insufficient financial expertise to run a business of the magnitude which printing demanded. Hence most of them ran into debt and many were taken over by entrepreneurs, who then chose the books for publication and farmed out the actual printing to the artisans, just as a modern publisher does. This did not happen in England's case because Caxton was a merchant who made a conscious decision to go and learn how to print in order to set up a publishing business. We have already seen that he probably engaged in bookselling activities from an early period of his career, and printing would form a natural continuation of this activity since he would have a much closer control over the merchandise. It is easy to impute lofty ideals to Caxton's move in becoming a printer, but we should not forget that the basic reason was economic: he saw here a good opportunity of developing his business in a profitable way. As a publisher Caxton remained a merchant, though the goods he dealt in now were exclusively books and manuscripts. The other side of his trading activities was run down.

III
THE BRUGES PRINTER

Our information about Caxton's decision to learn the art of printing comes mainly from his own additions to his translation of the *History of Troy*, the first book he printed. From it we learn that he began translating this book on 1 March 1469. As far as we can tell he had not undertaken any translations before this date, and the way in which he compares himself as a translator with 'blind Bayard' seems to confirm this view. In other words he started to translate the *History of Troy* with a view to printing it and that means his decision to learn how to print was made early in 1469 at the latest. But he goes on to say that after he had completed a few quires he put the translation aside for a couple of years. Something had arisen which made it difficult for him to realise his project at that time. The position may have been something like this. That he was making an English translation of the *History of Troy* presupposes that he wanted to sell the finished product in England, since there would be insufficient customers on the Continent who would want to buy an English translation of a book available in French. Something happened in England to thwart his ambitions and that can only have been the breach between Edward IV and the Earl of Warwick. Edward IV had managed, or so it seemed, to put an end to the civil strife of the War of the Roses. Although he had as yet no male heir, by 1469 he had been on the throne for eight years without any real opposition. But he had alienated the Earl of Warwick, the Kingmaker, and this breach became an open one in July 1469 when Warwick captured the King. Although Warwick was unable to keep the King in captivity for long, he made common cause with his hitherto bitter enemy, Margaret of Anjou, the wife of Henry VI. Edward's position became untenable and he fled to the Low Countries, and Henry VI was restored to the throne. Charles of Burgundy, Edward's brother-in-law, finally helped Edward equip a force to reconquer England. In March 1471 Edward sailed for England and defeated Warwick at Barnet on 14 April and Margaret at Tewkesbury on 4 May. Both

Henry VI and his son were killed. Edward was restored to power and Caxton could continue with his project.

He writes in the *History of Troy* that after this two-year delay he showed his work to Margaret of Burgundy, who ordered him to complete it. This statement has produced considerable speculation about Caxton's relationship with Margaret. Many scholars have thought that because Caxton describes himself as her 'servant' and because he received a fee from her he gave up the governorship of the English nation at this time and entered her service as some kind of librarian or secretary. We do not know when he relinquished his post as governor of the English nation at Bruges, but there is no need to assume that he did so till 1471 when he went to Cologne. His absence then of at least eighteen months would have precluded him from continuing in the position. As governor he would have had many opportunities for meeting Margaret, since both were working for the improvement of Anglo-Burgundian relations. But it is unlikely that he was in her household, since this view is based on a misunderstanding of his English and of fifteenth-century patronage. When he described himself as her servant he was merely using the typical language of the fifteenth century, for any member of the lower classes was a 'servant' of the aristocracy. And Caxton

10. *The Hall of the English, Bruges*

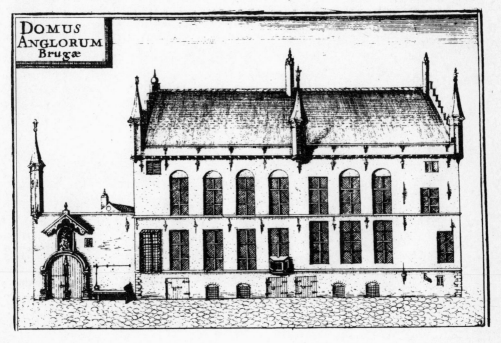

11. *Margaret, Duchess*
    of Burgundy

used the word often to indicate his status *vis-à-vis* many members of the aristocracy, and in these other cases there can be no question of his being in their employ. Similarly his fee from Margaret was not a salary so much as a token of her liberality and esteem. Caxton's frequent begging prologues and epilogues show that he expected all his patrons to reward him financially for linking their names with his books. They acquired general prestige and he gained the necessary cash to carry on his business. Patronage was a part of fifteenth-century publication and its purpose was not unlike that served by reviews today. We have already seen in the last chapter how Caxton made his talents seem as bad as possible. His praise of Margaret was the reverse of this. The patron bestowed on the book all the merit it had and her name would guarantee that it was fashionable and hence make it seem worth acquiring. It was for this reason that Caxton introduced the story about Margaret's comments on his English. She found fault with his translation when he showed her the first few quires that he had done, but she urged him both to correct and then to finish the translation. The story, which may have some foundation in fact, was no doubt elaborated by Caxton to emphasise that his style when corrected had the approval of such an important arbiter of taste as Margaret of Burgundy. Though from unpromising origins, claiming to have been born in the Weald of Kent, nevertheless his book should prove acceptable to the fashionable since it had the approval and patronage of Margaret. Its credentials were sound. In this way Margaret was useful to him in launching his new career, but he was not in her service and it is unlikely that she was in any real way connected with the translation or the venture of printing.

So after starting his translation in 1469 and abandoning it for two years, Caxton writes that he continued with it in Ghent and completed it in Cologne on 19 September 1471. That he finished his translation in Cologne raises the question as to why he was there. It is now accepted that he went there to learn how to print. Apart from the books possibly printed about 1470 in Utrecht, in 1471 the nearest printing presses were those in Cologne, for printing had otherwise not yet reached the Low Countries, let alone England. The first press had been established in Cologne in 1464 and others had followed in quick succession. Cologne was moreover the city which dominated the Low Countries. It was an important staging post on the Rhine and linked the South German towns with the Flemish and Brabant trading cities. It was an important and influential member of the Hanseatic League, though its pro-English policy had resulted in its temporary expulsion from the League at about this time. It was a university town to which students from the Low Countries mostly went for their further education, and it was the seat of the archbishopric which included Holland and Belgium within its province. A rich and thriving town, it might in some respects be considered the capital of the Low Countries. It was its pre-eminent position which had led printers to settle there so early, for until the 1470s it was the only Northern European town with a printing press. Whether Caxton had visited it before 1471–72 is uncertain, though it is quite probable since he had been employed by Edward in negotiations with the Hanseatic League. He may well have had contacts in the town since he started to make his translation of the *History of Troy* in Bruges in 1469 and this translation was started in the expectation that it would finally be printed. A man like Caxton would hardly go to Cologne unless he had some assurance that he would get what he was looking for. To go into printing was a sufficient gamble without assuming that he was so foolhardy as to embark on the project without some kind of encouragement.

Caxton's visit to Cologne was protracted. The Register of Aliens in the archives there records his stay. His residence permit was issued on four separate occasions. On 17 July 1471 he was given permission to stay a month. This permission was extended to Christmas on 9 August, and further extended to John the Baptist's day (i.e. 24 June 1472) on 11 December. The final renewal for a six-month period is dated 19 June 1472. It is unlikely that anything should be read into these renewals; they were an administrative formality. It does not follow that because his permission to stay was renewed so many times he expected his visit to be much shorter than it was. Since he took his translation with him and finished it only in September, he cannot have expected to be there for a brief visit. In the Register he is referred to simply as 'uyss Engelant' (from England); there is no reference to his position as governor of the English nation in Bruges, and this lends further support to the view that he had relinquished this job when he left for Cologne.

The history of the printing press in Cologne is not easy to disentangle, since there were a number of small, anonymous printers working there fairly early on. It is probable that what happened there is similar to what happened elsewhere. A number of artisans familiar with printing issued two or three books each. Then financial difficulties overwhelmed them and they were taken over by entrepreneurs who became the publishers, while the artisans did the printing. There is evidence of a merging of some presses which can best be understood in this way. The entrepreneur would have been a merchant like Caxton. Wynkyn de Worde, Caxton's assistant, wrote in his own edition of *De Proprietatibus Rerum* (*c.* 1495):

> And also of your charyte call to remembraunce
> The soule of William Caxton, first prynter of this boke
> In Laten tonge at Coleyn, hymself to avaunce,
> That every well disposyd man may theron loke.

There is indeed a Latin edition of the *De Proprietatibus* which was produced in Cologne about the time that Caxton was there. While he cannot, as de Worde says, have printed it, he may well have learned how to print by attending at the shop while the book went through the press. We need not assume that he became very expert as a printer, since he would normally leave the day-to-day running of the press to his workmen, but he would need to understand the principles involved. Otherwise he may have made some kind of financial contribution to this volume as a kind of joint publisher, since by this means he could get an entrance to the printing business. It would, however, be important for him to acquire a skilled workman and he probably recruited Wynkyn de Worde at this time. Caxton never refers to his own assistants and so we learn nothing about de Worde until he inherited the press from Caxton at the end of the fifteenth century. His name shows that he came from Wörth in Alsace, and no doubt he went to the city of Cologne to find work. He was to remain with Caxton for the rest of Caxton's life and he carried on the business after his death. In addition to his assistant Caxton would have acquired a press and type while in Cologne. The type he used was probably cut by Johan Veldener, who supplied several printers in the area, but this is a matter to be discussed more fully later.

Caxton arrived in Cologne about 17 July 1471. Since his residence permit was extended for six months on 19 June 1472, he may have left the city about November/December of that year. It is difficult to know whether seventeen months is a long time for the acquisition of all that Caxton wanted. Printing was still so much a new art that one could hardly acquire a press and type without some delay; there was as yet no ready supply. The *De Proprietatibus* is a long work which could have taken up to three months to print, and if Caxton had put any money into it he may have waited to get some return. Nevertheless

I think we may say that although Caxton went to Cologne with the intention of acquiring a press, and although he probably had some kind of guarantee that he would get one, his time there was almost certainly accompanied by frustration and delay. As a merchant his time there may have been unproductive financially, and this shows that he was now sufficiently well off to support himself over such a long period. When he refers to the great cost he was put to to learn the art of printing, it may well be his visit to Cologne he had in mind.

When he had got his press, type, and foreman he left Cologne. There is no direct evidence that he made his way to Bruges to set up his press, since the *History of Troy* has neither a date nor a place of publication. But he did not return to England until 1476 and Bruges is the most likely place for him to have spent the intervening years. He had some working arrangement with a Bruges scrivener called Colard Mansion, which may in fact date from before his visit to Cologne. For Mansion was a trained scribe who like many in his occupation also indulged in translating and bookselling. Shortly after Caxton returned to England Mansion started printing on his own account in Bruges, and his books are so similar to Caxton's that he almost certainly learned the art from him. Indeed he may have helped Caxton before he returned to England. Mansion's career shows how someone interested in bookselling and book production was naturally drawn into printing. Since Caxton dealt in manuscripts for sale in England, it may be that he had bought manuscripts from Mansion over a period of years. Mansion had sold books to the Dukes of Burgundy and was clearly producing the sort of material being read in fashionable circles which Caxton wished to acquire. His help would be invaluable to Caxton both in providing works for the press and possibly also in providing extra capital.

If it can be accepted that Caxton produced his first book, *History of Troy*, in Bruges, the date at which he did so is still uncertain. If he left Cologne late in 1472 he and the press could have been in Bruges early in 1473, since the transportation of the press by ship would have presented few problems. Everything could have been ready to begin printing in March 1473 at the latest. The translation had been completed in 1471 so there would be no delay on that score; and as Bruges was an important centre of book production, paper was plentiful. The only thing which would hamper him was the inexperience of his staff. Though Caxton may have recruited de Worde in Cologne, he cannot have been very old at this time since he lived till 1535. If the press could be ready by March 1473 we may assume that work commenced immediately. Caxton had been in Cologne since July 1471 and this would have been a financially unproductive time for him. He would surely wish to get on with the printing and see some return on the capital he had invested. There was no reason to delay. The *History of Troy* is a long book and, as it was the first text he printed, its production may well have taken longer than usual. Even so it could easily have been ready for sale before the end of 1473. So we may date the first book printed in English to the end of 1473.

This date is confirmed by the second book to be printed, Caxton's translation of the *Game of Chess*. The first edition of this work contains an epilogue which concludes 'Fynysshid the last day of Marche the yer of Our Lord God a thousand, foure honderd and lxxiiii' (i.e. 31 March 1474). There has been some controversy over the meaning of the word 'finished' and over the actual date he meant. He used the word 'finished' to refer either to the printing or to the translation of his books. When there is no indication which is meant, its meaning is uncertain, though in most cases it seems probable that the printing is intended. So it is on balance preferable to take 'finished' in this context to mean the completion of the printing. As for the date, Blades understood Caxton's 31 March 1474 to signify 31 March 1475, and he has been followed in this by most bibliographers. Caxton used two ways of calculating the beginning of the year, one from 1 January which has since become the standard method, and the other from 25 March or Lady Day which was the more normal method at that time. Blades, however, knew of a third method which was sometimes used in the Low Countries, but which was not very common even there. In that system the new year began at Easter, which would mean that '31 March 1474' was by our reckoning 31 March 1475. But there is no evidence that Caxton knew or used this system and as he was publishing his book for the English market it is unlikely that he would use a system unknown in England. By '31 March 1474' he meant 31 March 1474 by our reckoning as well. But if the *Game of Chess* was printed on that day, it would mean that it had been started early in 1474. This would imply further that the *History of Troy* was printed in 1473 and that Caxton was translating the *Game of Chess* while the *History of Troy* was being printed. This is a reasonable view, for as we have seen Caxton was a translator and publisher who took little part in the day-to-day printing.

So far things had gone reasonably well for Caxton. He had acquired a press and in the course of about twelve months he had produced two books in English. If he made a mistake it was in selecting such a large volume as the *History of Troy* as the first text to print. In its printed form it occupies just over

12. The chessboard

This chapytre of the fyrst tractate sheweth who fond first the playe of the Chesse   Capitulo ij

This playe fonde a phylosopher of thoryent Whyche was named in caldee Eperses or in greke philemet tor Whiche is as moche to say in englissh as he that loueth Justyce and mesure / And this philosopher was renomed gretly among the grekes and them of Athenes Whyche were good clerkys and phylosophers also renomed of their conynyng / This philosopher was so Just and trewe that he had leuer dye / than to lyue longe and be a fals flaterer with the sayd kyng · ffor whan he behelde the foul & synful lyf of the kyng · And that no man durst blame hym

700 pages. We should remember that the greatest expense in printing books was the capital investment of buying the paper. No return on this capital could be realised until all copies of the work had been printed and distribution set in hand. We cannot tell how many copies of the *History of Troy* were printed, but as at least sixteen survive today it is probable that the printing was reasonably large by fifteenth-century standards. If we assume that 250 copies were printed, it will be appreciated how large the investment in paper was. The strain on Caxton's resources would be considerable. As the *History of Troy* was available in French in manuscript form, the English translation would be sent to England for sale and this involved extra expense and further delay in getting any financial return. It is of course possible that Caxton himself went to England to promote his book, because the expenses of production and the difficulties of selling the finished product may well have been greater than he anticipated. Even the dedication of the *Game of Chess* to George, Duke of Clarence, the brother of Margaret of Burgundy, proved not to be of much help since the duke was soon to fall into disgrace.

At all events after these first two books there was a period of readjustment and stocktaking by Caxton. No more books were produced in English while he was in Bruges; and this fact is significant since he had started off his press with a view to capturing the English market. The next four books were all in French, and although they are now attributed to Caxton they may have been produced in collaboration with someone like Mansion. For while there is no reason to doubt that they were printed on Caxton's press and by his workmen, others may have taken a share in the publishing and financial risks. One of the texts was the French version of the *History of Troy* from which Caxton had made his English translation and which has close connexions with Colard Mansion, since he had written a manuscript of it for the Duke of Burgundy. The French-printed text was presumably for sale to the nobility and merchants of Flanders and the surrounding areas, and its production shows that the English text was not sold in this market. The other French texts were the French version of *Jason* which Caxton was to translate and print shortly after his return to England, and two religious works, one on the penitential psalms and the other on the four last things. The occurrence of *Jason* is interesting since it suggests that Caxton may already have been thinking of the future; the sale of the French version in Flanders may well have encouraged him to embark on its translation even before he returned to

England. One other text may have been issued in Bruges, the *Propositio Johannis Russell,* which is the Latin oration delivered by Russell, the future Bishop of Rochester, on the occasion of the Duke of Burgundy receiving the insignia of the Order of the Garter. It consists of only four printed pages and it may be described as an occasional piece which could easily have been paid for by Russell. It may be a commissioned rather than a commercial text, for Caxton was quite prepared to take on work of this type to keep his employees busy.

Before we pass on to consider Caxton's life at Westminster it is time to consider what sort of man Caxton was. It is easy enough for us today to think that his decision to embark on printing was an easy one. Nothing could be further from the truth. Up till this time printing had developed haphazardly. Artisans who knew the trade had made for the large cosmopolitan towns. They had set up their presses and most had run into difficulties. A merchant had then seen an opening and taken them over. Caxton acted differently. He realised the potential of the new trade perhaps before he had even seen a press, and he had gone out of his way to learn it. He did not simply exploit a situation on his own doorstep. Thus though Caxton was not an inventor, he did introduce a new attitude to printing and publishing. An important aspect of his project was the publication of works in the vernacular. He tried to create a monopoly of English books on the English market. He was aiming at a more popular clientele rather than at a learned audience in so far as his books were new, fashionable, and in the vernacular. Printing made literature available to others than the wealthy and the learned, but Caxton was the first to realise and develop its potential. The amazing thing is that he appears to have thought out this position even before he learned how to print, since he started translating the *History of Troy* before he went to Cologne. There was little in the contemporary printing scene to suggest this *modus operandi* to him. Most printers issued texts in Latin, still the *lingua franca* of the educated classes, and only the occasional book in the vernacular appeared. No one before Caxton had a conscious policy of producing a list consisting almost exclusively of vernacular texts. In this respect Caxton was an innovator. The closest parallel is with the producers of manuscripts both in England and in the Low Countries. Here we find bookshops specially geared to issue vernacular translations of popular works. Indeed some of the texts Caxton translated into English had already been translated into French from Latin and published

13. A page of Caxton's 'Jason'

Incontinent Whan Apollo apperçeyued & vnderstood this thinges & among all other he behelde him that Was thus come & had put him in the see. Certes he Was sore abasshid, but for to knoWe all the tydingis, he made to roWe ner him & foude that the Water Where he Was in, boilled by grete hete al aboute his body, The poure felaWe incontinent that he kneWe the king apollo his lorde, began passing pietouslp to escrie Vpon him Weping & saying. Ha A sire Apollo if hit be possible to the, helpe & deliuere me from this mortal daunger. Whan apollo saWe the poure felaW in suche desolacön the teeris fill doun from his eyen, & for asmoche as the Water boilled so aboute him he had grete pite, & demanded of him What eyled him so to crye & Wepe And from Whens that Water cam that so boilled aboute him, & axid spn Where Was zechi9. Alas ansuerde the pou ure felaWe Whiche labourid spuyng there to the deth in a dolour & payne inestymable. Praye ye sire for zechius & for his felaWes, for I haue seen all, one after another dye in a mortell destresse and so anguisshously, that Vnnethe that is creature spuyng that coude ferailp acompte and telle hit to pou

Whan Apollo herde speke of the deth of zechi9 and his felaWes he Was so soroufull that he Wist not What to do, but ansuerde to the poure felaW and saide by grete ad, myracïon, hoW maye that be fayr sire, for I saWe right noW zechi9 and all his felaWes that Were With him Whan they toke londe in colchos in descendyng from the shippe, Alas dere sire ansuerde thenne the felaWe, Hyt is Well reson that I recompte & telle pou the trouth & Verite of the manere of

in manuscript form. Caxton's innovation was to extend this principle to printing. It is an innovation showing considerable foresight, courage, and determination.

After all, in 1473 when he issued his first printed book Caxton was probably already at least fifty. He had been a successful merchant; yet he was prepared to embark on a new venture which had certain similarities with what he had done so far, but it also carried new risks. Not everyone is ready to undertake new projects so late in life. His determination is revealed by his willingness to delay the scheme from 1469 to 1471 when political conditions in England made it difficult to realise. Others might have become disillusioned and given up, or else carried on and gone bankrupt. Caxton had the determination to carry on and also to wait until conditions were more favourable. Similarly we have seen that the time he spent at Cologne had its frustrations and delays, which he put up with. Even when he returned to Bruges the distribution from there of books in English to England proved to be more difficult than anticipated; it resulted first in the issuing of French books and then in his permanent return to England. At any one of these stages a less determined and a less astute man might have sold the press and gone back to the sale of manuscripts and other luxury goods. Others, such as his collaborator Mansion, did this. He was still a member of the merchant class and it would be easy enough to give up the press. His actions show Caxton to be both prudent and determined.

What the financial rewards of printing were we can no longer tell. There was no shortage of those willing to try their hand at it despite the very high failure rate. Caxton was certainly a good financier and manager, and he must have reckoned that the risks were worth taking. He was able to organise his business so efficiently that his press remained productive till the end of his life, even though there were politically difficult times to come. His training as a merchant was invaluable.

Caxton did add little bits of information to the books he printed. These generally show that he had an acquisitive rather than an enquiring mind. He added details and stories from his own experience, but he never seems to have questioned what he learned or saw. He was orthodox in his faith and he accepted many of the fashionable panaceas of his time. A return to the age of chivalry would cure his contemporaries of their self-seeking. His reading of Chaucer, whose works he praised so highly, did not lead him to realise that what he complained of was the subject of complaint a hundred years earlier. His mind was not original; there was no new solution to the problems of the time. He repeated what was then current. His strength lay not in his thought or writing, but in his exploitation of a particular invention at a particular time.

IV
THE WESTMINSTER
PUBLISHER

Caxton returned with his press to England in 1476. The exact date is uncertain, but an indulgence issued by the Abbot of Abingdon to a Henry Langley and his wife is dated by hand 13 December 1476. This indulgence was printed by Caxton and must date from early December at the latest. It is of course possible that he returned to England before 1476, but this is unlikely in view of various documents relating to the negotiations between England and the Hanseatic League dating from 1475 in which it appears he was still resident in Bruges. The earliest date of his return to England is late 1475, but 1476 is the more realistic

14. *The earliest piece of printing in England*

suggestion. The indulgence need not be the first thing printed in England, though many scholars assume that after his return he started by printing a variety of small works. This view is based on what Robert Copland, who may have been an apprentice with Caxton, wrote in his preface to *King Appolyn of Tyre*, printed by de Worde in 1510:

My worshypfull mayster Wynkyn de Worde havynge a lytell boke of an auncyent hystory of a kynge, sometyme reygnynge in the countree of Thyre called Appolyn, concernynge his malfortunes and peryllous adventures right espoventables, bryefly compyled and pyteous for to here, the which boke I Robert Copland have me applyed for to translate out of Frensshe languge into our maternal Englysshe tongue at the exhortacyon of my forsayd mayster, accordynge dyrectly to myn auctor, gladly folowynge the trace of my mayster Caxton, begynnyng with small storyes and pamfletes and so to other.

Copland's words are ambiguous. Since he was the translator and not the printer of *King Appolyn*, his words are best understood to refer only to Caxton's translating activities. And *King Appolyn* itself is hardly a small item in the sense that many commentators appear to understand Copland's words. We cannot attach too much importance to them and we need not assume that in its first year the press published only smaller works. The one point which is worth emphasising about the 1476 indulgence is that so soon after his return Caxton was employed by such an important ecclesiastic as the Abbot of Abingdon to print an indulgence. Either this contract was secured through the good offices of the Abbot of Westminster or Caxton himself had tried to acquire work of this sort, perhaps before he came back. What is significant, though, is that he failed to capitalise on this contact, since he did not in general publish for a religious audience. It would seem as though he could have concentrated on this audience if he had wanted to.

In the previous paragraph we noted that Caxton acted as one of the English negotiators in the discussions with the Hanse in 1475. He was such a seasoned diplomat that he could not escape from public service. Even after his return to England there are records of payments to him from the royal treasury almost to the year of his death. It is not certain what these payments were for, but probably they were for his expenses incurred in diplomatic missions. For it is wrong to imagine that his life altered profoundly as a result of his becoming a publisher in England. He remained predominantly a merchant selling goods, though these

15. *Edward IV at Caxton's press*

were now books and manuscripts rather than anything else. His expertise in negotiations and his knowledge of Continental rulers led to his employment not only by Edward IV, but also by Henry VII. His return to England was not a kind of retirement or a way of escaping from an active life, for there was very little change in the mode of his life.

In Westminster he was a publisher having books he chose printed and a bookseller handling both his own printed books and many manuscripts. The bookselling side of his business is easily overlooked, but hints of it are found here and there. He refers to a manuscript of *Blanchardin and Eglantine* which he had sold to Margaret, Duchess of Somerset, before he made his translation of this work. Customs records show that he imported

16. *Henry VII*

SOVVENT ME SOVVIENT

17. *Margaret, Duchess*
of Somerset

18. *Caxton and the
Abbot of
Westminster*

books from the Continent and some of them were probably manuscripts. There was no sharp division between books and manuscripts, and a man who dealt in the one would certainly handle the other. He may have had manuscripts made of some of his translations either as presentation copies or for sale. The so-called Caxton Ovid survives only in a manuscript which may have been made for Caxton either to sell or to present to someone. Many French manuscripts passed through his hands for his translating activities alone and presumably he disposed of them by sale after he had finished with them. In his prologue to *Eneydos* he refers to his study which contained 'many dyverse paunflettis and bookys', and this study was no doubt his shop where these volumes were kept for sale. He also frequently refers to the conversations he had with his clients and patrons about books. It is unlikely that they would visit a printing shop to discuss literary matters; it is more reasonable to suppose that they called in to inspect a bookseller's wares, both manuscripts and printed books. Visits of this type would pass naturally on to the consideration of what should be translated and printed.

Although all of Caxton's adult life in England had been spent in London, when he set up his printing establishment he chose Westminster as its location. It used to be thought that he was prevented from settling in London because of the opposition of the professional scriveners who feared for their livelihood. But this is unlikely, for not only did he enjoy good relations with the scriveners in Bruges like Colard Mansion, but also Westminster Abbey was the home of a very important monastic scriptorium. He could not escape professional scribes there. Indeed he was on good terms with the Abbot and there is evidence that he made use of the services of the scribes in the scriptorium. By and large there was little animosity between the practitioners of the old and the new trade; and the history of printing shows that among those who became printers there were many scribes. Caxton's reasons for settling at Westminster were positive rather than negative. Although he was there some way from the main trade routes for the distribution of books, many of the people for whom he printed had cause to visit Westminster, which was the home of the monarch and the seat of the legislature and the judiciary. Instead of distributing his books throughout the country, his customers came to him. In this connexion it is worth noticing that in the accounts of 1488–89 the charge for an extra room for a week in which Parliament was sitting is listed. This was no doubt to cater for all the extra people who would be at

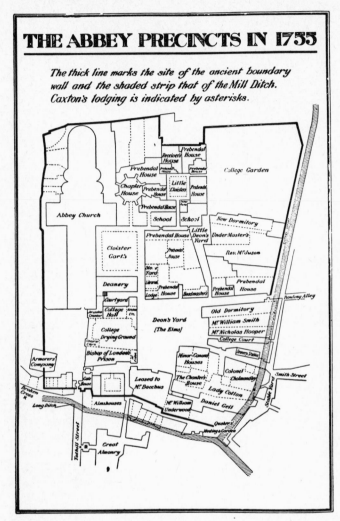

THE ABBEY PRECINCTS IN 1755

*The thick line marks the site of the ancient boundary
wall and the shaded strip that of the Mill Ditch.
Caxton's lodging is indicated by asterisks.*

Westminster at that time, and the additional space would be
used to mount a bigger display than usual. It is partly because
his shop was at Westminster that he published so many books of
the same kind. It was essential to produce books which appealed
to the people who lived in or visited Westminster—courtiers,
lawyers, merchants and country gentlemen. It is true that the
Abbey was an important religious centre and many ecclesiastics
visited it. But they probably formed a small percentage of all
the visitors to Westminster, and many of them thought and
behaved more like courtiers than like clerics. Caxton could afford
not to concentrate on serious religious or learned treatises.

Jf it plefe ony man fpirituel oꝛ temporel to bye ony
ꝑycs of two and thꝛe comemoracios of Salifburi vfe
enprynted after the foꝛme of this prefet lettre whiche
ben wel and truly correct, late hym come to weftmo;
nefter in to the almonefꝛye at the reed pale and he fhal
haue them good chepe .·.·

Suplico fet cedula ·

The location of his press within the precincts of the Abbey
has been the subject of dispute. The accounts of the Abbey were
kept by various officers including the prior, the sacrist and the
almoner. Unfortunately it is not clear what the relationship
between their accounts is, for the picture they give of Caxton's
tenancy is far from straightforward. The sacrist's accounts, for
example, show that he rented a room in the Abbey from 1476
onwards and that this room was paid for by de Worde after his
death. These accounts provide further evidence that Caxton did
not return to England before 1476. The almoner's accounts, on
the other hand, record payment by Caxton for a room over the
outer door *(supra portam exteriorem)* only for the financial year
1482–83. As this room was presumably in the almonry, the
almoner's domain, it has been suggested that he had his shop
at the sign of the Red Pale in the Almonry only from 1482
and that his main premises were in the Abbey precincts near
the Chapter House. Indeed a room above the outer door would
be an ideal place to exhibit a sign to attract customers. But Caxton's *Advertisement,* which though undated is thought to have
been issued to sell the *Ordinale,* is attributed to the year 1477
and in it Caxton urges those who want to buy 'ony pyes of
two and thre comemoracions of Salisburi Use' to come to Westminster 'into the Almonesrye at the Reed Pale'. If 1477 can be
accepted as the date of the *Advertisement,* he must have rented
a room in the almonry right from the beginning of his stay at
Westminster. It is possible that he rented space in more than
one part of the Abbey, for the press did not have to be next
to the shop; but this does not help us to locate the premises
he may have rented. The wording of the accounts does suggest
different places. In the prior's account Caxton has a *tenementum*

or *domus*; in the sacrist's account it is a *shopa*, which can be
either a shop or a workshop; and in the almoner's account it
is simply a *camera*. Though we cannot say exactly where his
premises were, by the time of his death they were evidently extensive. His business prospered. What also emerges from the
accounts is that other merchants rented space in the Abbey buildings. In view of its location near the Palace of Westminster it
was a prime site. By setting up his business there Caxton was
simply capitalising on its advantages, for the idle and the curious
would come to visit all the shops. He was merely one of many
shopkeepers who traded in goods suitable for the clientele who
paraded in those parts.

21. The Almonry

In his publishing business Caxton needed assistants to run the press, fellow merchants to finance it and patrons whose names would help to sell the books. We do not know how many helpers he had, for he never makes any reference to them in his books. Wynkyn de Worde he recruited in Cologne, and Robert Copland mentions that Caxton had been his master and so he may well have been apprenticed to him at some time. Indeed others who later became printers in their own right may have learned the

*22. The Caxton
     window*

art from Caxton, though we cannot be certain of this since he makes no mention of them in his prologues and epilogues. The additions he made to his books were designed to promote them, and the names of his assistants would not be of any help in that respect. As a general rule only authors, members of the nobility, and merchants are named in his writings.

Margaret, Duchess of Burgundy, was the patron of his first book, but as she was resident in the Low Countries she would be of little use to him when he started selling books at Westminster. Even before he returned to England he had used the name of George, Duke of Clarence, in the first edition of the *Game of Chess*. Significantly Caxton says that he was unknown to the Duke, for the dedication of books was not a personal matter and there is no need to assume that all the people mentioned in his books were known personally to Caxton. The only important thing was that the patron should be a well-known member of the nobility, for this would guarantee the book's quality to potential buyers. Margaret of Burgundy may have suggested to Caxton that he use the Duke of Clarence's name in the *Game of Chess*, since he was her favourite brother. Unfortunately he fell into disgrace and when Caxton returned to England he had to find another patron.

His first book with a dedication published in England was probably *Jason*, the French version of which had been published in Bruges by Caxton and Mansion and the translation of which may have been ready before Caxton's return to England. This dedication refers first to Margaret of Burgundy and to his own translation of *History of Troy*, for not only is *Jason* a continuation of the *History of Troy* but also Caxton may not yet have found a suitable patron in England. For this volume was dedicated to Edward, Prince of Wales, who was at the time about seven years old. Caxton cannot have known him and in fact he addresses him through the good offices of the King and Queen, who are also referred to in a formal way. The formality implies he is hoping to arouse interest and he is uncertain of his reception. This volume follows the pattern set by the *Game of Chess*: Caxton dedicates his work to members of the royal family even though he is not acquainted with them.

At this point in his career he had a lucky break in his search for a patron. Anthony, Earl Rivers, the King's brother-in-law, sent him his translation of the *Dicts or Sayings* to look over and then to print. Caxton says that 'it liked him [Earl Rivers] to sende it to me', and this suggests that the Earl did not come in person

23. George, Duke of
    Clarence

but sent his secretary or some other official with the work. We
know that he had a secretary for he is mentioned in Caxton's
addition to the *Moral Proverbs*, another of the Earl's translations.
On receiving the *Dicts or Sayings* Caxton decided to see the Earl
to talk things over and to praise him for his translation. The
implication is that he seized this fortunate opportunity to get
to know the Earl and to enlist him as a patron. It remains a
possibility that he had met the Earl earlier, possibly in Bruges,
and that Rivers encouraged him to come to England. But there
is no evidence for this, and a close reading of Caxton's words
in the prologue to the *Dicts or Sayings* and his choice of patrons
early on in his career make it unlikely. It was this text which
led to their meeting and they found they could help each other:
Rivers liked to have his books widely disseminated through print-

ing and Caxton needed the Earl's patronage, for the publication of works translated by an earl would stand him in good stead. Since Earl Rivers was originally a Lancastrian and was regarded as an upstart by the older Yorkist nobility, including Margaret of Burgundy, an agreement by Caxton with him represented an important change in his policy of patronage. It was a successful change for Caxton, even though Rivers was named as patron only in those books which he had translated or directly recommended. But he did provide the press with numerous works and his name added tone to the press's output. Caxton had at least one member of the aristocracy who took an interest in his work.

Caxton printed three works by Rivers, *Dicts or Sayings, Moral Proverbs* and *Cordial.* The *Curial,* published after Edward IV's death, was probably translated and printed at the Earl's request as well, though it is surprising in some ways that Rivers, who thought of himself as a literary man, should not have made the translation of this work. The French text would have been given to Caxton before 1483 and Rivers could not foresee that Edward IV was going to die so suddenly and that his own fortunes should take such a change for the worse. Indeed the political upheaval following Edward's death put a speedy end to this partnership between the Earl and the printer, for Richard III had Rivers beheaded. The Queen, Rivers's sister, fled into sanctuary where Caxton dedicated a volume to her, though he did not do so openly for she is not named. This book, *Knight of the Tower,* is the only one which can be associated directly with Elizabeth Woodville, for in a book like *Jason* her name is merely inserted with that of the King as the parents of the Prince of Wales. It may be that Caxton in his desperation for patronage turned to her after the death of her brother, even though she was in unfortunate straits at the moment. He had to look somewhere for his patronage, and Elizabeth was still an important person. For otherwise before 1483 Caxton had referred only to 'diverse gentlemen' as the people who had requested works to be published and this phrase is probably a euphemism for his hope that such people would read these books.

The years following 1483 were difficult ones. He may well have thought that he had established a flourishing business with the active, if possibly selfish, interest of a patron like Earl Rivers. With the accession of Richard III and the eclipse of the Woodville faction Caxton lost both his best patron and possibly many customers. Once again he had to start looking for support and as we have seen this is probably the reason why he looked to the

ELIZABETH · REGINA · REGIS · EDWARDE · 4 · ANGLIE

Coll. Regin.
Fund. altera
A.D. 1465.

24. *Elizabeth*
    Woodville

Queen. But he did not refer to her by name and the years 1483–85 are notable for this anonymous patronage as well as for the search for new patrons. The anonymous patrons are those who could not be named because of the political conditions of the time, but whose rank could be mentioned since an earl would help a book's image even if the earl was not identified. Thus the *Curial* was asked for by a 'noble and vertuous erle', almost certainly Earl Rivers. Even *King Arthur* may have been requested by Rivers, since the prologue refers to an unnamed gentleman who discussed Arthur with Caxton. The *Order of Chivalry* was requested by a squire, and the second edition of the *Canterbury Tales* by a gentleman. New named patrons, on the other hand, included the Earl of Arundel and William Daubeney. The Earl of Arundel, whose patronage extended only to the *Golden Legend,* was naturally the best catch, though it cannot be shown that he ever met Caxton as their business was conducted through an intermediary. But Arundel was in favour with the new regime and Caxton may have wished for a long relationship; he even went so far as to include the arms of Arundel as a woodcut in this volume. Unfortunately Arundel's interest in the press was short-lived. Daubeney is quite a different kind of patron, for he is referred to as 'a good and synguler frende of myn' in the epilogue to *Charles the Great,* which Caxton claims Daubeney asked him to print. Daubeney may be described as a civil servant who had held the position of Searcher of the Port of London under Edward IV. As a merchant who imported books through London Caxton may have become acquainted with him through this job. His patronage marks a significant shift in the sort of people acknowledged in the prologues and epilogues. Up till now Caxton had admitted only to aristocratic patronage, though one assumes merchants and other members of the middle classes also read his books. With the uncertainties of the political situation and the dangers of aristocratic patronage, Caxton acknowledged the people whom he had chosen to ignore hitherto in his writings. His *Caton,* of about the same date, is addressed to the City of London. (*Caton,* a translation of a French prose text by Caxton, should not be confused with *Cato,* a poem by Benedict Burgh which Caxton issued three times.) It may be significant that his edition of Chaucer's *Boethius,* issued about 1478 and long before these political uncertainties, was printed 'atte requeste of a singuler frende and gossib of myne' who is unnamed. This friend may well be William Pratt, a fellow mercer. Amid the difficulties of 1483–85 Caxton may have become disenchanted with aristocratic patronage or realised that he was safer in emphasising his merchant connexions. So he was quite happy to mention Daubeney in *Charles the Great* and to mention Pratt, unnamed in *Boethius*, in the *Book of Good Manners* from 1487.

It is only for people like Daubeney and Pratt that Caxton uses terms of affection and friendship. The aristocrats were his patrons with whom he had dealings from time to time, but merchants and officials were his friends. The point is worth emphasising because it is often thought that by settling at Westminster he became a kind of courtier and cut himself off from his former acquaintances. This is not so. He probably met few of the nobility, for much of his business was conducted through third parties. If he met kings it would have been at an audience rather than on a personal basis. He remained a merchant and no doubt felt most at home among his fellow merchants. We should also remember that some of them may have been business partners as well as friends. People like Pratt and Daubeney may have been co-publishers of the volumes in which they are named. The mercer Hugh Bryce who asked for a translation of the *Mirror of the World* to present to William, Lord Hastings, would have made a substantial contribution to the costs of the edition.

Whatever Caxton's feelings towards the nobility and their patronage may have been in the period 1483–85, as soon as more stable conditions prevailed he made another bid to win aristocratic support. He was once again fortunate in that he managed to attract the attention of John de Vere, Earl of Oxford, who was one of the most important members of the new government. Oxford was not a translator like Rivers and his interest had to be aroused by the translation of the life of Robert of Oxford, one of his ancestors. This translation was undertaken at the Earl's request, and since he presumably knew French (he had been in exile in France for some years) the translation must have been intended for wider dissemination. No doubt it was printed, though no copies survive, for Caxton's reference to the miracles it contained suggests that it could have had a wide appeal. Oxford was also responsible for presenting Caxton to Henry VII and for gaining the royal commission for the translation and publication of the *Feats of Arms*. But he was evidently not so interested in literary matters as Rivers had been and in this he was probably no different from most other courtiers. In general their interest could be aroused for a time, particularly if their vanity was engaged, but then they forgot the printer. Even Rivers was not such a disinterested lover of literature as he is often

25. *Arthur, Prince of Wales*

ELIZABETHA ♂ VXOR
HENRICI VII

26. Elizabeth of York

portrayed, or at least he took an interest only in those books he translated. Thus throughout his entire career Caxton could never be certain of gaining the patronage he wanted. Henry VII took as little interest in the press as Edward IV, for Caxton was obliged to dedicate *Eneydos* to his son, Arthur, Prince of Wales, just as he had dedicated *Jason* to a former Prince of Wales. And this dedication was designed to ingratiate him with the monarch; it was not the fruits of any personal relationship. He even managed for a time to win the patronage of Henry VII's mother and of his wife. The former had bought manuscripts from him and had acquired a large library, for she was interested in books. But her patronage, coming as it did in 1489, was too late to be of much assistance to Caxton.

Caxton printed a larger number of books of a religious nature towards the end of his life and it has been suggested that he became more devout as he grew older. This suggestion is possible, but perhaps unlikely. He had always been devout, but the books he translated at the end of his life are no more religious than those he translated earlier. It is necessary to remember that he could not survive simply by printing his own translations because he could not translate as quickly as his men could print. In order to keep his workmen busy he had to print material he had not translated and thus throughout his career he was looking for works to print. As he became older and his energies waned, his output of translations may well have fallen so that the need for other material was greater. But in his early career as a printer he had already published a large amount of the courtly poetry available so that there cannot have been too much poetry left which he thought worth printing. Similarly at the end of his life he had no member of the aristocracy who wanted him to publish what he had translated and Caxton did not recruit anyone else to make translations for him. He could easily have employed a scribe or even some indigent gentleman to make translations, as de Worde was to do; but he chose not to. Hence he would of necessity be forced to print more religious material if for no other reason than that this type of writing was so plentiful at that time. It may have been an added attraction to him that many of these pieces were relatively short and so the capital outlay needed for their printing was limited.

The picture we get of Caxton from his prologues and epilogues is of a man at the centre of a busy literary circle. This view is one-sided. There does not seem to have been a single patron of his who took a selfless interest in the press or in literature in general. No patron came forward who had a real love of literature and no English humanist seems to have taken any interest in what he was doing. Only two visiting Italians commissioned him to print texts which they wanted to see in print. While it is unlikely that he invented the stories about his literary conversations, they may have been infrequent and perhaps conducted with merchants as much as with gentlemen. They can have occupied little of his time. He spent most of that translating or attending to the financial side of his business. As a publisher he imported books and he had books printed for him on the Continent. So he may have visited London frequently. The sale of his books may well have been his own particular responsibility. He was also employed on official business from time to time. So his life was a full one right to the time of his death.

The exact date of his death is uncertain. His burial is recorded in the churchwardens' accounts of St Margaret's parish for 1490–1492. Six shillings and eightpence was paid for the torches and sixpence for the bell at his funeral. The shop he was renting in the Abbey was taken over by de Worde on his death and this transfer is noted in the sacrist's roll at Westminster Abbey in the financial year 1491–92. Blades preferred the date 1491 for his death, but there is nothing to prevent it from being placed in early 1492. Caxton was married, though absolutely nothing is known of his wife who is never mentioned in his writings. But they had a daughter Elizabeth who survived him. She was married to a Gerard Crop, a tailor, who took Caxton's executor to court for the non-payment of certain monies which he claimed were due to him under Caxton's will. We are unable to disentangle the complexities of this lawsuit because no will has been found. But Elizabeth and Gerard agreed to part company and this decision is recorded in the Chancery Proceedings. It is a possible, but not necessary, assumption that he had no surviving son at his death because the business was taken over by de Worde. As we have seen, de Worde started paying for Caxton's shop at Westminster as soon as he died. Naturally the business would change and develop under this new management, and we shall review these changes in the coming chapters.

V
THE BOOK AND ITS
PRODUCTION

If you were looking at a Caxton volume and an ordinary fifteenth-century manuscript the first thing to strike you would be how alike they are. Indeed a page of the Caxton Ovid, a manuscript which was presumably written for Caxton about 1480, could at first glance be mistaken for one of his printed books (see plate 27). This is natural enough, for the early printers had no other models except the manuscripts they were used to seeing and working from. With most discoveries there is a time-lag before the new invention breaks out of the constrictions of the old format and can realise its full potential. This happened with printed books, and with Caxton the similarity between books and manuscripts extended to the size of paper, the design of type and the whole layout of a given page.

Generally Caxton printed his books in folio, which means that a sheet of paper is folded only once and so produces four sides of printed text. But of course sheets were not bound individually; they were collected into bundles which were then bound. Such bundles are called 'gatherings' and may consist of three, four or five sheets, known respectively as ternions, quaternions and quinternions. The importance of this method of binding is that what is printed on one half of a sheet of paper will not necessarily be the next consecutive passage of the text of what is printed on the other half. Consider for example the gathering of three sheets as presented in plate 28. There are three sheets A, B and C, but as each is folded once there are 12 sides of text. But sheet A will have text pages 1 and 12 on one side and pages 2 and 11 on the obverse. Sheet B will have pages 3 and 10 on one side and 4 and 9 on the other. As it seems probable that the two pages of text on a folio sheet could be accommodated in the press together and were printed at one pull, when sheet A was laid in the press pages 1 and 12 would already have had to be set up in type. While it is possible that the compositor did set up pages 1 and 12 following their order in the text, this system would have had two disadvantages. The pressman would

to god Bachus
¶This is to vn-
derstond that for to
fylle theyr belyes &
appetytes dranke so
moch wyn that pey
were oute of theyre
wytte & frantyke.
Pentheus dyde doo
take Acotes the
tauerner that had
broughte the wyne
and wolde haue
put hym to deth.
But Acotes haue
to the sergeantis &
seruauntes so moch
to drynke that pey
shulde brynd hym
in such wyse that
they wyste not
where they were &
suffred hym to vn-
bynde hym felf &
lefte the dores open
And thus escapped
Acotes fro the dron-
kardes by the force &
vertu of the wyne
and wente quyte &

delyurd wythoute
ony empesshement
¶Penthe? that
knewe that his pry
soner was escaped
ran after for to take
hym achirn and to
put hym to deth.
But he was mett
& recountred wyth
the dronkardes and
by them slayn and
after difmembrid
hym piece fro pece
in vengeance of hym
that empesched and
blamed them to
drynke wyne.

Thus en-
deth the iij.e booke.

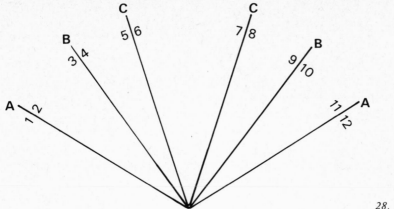

28. *A ternion*

have to wait until twelve pages were in type before he could start page one, and twelve pages would have to be in type at the same time. This in its turn would mean a greater investment in type, for there would have to be sufficient type to set up all these pages. In fact what seems to have happened is that the supervisor broke up the text into what he thought would be the pages of type so that the compositor could set up pages 1 and 12 first and then pages 2 and 11. An added advantage of this system was that two compositors could work on the same text at the same time. This was necessary because a pressman could print 250 copies of a sheet more quickly than a compositor could set up the material for that sheet. So unless the pressman was going to have a long rest at the end of pulling the requisite number of each sheet, it was essential to have at least two compositors.

This system worked well, though occasional mistakes were made. It is from these mistakes that one can deduce what system was used. There are thus examples where the logical order of gatherings is interrupted, which is best explained by a mistake in breaking up the text. When the second edition of Mirk's *Festial* was printed about 1491 it had the following gatherings, a–p⁸ q² r⁸ s⁶. In other words the gatherings were normally quaternions of four sheets or sixteen pages each. But one gathering, 'q', consists of only one sheet or four pages, although the next gathering has the normal pattern. It seems as though the compositor made a mistake in allocating the different sheets to each quaternion so that when one compositor came to set up 'q' he found he had insufficient material to fill a whole quaternion and that there was nothing he could do about it since his fellow compositor

had already started on 'r'. An even more instructive example
is found in *Reynard the Fox* printed in 1481. The collation of
this text is a–h⁸, π, i⁸, k–l⁶, in which π is a half-sheet bound
in between gatherings 'h' and 'i'. A normal page of type in this
volume consists of 29 lines. As the half-sheet has 15 lines on
one side and 14 on the other, it is difficult to escape the conclusion
that this represents a page of type which was miscounted in some
way. Probably when the compositor finished the 'h' gathering
he discovered that 17 pages had been allocated to it instead of
the desired 16. Since this page was not included in gathering
'i', it must be that this gathering was already being set up in
type. The only solution was to insert a half-sheet rather like
a modern erratum slip. A similar mistake was made in the *Polychronicon* printed in 1482.

Another problem that would arise if a text was divided into
pages before being set up in type was how to accommodate
all the allocated writing on the particular page. At first this may
not have been a pressing problem since the lines of type were
of an irregular length and could no doubt be adjusted accordingly.
In other texts the gaps left for the paragraph marks to be filled
in by hand could be expanded or contracted to even out the
page. And since fifteenth-century orthography was fluid, it would
also be possible to alter the spelling to fill out or to contract
certain lines. But it remains true that in his English texts Caxton
used contractions most frequently at the bottom of a page, and
this may be a sign that the compositor was trying to cram things
in, that he was trying not to let his allocated text go beyond
the page allowed. This can be seen strikingly in the use of the
ampersand. Thus if one considers page b3ʳ of the first edition
of *Reynard the Fox* it will be seen that of the seven ampersands
on the page six occur in the last six lines. There are no examples
of 'and' in full in these six lines, though there are twelve on
the rest of the page. The same applies to other types of abbreviation. On page h2ʳ the only two abbreviations for omitted letters
are in the last line. Throughout the book the use of the complete
word *capitulo* or one of its abbreviated forms in each chapter-
heading is determined by the need not to let the headings spill
over into a further line, as though each had been allocated a
certain number of lines. Plate 29, which shows a page of the
first edition of *Quattuor Sermones* (a3ᵛ), exhibits the same
features. The ampersand occurs only in the last five lines on the
page. The abbreviation $Þ^e$ for 'the' is found in lines 35 and 37.
And the other abbreviations at the bottom of the page include

in body and soule to gyder to blisse for euermore / Of this blisse
spekith saynt Mathewe in the last article / The twelfthe is Et
vitam eternam amen / I beleue in euer lastyng lyf / Thes ben
the articles of the feyth /the whiche but euery man truly and sad
ly beleue / may not be saued / For with out feyth / hit is not
possyble to plese god / Thise be the x commaundementis of god
The thyrd thyng that thou sholdest knowe god by / by his ten
commaundementis / whiche he hym self wrote in two tablis of
stoon / And toke them to moyses to teche them his peple /promy
syng them that wolde kepe them / his blessyng /welth /and wel
fare / And to them that wolde not his curse / grete sorowe and
myschefe / A man askyd of Crist / what he myght doo to haue
euerlastyng lyf/ And he answeryd and sayd yf thou wolt entre
euerlastyng lyf / kepe the commaundementis / This preuyth yf
thou kepe his commaundementis / thou fulfillest alle the lawe of
god and shalt haue euerlastyng lyf / The first is he commaun
dyth that thou haue no god / but hym / Ne that thou worshyp
serue ne peue thy trust to none other creature / ymage ne thynge
graupn but oonly to hym/ In thys is forboden malwmetry/fals
enchauntementis / wytchecrafte/ fals charmys and dremps and
mysbeleups that ony man or woman hopith helpe in wythoute al
myghty god/ In thys ye synne dedely that for sekenes or losse
of goodes /put your feyth and byleue that ye shold haue in your
lord god / by the deuyllys mynystris fals wytches / the whyche
brynge many a soule to the deupl / For they beleue more the
wytches wordes / thenne Inne the wordes of scripture that the
preest techyth them / Alle suche haue goddys curse at the leste iiij
tymes a yere in the grete sentence / And euery day in our pryme
As for ymagys / Also ye shul vnderstonde that as clerkys
leyn in theyr bokys holy they shold lyue and doo/ so shold lewd
men lerne by ymagis whom they shold worshyp and folowe in
lyuyng /to doo goddys worship to ymagis euery man is forbede
Therfore when thou compst to the chirche first beholde goddys body
vnder fourme of brede in the auter/ & thanke hym that he vouchesauf
euery day to come fro þ holy keupn aboue for þ helth of thy soule
loke thou on the crosse & therby haue mynde in the passyd that he
theron suffrid for the/ thene to þ ymagis of the holy saintis not be
keupng on the/but that by the sight of the thou may haue mynde

the macron to indicate the omission of a nasal. The top three-quarters of the page are entirely free of any such abbreviations. The reverse is also true. When insufficient text was allocated to the page this led the compositor to leave spaces and to spread out his words. On folio cl^v of the first edition of *Quattuor Sermones* there is a long gap in line 31 and the last line is noticeably spread out with largish gaps between some words. All these features suggest that the pages of type were carefully calculated in the copy before typesetting commenced, though it is something which has not been properly investigated as yet.

A further indication that the pages of the edition to be printed were marked off in the copytext is provided by *Feats of Arms* printed in 1489. In all extant copies of this edition there is a mistake in the make-up of signature 'o', for the text which should appear on 03^v is in fact found on 06^r and vice versa. These two pages are those which lie side by side in a sheet of a quaternion, the regular gathering in *Feats of Arms*. The two pages must have been set up in type at the same time and were then laid incorrectly in the forme so that they appeared in reverse order in the book. Since neither page has a signature the mistake was not discovered. But it is one which is best explained on the assumption that the pages in the book were not set up following the order of the text in the book since in those circumstances a mix-up of this sort would be unlikely to occur. It is only if the pages are set up according to the convenience of the printer and hence become divorced from their regular sequence that an error like this will occur.

Another aspect of the preparation of the text is worth comment. We saw that the normal progress of the gatherings was occasionally interrupted as though a mistake in allocation had occurred. As a general rule Caxton texts are arranged in quaternions except naturally that the pages at the end of a book which cannot be so grouped are arranged in the most convenient fashion. A standard collation for a Caxton text would be something like a–g^8 h^6, and where this pattern is not found one should look for the reason to explain the divergence. Thus as already noted the collation of the second edition of Mirk's *Festial*, a–p^8 q^2 r^8 s^6, may be explained by faulty allocation, and the same may well apply to the first edition of the *Directorium Sacerdotum* which has the collation a–q^8 r^{10} s–t^8. Both the French and the English versions of the *History of Troy* are arranged in quinternions. Since the English version is Caxton's first printed text and since the French one cannot have been much later, this arrangement can be accounted for by what he had learned in Cologne. The *De Proprie-tatibus Rerum* printed in Cologne in 1471, the text on which Caxton almost certainly learned how to print, is arranged in quin-ternions. In other words he started his career by following the method he had learned in Cologne, but soon changed to printing in quaternions. The reasons for this change are not clear, though there are possible practical advantages in using quaternions. But more importantly perhaps quaternions were normally used in English manuscripts of this time. With some of his texts there is an unusual gathering at the beginning. Thus *Eneydos* has the collation $A^4 A3^2 B–L^8$. The first six sheets ($A^4 A3^2$) contain the prologue and the table of contents. No doubt the signature letter 'A' was left free and the material for it was printed at the end, presumably because Caxton had not yet written the prologue. As there was more material than could be accommodated in a quaternion, the edition came to have a confused initial signature. A similar explanation may apply to the *Siege of Jerusalem, Knight of the Tower* and many other texts. Another text with an unusual collation is the *Nova Rhetorica* by Traversagni. As this text was apparently seen through the press by the author, the arrangement here could reflect his whim rather than Caxton's practice. Some composite texts have a mixture of signatures. The *Book of Divers Ghoostly Matters,* which contains the three texts *Horologium Sapientiae, The Twelve Profits of Tribulation* and the *Rule of St Benedict,* has the collation $A–M^8$, $A–D^8$, $a–b^8 c^4$. The three dif-ferent collations correspond to the three texts. They were no doubt set up separately and may originally have been intended for separate publication. But then before they were issued, they were linked together and a table of contents included at the end. In the case of the composite volume *Of Old Age* only the first of the three texts has an individual collation. Conversely when several texts are in one volume with a uniform collation, as is true of some of the Chaucerian texts printed by Caxton, it is probable that all the poems in a given volume were found together in the manuscript that was used as the copytext. The occurrence of these texts together does not reflect editorial activity on Cax-ton's part, but merely reflects what had already been united by someone else. But another volume of Chaucer presents an interesting problem. The second edition of the *Canterbury Tales* printed about 1483 has the collation $a–t^8 v^6 aa–hh^8 ii^6 A–K^8 L^4$. It has what would be three normal collations if they were not all in the same text, for there are three groups each with a different signature letter (lower case, double lower case and

fayn wolde I satysfye euery man/ and so to doo toke an olde
boke and redde therin/and certaynly the englysshe was so ru
de andbrood that I coude not wele vnderstande it.And also
my lorde abbot of westmynster ded do shewe to me late certayn euydences wryton in olde englysshe for to reduce it in to
our englysshe now vsid/And certaynly it was wreton in
suche wyse that it was more lyke to dutche than englysshe
I coude not reduce ne brynge it to be vnderstonden/And certaynly our langage now vsed varyeth ferre from that.Whi-
che was vsed and spoken whan I was borne/ffor we englysshe men/ben borne vnder the domynacyon of the mone.
Whiche is neuer stedfaste/but euer wauerynge/wexynge o-
ne season/ and waneth & dyscreaseth another season/And
that comyn englysshe that is spoken in one shyre varyeth
from a nother.In so moche that in my dayes happened that
certayn marchauntes were in a ship in tamyse for to haue
sayled ouer the see into zelande/and for lacke of wynde thei
taryed atte forlond.and wente to lande for to refresshe them
And one of theym named sheffelde a mercer cam in to an
howes and axed for mete .and specyally he axyd after eggys
And the goode wyf answerde.that she coude speke no frenshe . And the marchaut was angry.for he also coude speke
no frensshe. but wolde haue hadde egges/ and she vnderstode
hym not/ And thenne at laste a nother sayd that he wolde
haue eyren/then the good wyf sayd that she vnderstod hym
wel/Loo what sholde a man in thyse dayes now wryte.eg-
ges or eyren/ certaynly it is harde to playse euery man/ by
cause of dyuersite & chauge of langage .For in these dayes
euery man that is in ony reputacyon in his countre.wyll vt
ter his comynycacyon and maters in suche maners & ter-
mes/that fewe men shall vnderstonde theym/ And som ho-

capital) and each finishing with a gathering which is less than a quaternion. Since the compositors of the second edition were working from the first printed edition and since the text was a poetic one which could easily be broken down into the requisite pages of type, the most reasonable explanation of the collation of the second edition is that there were three presses working on it at the same time. Each press with its own compositors was given a section of text and a different kind of signature letter to use. If this did happen, it is the only direct evidence we have that Caxton used more than one press, though by this date they need not all have been in his own shop. This example shows how detailed study of Caxton's texts may help us to understand the organisation of his shop and the methods he used.

Not all of Caxton's books were printed in folio. He also issued some in quarto, by which a sheet has two folds and produces four pages or eight sides of printed text. As a general rule works of a religious nature are printed in this format, as are small volumes of poetry and books of a more technical nature. Thus all editions of the *Horae*, the *Ordinale*, the *Psalter*, *Ars Moriendi*, the *Fifteen Oes*, the *Book of Divers Ghostly Matters*, and the *Festum Transfigurationis* and *Festum Visitationis* are in quarto, though the *Directorium Sacerdotum*, the *Art of Dieing* and *Quattuor Sermones* are in folio. Poetic texts in quarto include *Anelida and Arcite*, *Parliament of Fowls*, *Book of Courtesy*, *Churl and Bird*, *Horse, Sheep and Goose*, *Stans Puer*, *Temple of Glass*, and the first two editions of *Cato* but not the third. The third edition was printed in two different types and also contained woodcuts, so that Caxton may have felt the larger format more suitable. Some short poetic texts, like the *Moral Proverbs* translated by Earl Rivers, are printed in folio, though whether this is to make them seem grander and hence a more fitting monument for the translator is not clear. The remaining texts in quarto are those of a more technical nature like *Sex Epistolae* and *Governal of Health*. The two texts which occur in sizes that are unexpected are the *Order of Chivalry*, the only book of a courtly nature to be in quarto, and the *Life of St Winifred*, which is in folio. It is difficult to think of any reason to account for the size of the first book; the second may have appeared in folio because though a short text it was associated with the *Golden Legend* and was not looked upon as a service book. In most respects, though, Caxton simply followed tradition in choosing the format of his books, since most manuscripts in the fifteenth century were in folio except service books and books of a technical nature.

The materials needed to make paper were few and easily available, so that it is perhaps surprising that the earliest reference to papermaking in England is John Tate's mill of the 1490s. Tate, a mercer, established his mill at Hertford and it is mentioned by de Worde in his edition of the English version of *De Proprietatibus Rerum* (*c.* 1495), who no doubt purchased paper from Tate; but his mill seems not to have flourished. There is no evidence that Caxton bought English paper, and most of the watermarks in his books are those used by Continental papermakers; he apparently satisfied his needs by importing paper. It is worth remarking therefore that the size of paper in his books printed in Bruges is a little different from that found in the Westminster ones. The former all measure approximately 185 × 130 cm, whereas the latter are a little taller and narrower, about 190 × 120 cm. Three books alone are larger than this: *Golden Legend* (269 × 165 cm), *Confessio Amantis* (218 × 151 cm) and *Vocabulary* (211 × 149 cm). The first two are particularly long books and the first with its extremely large pages may have been intended for use at a lectern or reading desk. All three are printed in double columns, though they are not the only texts to have this feature. Presumably a single line of text stretching across such a wide page would not be attractive and so he used double columns for *Golden Legend*. *Confessio Amantis* is a poetic text and the size of page may have been determined by the need to accommodate two columns per page. The *Vocabulary*, which is a kind of phrase book with a column of French text and a parallel column of English translation, falls naturally into two columns and so again would need wide paper. Its size does, however, make it too large to carry about, and it is less practical than the text books in quarto.

Apart from paper, vellum was also available as a suitable material to make books out of, though it was more expensive. But with some indulgences the only extant Caxton book on vellum is a copy of the *Doctrinal of Sapience*. This copy contains a chapter on the misdemeanours at mass not found in the other copies and it would seem as though it was meant for clerical use only. So in this case the use of vellum may have been designed for long life or it may even reflect the traditional use of vellum in ecclesiastical books. It is surprising that no vellum copies of any courtly texts are extant and this suggests that Caxton did not produce a few de luxe examples of a text on vellum in addition to the paper copies, as some printers did. It may be that his presentation copies were handwritten manuscripts, like the Caxton Ovid, rather than printed copies on vellum.

❡ Here begynneth a lytyll treatyſe ſchortely
compyled and called ars moriendi/that is
to ſaye the craft for to deye for the helthe of
mannes ſowle.

When ony of lyklyhode ſhal deye/thenne
is moſte neceſſarye to haue a ſpecyall
frende/the whiche wyll hertly helpe and praye
for hym ⁊ therwyth counſeyll the ſyke for the
wele of his ſowle/⁊ more ouer to ſee that alle
other ſo do aboute hym/or ellys quyckly for to
make hem departe. ❡ Thenne is to be remem
bred the grete benefyctes of god done for hym
vnto that tyme/and ſpecyally of þ paſſyon of
our lorde/and thenne is to be rede ſomme ſtory
of ſayntes or the vij pſalmes wyth þ letanye
or our lady pſalter in parte or hole wyth other
And euer the ymage of the crucyfyxe is to be
hadde in his ſyght wyth other. And holy wa
ter is oftymes to be caſt vpon and aboute hym
for auoydyng of euyll ſpirytes þ whiche thene
be full redy to take theyr auauntage of the
ſowle yf they may. ❡ And thenne and euer
make hym crye for mercy and grace ⁊ for the

A j

The watermarks in the paper used by Caxton are those associated with Continental mills. In general a printer bought as much paper as he needed for a book before he started printing and when there is a difference in the watermarks a special explanation may be sought. Thus the *History of Troy,* the first book Caxton printed, has at first paper with the shield of France watermark, but the later sheets have either unicorns or bulls which can be identified with marks originating from Troyes. In this case we can assume that as it was the first book he printed he miscalculated how much paper he would need and ran out of the first lot during the course of printing. When only a single sheet contains a different watermark, the usual explanation will be that it is part of some sheets left over as surplus from the previous book which were added to the new stock. This explanation would apply to *Reynard the Fox,* in which all copies have sheets with the shears-type mark except one sheet of the Pierpont Morgan copy which has the hand with fleur-de-lis mark. Allan Stevenson, who made extensive studies of paper, has shown that the printers used the same sort of paper as the manuscript makers; a special paper was not produced for printed books. Thus the unicorn mark in Caxton's *Siege of Jerusalem, Description of Britain* and second edition of *Chronicles of England* is identical with that found in contemporary manuscripts. Most of this paper came from Normandy, though it may well have been shipped first to Bruges before coming to England. It is possible that further investigation of watermarks will help us to date Caxton's works more closely. Thus the banded unicorn found in Caxton's *Jason* is found there for the first time in a printed book, and as we learn more about papermakers and their marks we may learn how and where Caxton acquired his paper. His first editions of *Churl and Bird, Horse, Sheep and Goose* and *Canterbury Tales* all have the same watermark, a pair of unicorns of which one is fat and the other lean, which has been attributed to Essones near Paris. All these texts are undated though they belong to the first period following Caxton's return to England. As they are all printed on paper from the same mill, it is likely that they were printed one after the other from the same batch of paper. Among other things this information tells us that the second editions of the first two works, which are also early but undated, were not produced immediately after the first editions.

As we have seen, the printed texts were arranged into gatherings which were then bound together. To make sure that the sheets were in the correct order some indication had to be pro-

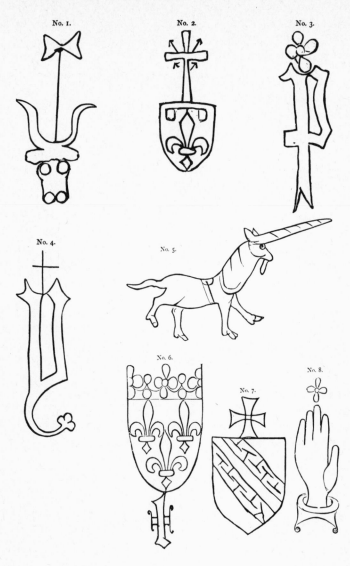

32. Some watermarks

vided for the binder. In manuscripts catchwords were frequently used, that is the scribe wrote in the bottom margin of the page he had just completed the first one or two words which were to follow at the top of the next page. The binder simply had to marry these words to be certain the order of pages was correct. Caxton never used catchwords in his books, though his successors were to do so. At first his books contained no sign for the binder as to the right order of the pages. The first dated book to use signatures is the first edition of the *Chronicles of England* printed on 10 June 1480. Caxton probably adopted the use of signatures from Continental books where the system was well established. Although he printed the *Description of Britain* on 18 August 1480 without signatures, by 1481 they had become a standard feature of his books so that any without them must be dated before then. The normal method of signatures was that each gathering is indicated by a separate letter and each page within a gathering by that letter and a separate number. If the first gathering is designated 'a', then the first page will be 'a1', the second 'a2', and so on. But as, for example, a quaternion consists of four sheets which are folded to give sixteen pages, it was necessary only to indicate the order of the first four recto pages for all sixteen to be in the correct order. Caxton's system of signatures shows some developments over the years.

In the first book with signatures, the *Chronicles of England*, they consist of lower-case letters and Arabic numerals. Other books of about the same time, such as the third edition of *Cato*, have lower-case letters with Roman numerals. The use of lower-case letters with Arabic numerals is confined to five books from the period 1480–81 and it was then abandoned in favour of lower-case letters with Roman numerals. But in 1481 the *Siege of Jerusalem* contains yet a different system, for only Arabic numerals are used for the signatures. The first gathering is designated '1', so the first page is '1.1', the second '1.2', and so on. The same system is found in *Polychronicon*, printed in 1482. These are the only two texts with this numerical system. It is possible that these differing systems indicate experiments or that they are the marks of different compositors before finally a house style with lower-case letters and Roman numerals prevailed. This latter alternative is supported by the emergence of a new type of signature about 1489 as though it was the sign of a new compositor. From that date as many books appear with signatures composed of capitals as with those of lower-case letters. Since so many of Caxton's later books are undated it is not certain which is the first to use the signatures with capitals, but it may well be the *Feats of Arms* from 14 July 1489. A text worth remarking in this connexion is the *Book of Divers Ghoostly Matters* which we have already noted consists of three different texts each with its own signature. The first two of these texts have signatures with capitals and the latter signatures with lower-case letters. These lower-case signatures are themselves unusual in that the pages of the first gathering, for example, are marked aa, aii, aiiii respectively. It does look as though two compositors were responsible for setting up this text.

Naturally when a book was so long that the alphabet was exhausted, the lower-case type gave way to an alphabet of capitals or of double lower-case letters. In some texts the ampersand is used to follow 'z', and the *Golden Legend* even includes the abbreviation '9' (*con-*) as a signature sign.

Of course such signatures were for the convenience of the binder, not the reader. Although some fifteenth-century manuscripts contained foliation or pagination, Caxton rarely numbered his pages. Indeed only five texts, all in the period late 1482 to early 1484, have their pages numbered—they are *Polychronicon, Pilgrimage of the Soul, Confessio Amantis, Golden Legend* and *Aesop*. All are in type 4 or 4* and followed one another quite quickly. Three of them are long texts and contain indices for which foliation was of course essential. The indices at the beginning of each text have irregular signatures and were clearly added after the rest of the text was in print. These pages are not numbered, the foliation beginning with the first page of text. The case of *Confessio Amantis* is interesting since it looks like an experimental volume. The first quaternion which contains the index was printed last and has a different signature from the rest of the book. The next gathering, the first to be printed, has no signatures, but the folios are numbered. The third gathering, the second to be printed, has no folio numbers, but it has the signature 'b'. The succeeding gatherings have both signatures and folio numbers. William Blades is probably correct in his assumption that as the book was going to have folio numbering the compositor thought signatures unnecessary, and that when he realised that signatures were needed he dropped the folio numbers instead. It was only after these attempts that he was persuaded to include both. This example shows that the compositors were not used to dealing with page numbers. In all these books the foliation is very erratic and was probably added by the compositor as he went along. Neither the *Pilgrimage of the Soul* nor *Aesop* is a large book by Caxton's standards. That both have numbers can be explained only by the particular date at which they were printed, for many larger books printed later, such as *King Arthur*, have no folio numbers. It seems as though numbering was adopted for the sake of the indices and was then extended to other books being issued at that time. But it was evidently inconvenient for the compositors to number the pages, for they were not set up in strict order, and so the system was abandoned. The convenience of the readers was evidently not considered.

Another experiment which was also to be abandoned was started about this time. As we have seen, some texts have two columns of type per page. This is essential in the *Vocabulary*, which has parallel columns of French and English, and is necessary in *Confessio Amantis* to prevent the book from becoming too unwieldy. But three prose texts use double columns as well. In the *Golden Legend* it was adopted because the size of the paper would have made a single column of type too ugly. But two other texts, both printed in December 1485, use double columns; they are *Charles the Great* and *Paris and Vienne*. These texts use the normal folio size of paper and are courtly works like so many others produced by Caxton. There would seem to be no reason why they were treated separately unless they are the evidence of experimentation by a particular compositor which was soon halted. Double columns were commonly found in manuscripts and they were to be used by de Worde frequently, so there were plenty of models available. The second edition of Mirk's *Festial* and the third edition of *Quattuor Sermones*, which are attributed to Caxton though they must date from the last year of his life, also have double columns. They are thus very similar to many of the texts which de Worde was to print immediately after his master's death, for *The Chastising of God's Children*, *A Treatise of Love* and *The Life of St Katherine* are all set in double columns. This spate of books produced in this way indicates that it was Caxton himself who preferred single columns and insisted on them for his books. When he died this restraint was removed and different layouts were tried.

The type used by the early printers is naturally one of the most conspicuous features of their books. As a general rule it may be said that the early typesetters imitated the scripts fashionable at the end of the fifteenth century not only in the shape of the letters but also in the number of sorts or different letter forms and combinations. By this time calligraphy was an old-established art which had developed conventions of its own. Most of these were taken over by the typefounders and only gradually abandoned as it was realised that type could be set up more efficiently without them. The need to let the pen run along without being lifted from the page too often had produced different letter forms and a variety of double and triple letters. Thus in some scripts 'r' was shaped like *r* or like z according to its position in the word, the latter being more frequent at the end of the an hous there as is a corps and wepyng thā to go to an hous the re as is grete reuel & moche myr the for suche thiges make a man to forȝete his god & himself both But there as is a sight of a corse maketh a man to thinke on his deth/that is the special thynge to put away sinne & vanyte of the worlde/For salamon sayth thus to his sone. Fili memorare no uissia tua.& ineternū nō peccab. Sone haue in thy mynde that ȳ shall deye & thou shall neuer sin ne dedely. thus holy chirche hauȳ ge grete compassiō of her childrē ordeyneth in maner of salues to helpe and to hele her childern that ken to thynke on dethe inwardly to labour besily / and to chastyse the body resonably/the first is to thynke on deth iwardly.holy chir che peuyth ensaple this day in the office of the masse Circūdederūt me /the siknes of deth hath biclip ped me/thus saith he techyng eue ry good childe to haue in mynde how harde he is bestad wyth deth on eche side/ in somoche ȳ he maye not scape noo way/ but euer deth sueth hym with a bow drawen & an arow euer therin redy to shote hym/ he wote neuer what tyme ȳ this is a pryncipall salue to eue

ry man ȳ taketh it to herte to put away al maner of vanyte and vayne myrthe/But for to vnder stonde this the better I shew this by ensample /

¶ Narracio

¶ I rede of a kynge that e uer was in heuy sorowe. and he wolde neuer laughe ne make me ry chere/but euer was in mornȳ ge and in heuynes. therfore hys meyny & all other men were gre ued. therwith thei yede to the kin gis broder / prayng hym to speke to the kynge/and sayd he greued all thoo that were aboute hym wyth his heuy chere/and counsep led hym to leue it and make lig hte chere in tyme cōmyng/Theke was this kynge wyse and tho ught to chastyse his broder by a wyle and wrothly bad hym goo home and do that he had to do. Thenne was the maner of the countrey that whan a man shold be done to deth/sholde come trom pettes and trompe afore his gate . Thenne sayd the kynge byd dynge theym goo trompe afore his broders gate. and men goo wyth theym to areste hym/ and brynge hym byfore the kynge/and in the meane while . the kynge

33. Caxton's second edition of the 'Festial'

fee that thou be compelled by do/
me/ and that it be right. not for
enupe loue nor drede . but oonly
for rightwysnese in declarynge
of trouth. and yf ony ony of thi/
se fayle it is periury. beware ther/
fore ye that vse questis or consil/
tory & bereth what parcel ye ston/
de in/ that wyttyngly be forswor/
re on the boke. The boke betoke/
neth all holy scrypture & the suf/
fragies of the chirche / the whi/
che there thou forsakest whan þ
forswerpst the/thy hondis al the
good werkes þ euer thou dides
&/þ whiche thou forsakest whā
thou wythdrawest it/ thou for/
sakest also god almighty.our la
dy saynt mary/al the saynces of
heuen/and the merites of the ho/
ly sacrament .and hooly betakest
thyselfe to the deuyll of hell / but
thou amende the or thou goost
hens/If they thenne shold be puny
shed thus for swezing.how shal
they be that blaspheme & dysmē
bre hym. swerynge by his herte.
naylkes woundes.& suche other/fo
me whan they ben repreued herof
sayne / It is good to haue god
in mynde/ and wyth suche lewd/
nes they kepen styll their othes/
And thy seruaunt dyde ayenste

thy byddyng/sayeng that he dide
it to haue þ in mynde/wolde thou
not be wrothe wyth hym. moche
must more god thā with þ/whā
thou dost ayenst his byddynge
and some sape.I may well swe/
re/for I swere soth/this is a fal/
se excusacōn For & thou sholdest
swere allwaye whan thou saydste
sothe/ thenne wold not crist haue
forbede swerynge/but for in mo/
che swerynge.is ofte forsweryng
Therfore he sayth . he that moche
swereth/shal be replete wyth wy/
kedncs & sorow. ne vengaunce
shall not departe from his hous
Some sayn also that noo man
wyll byleue theim.But they swe/
re/ this is a subtyll excusacōn
For therbi a fals man may swe/
re as wel as a true man. and so
sholo be as wel be byleued as the
true man/ For the falser he is/the
more he swereth and forswereth
& foo bekplith. Therfore yf thou
wylt be byleued wyth oute ony
sweryng/be true of thy worde &
lete it be/ye ye/and nay nay. In
token that thou sayst wyth thy
mouth.thou sholdest say it wyth
thi hert/and not say one & thinke
a nother/ The thirde is/haue in
mynde to halow thy holy dayes

word. Even today people are familiar with the long and short forms of 's' from seventeenth- and eighteenth-century texts. When they occurred finally some letters developed a flourish in manuscripts and these flourishes were reproduced in early type so that there were different forms of 'd', with or without a flourish. Some double letter forms are still found in modern type, particularly 'fi'. This means that the compositor has a single piece of type with 'fi' on it, instead of choosing two pieces one with 'f' and another with 'i'. In early type these double letter forms were far more frequent. It was also common in manuscripts, particularly those used in the liturgy or which contained Latin texts, to introduce a great variety of abbreviations. No doubt the original reason had been to cram as much text as possible into a line so that the vellum, which was expensive, could be used as economically as possible. Although with the more wide-spread use of paper such economy was not strictly necessary, many abbreviations had become so traditional that they were still employed in many manuscripts and some were taken over by the early printers. But like his fellow printers Caxton employed few abbreviations in his vernacular texts. Nevertheless his type contained many letter forms with different marks of abbreviation. Of these the superior stroke indicating the omission of a letter, usually a nasal, was the most common, and all his type contained vowels with and without the superior stroke.

The result is that a Caxton fount may contain as many as 250 sorts, and some of them contained more. In type 2, for example, there were the following sorts associated with the letter 's'. There are the long and the short forms of the lower-case letter as well as the upper-case form. The double and triple letter forms, all made with long 's' since the short form was used only finally, include *sa, sc, se, sf, sh, sl, so, sp, st, su, ss, ssa, sse, ssi, sso* and *ssu*. Some letter forms may not have been regarded as signifi-cant and so they may have been kept together in the same box. Thus some of Caxton's types have two forms of 'a', one with a medial bar as in the type of this book and one without as in the handwriting of most people today. It cannot be shown that the compositors used these forms in different words or in different places in individual words. But the various forms of 's', 'r' and 'd', for instance, which were used in different places, were presumably stored separately. All this means that the com-positor of Caxton's day would have had a tray of type in front of him which had at least 250 compartments, each one of which held a separate piece of type. When one considers how small

A	B	C	D	E	F	G	H	J	K	L	M	N	O	P	Q	R	S	T	V
ā	b̄	c̄	dξ	ē	fa	g	ħ	J	k	la	m	η	ō	p	q	r	ſa	ta	v
ãõ	ba	ca	ð	ee	fe	ᵷ	ha	ī	j	le	m̄	ñ	œ	p	q̄	ꝛ	ſe	te	ū
1	be	cc	da	ei	fi	ffl	he	ü	ÿ	ti	mi	ŋ̃	°	p̄	ꝗ	ꝛ̣	ſe	th	9
2	bo	ce	de	en	fl	ffo	ho	in	im	ll	lo	ni	·	ṗ	ꝙ	ra	ſh	ti	va
3	bꝛ	ai	do	eɲ	fo	ffu		iɲ	iɲ	tt	lu	nu	/	p̄	ꝙ̄	re	ſi	to	ve
4		co	dꝛ	er	fr		b	c	d	e	i	f	s	:	pa	ꝗ̇	ri	ſl	tr	vo
5		cr	W	et	fu										pe	un	ro	ſo	tu	ſſ
6	Y	ct	w	eu	ff		m	n	y	o	a	h	ſ	/	po	wꝛ	rr	ſu	ſſi	ſſa
7	X	cu	wa	ex	ffa										pp		ru	ſſu	ſſo	ſſe
8	x	Z	we	eʒ	ffe		u	r	t	l	En Quads and Spaces				ẙ	&	¶		Em Quads	
9	O	ʒ	wo	e	ffi									·	yᵗ	ÿ	⸗			

35. A suggested layout of a compositor's case

the individual pieces of type were and how dirty they must have been after they had been inked many times, it is hardly surprising that when a page of type was broken down some sorts ended up in the wrong compartment. This would naturally mean that when the next page of type was set up there would be typographical mistakes from the faulty distribution of the type as well as possibly from the compositor putting his hand into the wrong compartment. It is amazing not that there are typographical mistakes in incunabula, but that there are so few of them.

The shape, size and number of sorts distinguish one set of type from another. It is now usual to divide Caxton's types into ten groups numbered from 1 to 8, but groups 2 and 4 each has a variant set labelled respectively 2* and 4*. The sets 2* and 4* were recastings of 2 and 4, but they do not always contain the same letter forms and double letters. It is possible to divide these ten sets of type into two major groupings according to the style of the handwriting which is imitated. The larger group consists of those sets modelled on the Flemish bâtarde script, that form of the Bastard Secretary hand predominant in Flanders at this time. Types 1, 2, 2*, 4, 4* and 6 are based on this script. These types were used by Caxton for his courtly books whether in prose or verse and are thus found in the greater part of his output. The smaller group, consisting of types 3, 5, 7 and 8, are lettre de forme types which resemble the Gothic script of the Mainz printers rather than the Flemish scripts, though the latter three are more English than German in their affiliation. None of these types was used frequently and indeed Blades, the great nineteenth-century biographer and bibliographer of Caxton, failed to recognise types 7 and 8. These four types were for the most part confined to headings in courtly books and to religious and grammatical works. Type 3, for example, was used in a complete work only in the *Ordinale* (with the *Advertisement*), the *Psalter* and the second edition of the *Horae*, though it was also used for the chapter-headings in such works as the *Boethius* and the *Golden Legend*. Type 5, on the other hand, was used in three books translated by Caxton, the *Doctrinal of Sapience*, the *Book of Good Manners* and the *Royal Book*. While three texts are not very many, nevertheless that he did use this type for them suggests that in later life he may have overcome his prejudice against non-Flemish scripts for courtly literature. Type 5 was principally used for religious texts as in the third and fourth editions of the *Horae* and both editions of the *Speculum Vitae Christi*. The final two types were used infrequently. Type 7 occurs only in two indulgences and type 8 was used only for the Latin quotations and for the headings in several books produced right at the end of Caxton's career.

One has only to notice how frequently some of the *bâtarde* types were used to realise how popular this script was with Caxton as compared with the *lettres de forme*. Thus type 2 was used for the following: *Cordial* (French text), *Dicts or Sayings* (first edition), *Moral Proverbs, Boethius, Book of Courtesy, Cato* (two editions), *Canterbury Tales* (first edition), *Anelida and Arcite, Parliament of Fowls, Horae* (first edition), *Infantia Salvatoris, Jason, Churl and Bird* (two editions), *Horse, Sheep and Goose* (two editions), *Stans Puer, The Temple of Glass* and John Russell's *Propositio*. That the French version of the *Cordial* was printed in type 2 shows that he had acquired this type before he came back to England, and as no books printed in England used type 1 it is accepted that he had disposed of this type while still in Bruges.

Type 3 was almost certainly acquired by Caxton while he was in Bruges, for it is used for seven letters of the indulgence discovered by A. W. Pollard. Since this indulgence contains the date 13 December 1476 written in by hand, it must have been printed before then. The indulgence was certainly printed at Westminster and was no doubt one of the first things, if not the very first, printed by Caxton after he had set up his workshop there. The rest of the indulgence is printed in type 2. So probably both types 2 and 3 were acquired by Caxton in Bruges and brought

Epitaphiũ Galfridi Chaucer.per
poetam laureatũ Stephauũ surigonũ
Mediolanenſẽ in decretis licenciatũ

P   perides muse ſi poſſunt numina flct9
        Fũdere.diuinas atqʒ rigare genas
Galfridi vatis chaucer crudelia fata
    Plangite.ſit lacrimis abſtinuiſſe nephas
Uos coluit viuẽs.at vos celebrate ſepultum
    Reddatur merito gracia digna viro
Grande decus vobis.ẽ docti muſa maronis
    Qua didicit iheli9 lingua latina loqui
Grande nouũ qʒ dec9 Chaucer.famãqʒ pauit
    Heu qʒtum fuerat priſca britãna rudis
Reddidit inſignem maternis verſibʒ.vt iam
    Aurea ſplendeſcat.ferrea facta prius
Hunc latuiſſe virũ nil.ſi tot opuſcula vertes
    Dixeris.egregiis que decorata modis
Socratis ingenuum.vel fontes philoſophie
    Quitquid ʒ archaini dogmata ſacra ferunt
Et qʒcunqʒ velis tenuit digniſſimus artes
    Hic vates.puo conditus hoc tumulo
Ah laudis qʒtum preclara britannia perdis
    Dum rapuit tantũ mors odioſa virum
Crudeles parce.crudelia fila ſorores
    Non tamen extincto corpore.fama perit
Uiuet ineternum.viuẽt dum ſcripta poete
    Uiuant eterno tot monimenta die
Si qua bonos tangit pietas.ſi carmie dign9

back by him to England. The seven letters in type 3 in this indulgence, namely '[I]Ohannes', were used to make the name more prominent and suggest that from the very beginning Caxton intended to use this *lettre de forme* type only for occasional use, such as headings and quotations. Thus the first edition of the *Horae* is printed in a *bâtarde* type, even though he already had type 3. But the second, third and fourth editions are in *lettres de forme*. Possibly Caxton, whose principal affection seems to have been for the *bâtarde* script, responded to conventions then current in England by producing liturgical and technical books in a different script, and it may be that books printed in *lettres de forme* were intended for a different audience. It seems likely that all texts printed in a *bâtarde* type were regarded as courtly by Caxton, even though some of them might seem to us to be more in the nature of religious works. Thus it is natural that the *Fifteen Oes*, a series of Brigittine prayers, was printed in *bâtarde* type since the book had been requested by Henry VII's wife and his mother. Similarly the *Art of Dieing*, which was translated by Caxton, may have been considered more as a consolatory text to be read by aristocrats and merchants than as a religious text for clerical use, for it too has a *bâtarde* script. The *Life of Saint Winifred* is in type 4* and is thus to be equated with the *Golden Legend*, also in type 4*, rather than with the liturgical and narrowly religious books; and we may remember that the *Golden Legend* was issued under the patronage of the Earl of Arundel. On the other hand, a text which was printed in *lettres de forme* should not necessarily be considered religious. The reason for this may simply have been that as his output consisted mainly of courtly texts rather than of religious books, there would be times when he had spare *lettre de forme* type, whereas the reverse is not likely to have happened. Let us consider the case of type 5. It was in use for religious and technical texts not later than 1486, though it could have been available earlier. Thus the translation of the *Royal Book* was finished on 13 September 1484. Because it is in type 5 most bibliographers consider that it was not printed until about 1487, because they feel type 5 was not available until 1486, even though a delay of this length between translation and printing cannot be proved for any other of Caxton's works. But 1484 and 1485 were busy years for the press and many books were issued at that time. So it may be that type 5 was used, which would mean that all the available courtly *bâtarde* type was already committed to other works. Thus although a courtly text, necessity may have made it appear in *lettres de forme.* The *Book of Good Manners* was printed on 11 May 1487 and the other courtly book issued in type 5, the *Doctrinal of Sapience*, was translated only on 7 May 1489 and so cannot have been published till late that year at the earliest. This staggering of courtly books in this type does suggest an occasional use forced on the printer by the pressure of circumstances. Although intended for headings and for religious and technical books, type 5 was used for courtly works whenever all his *bâtarde* type was committed to works already in hand.

It is generally accepted that to start with Caxton did not make type in his own workshop, but bought his sets of type from a supplier. When Caxton went to Cologne in 1471 to learn how to print, it is assumed he acquired a press and type while there which he then transported to Bruges. We know from Wynkyn de Worde, his foreman, that he assisted at the printing of the *De Proprietatibus Rerum* by Bartholomaeus Anglicus in Cologne. This was issued by the printer who is referred to by modern bibliographers as the Printer of the Flores Sancti Augustini from one of the works he printed. The evidence now indicates that this printer was Johan Veldener. Veldener came from Würzburg in Southern Germany. The first text which can definitely be assigned to him is the *Lis Belial* printed in Louvain, for the writer of the preface of that work, Gervinus Cruse, mentions the printer and refers to the date 7 August 1474. So this book was presumably printed towards the end of 1474 in Louvain, in whose University Veldener had enrolled as a medical student on 30 July 1473. However, an edition of Boccaccio's *Genealogia Deorum* which was formerly attributed to the Printer of the Flores Sancti Augustini at Cologne is now thought on the basis of its paper and type also to have been printed in Louvain by Veldener between 30 July 1473 and the publication of the *Lis Belial* in 1474. But since the *Genealogia Deorum* is almost certainly the work of the Printer of the Flores Sancti Augustini, the only possible conclusion is that Veldener was a printer at Cologne (indeed the Printer of the Flores Sancti Augustini) before he moved to Louvain and that it was from him that Caxton acquired not only the knowledge of how to print but also the necessary equipment for printing such as the press and type. Shortly after Caxton left Cologne in 1472, Veldener himself left and went to Louvain to start printing there. So it may well be that Veldener rather than Caxton was the first printer in the Low Countries.

Besides being a printer Veldener was a typecutter. He certainly supplied Caxton with his types 2 and 3, for he himself used these types in his own printed works as well, and so there is every reason to suppose that he likewise supplied him with his type 1. Veldener's move to Louvain would explain the hitherto puzzling fact that Caxton should have gone there rather than back to Cologne for his second and third sets of type. Type 2 was in fact based on the typical Bruges book-hand of the late fifteenth century and it has been called 'the book-hand of the Burgundian literature of the day'. Its attraction for Caxton lay in these associations. Veldener also supplied others besides Caxton with type, notably the Brothers of the Common Life who set up a press in Brussels in 1475. In both cases it is probable that Veldener advised his clients on the running of a workshop as well as providing them with the necessary equipment. It certainly seems as though Veldener may be the key to several of the puzzling features of the development of printing in the Low Countries.

While it may be taken as proved that Veldener supplied Caxton with his first three types, there is no evidence that the two men had any dealings after Caxton's return to England, though it remains possible that they did remain in touch. But Caxton's type 2* is thought to have been made from matrices formed from trimmed-up letters of type 2 and this work would almost certainly have been carried out in England, probably at Caxton's shop. It is interesting to note that types 2 and 2* are never used in the same texts and were never mixed together. This may be explained by the hypothesis that the original type was destroyed in forming the matrices for the new type. This explanation, however, seems insufficient since some of the sorts in 2 are not found in 2*. So it may be that the compositors thought of them as separate and so kept them distinct. Type 6 is also a modified version of type 2 and it too may have been made in England. Type 4, on the other hand, is a completely new set of type which was cast afresh. William Blades was of the opinion that the same hand which cut type 2 also cut type 4, for type 4 is also a Flemish *bâtarde*, although smaller than that of type 2. If Blades is right, then Caxton purchased type 4 from Veldener as well. This is quite likely, for during his various moves around the Low Countries Veldener continued to supply type to various printers there as well as to London printers such as Machlinia. Type 4* is a recasting of type 4 on a larger body, and this again was probably done in England like type 2*. So the pattern which emerges is that when Caxton wanted a completely new set of type he went to a supplier on the Continent, either Veldener or someone else. But otherwise he made running modifications and improvements to those sets of type he already had in his own workshop.

One further point that has to be considered in relation to the types used by Caxton is whether the books can be dated from the type. In this connexion we should remember that the type represented an important capital investment which was too valuable for the printer simply to throw away. Usually the type would be sold to another printer, remodelled or put on one side. Thus Wynkyn de Worde, who inherited Caxton's workshop, used Caxton's types 3, 4*, 6, 7 and 8 in his printed works from 1491 onwards. Although there is no evidence that Caxton himself used type 3 after 1484, it was evidently put to one side and stored. It was thus available for Wynkyn de Worde when he took over the business. So unless there is evidence to suggest that a type was disposed of or remodelled, it is dangerous to assume that it was not used by an individual printer after a given date. The evidence of the type by itself is not sufficient proof for dating. On the other hand, it is sometimes possible to say that a certain type was not used before a certain date. Even this cannot usually be posited with confidence since our knowledge of when the type was acquired is often so uncertain. Thus we now think that Caxton acquired his type 3 while he was in Bruges. But until A. W. Pollard discovered the 1476 indulgence, the first dated text using type 3 came only from 1479, though it may have been used in undated texts before then. It was natural before the discovery of the indulgence to assume that type 3 was acquired by Caxton in England, and possibly only shortly before his use of it in 1479. In other words a set of type was available to Caxton from 1476, but it seems to have been used infrequently for the first two or three years. Because of this infrequent use, without the indulgence we would certainly want to date works in type 3 later than they are now dated.

The reason for the infrequent use of type 3 at the beginning may be attributable to Caxton's attitude towards different sorts of handwriting. Type 3 is a *lettre de forme* type and Caxton evidently preferred the Flemish *bâtarde* script. It may be that he wanted his courtly clientele to identify his printed works with the fashionable Flemish handwriting rather than with the traditional ecclesiastical hands. It is interesting to note that when Wynkyn de Worde inherited Caxton's workshop and type, he took over two *bâtarde* types, 4* and 6, as well as three *lettre de forme* types, 3, 7 and 8. But he used types 4* and 6 only in a few of his early texts. He soon abandoned them and used

¶Here begynneth the lyf of saint
katherin of senis the blessid virgin

¶Andi filia et vide

Ere dou=
ghter & see
fructuous
example
of vertu=
ous liuin
ge to edy=
fycacion of
thy sowle
and to cō=
forte and

encrese of thy gostely labour in all werkis
of pyte: For as I truste by the gracious
yeftes of oure lorde Ihesu / thy wyll is
sette to plese hym and to do hym seruyce
in all holy excercise by the vertue of obe=
dyence vnder counseyll and techinge of
thy gostely gouernours / And for as
moche as I fele by longe experyens the
inward affeccions inclynyng wyth py=
te to comforte of all that haue nede bothe
lyuyng and dede therfore to strengthe &
cōforte of thy wil & of al other of thi gos=
tely susterē whiche our lord hath gracious
ly chose to serue hym nyght & day in pra
yer & meditacion and to laboure bodely in
tyme of nede to socour and helpe of the se
ke and the poure / Here I purpos by
our lordis mercy only in his worshyppe
wyth truste of his grace and leue by hel=
pe of your prayers to translate in eng=
lysshe tongue the legende and the blessid
lyf of an holy mayde and virgyn whiche
was and is callyd Katheryn of sene.
This legende compyled a worshypfull
clerke fryer Reymond of the ordre of sa=
ynt dompnik doctor of deuynyte and cō=
fessour of this holy virgyn / But in this
translacion I leue of the two prologues
whiche in the begynnyng the same clerke

made in latyn. The whiche passeth your
vnderstondyng / And to touch alle ma=
ters only that longeth only to your ler=
nyng by cause that moche maner of her
vertuous lyuyng shall be rehersyd in es=
pecial in chapytres of this boke : Whiche
in generall wordes he toucheth shortly in
his prologue: I leue of also poyntes of
diuynyte whiche passeth your vnderston
dyng & touche only maters y longeth to
your lernyng / Now thā as I saye in the
begynnyng / Here doughter and see what
thou thyrst or redest of this holy mayde &
virgyn. And that thou yeue full creden=
ce to that I shal wryte /   The berypte
may be preuyd wythout ony feynyng bi
scryptures of her confessours and verefy
eng of creatures whiche late lyued in er=
the / Also the vytnes I purpose to put in
at the ende of eche chapytre / as that wor=
shypfull clerke dide /   Whiche compyled
this boke in latyn. Therfore that all our
werke begynne and perfourmed in the
name of the holy trynyte :   This boke
shall be deuyded in thre partyes and eche
parte of the boke shal be departed in to di
uerse chapytres / whiche chapytres been
compyled to gyder in the begynnyng in
manere of a kalendre that ye mowe re=
dely fynde : What matere in the boke ye
desyre to here or rede :
¶The fyrst parte of the boke shal be the
byrth and the holy werkis of that may=
de from her chyldhode and tendre age In
to the time that she was spoused meruey
lously and gracyously to our lord
¶The seconde parte conteyneth the ma=
ner of her conuersacion from the tyme of
her despousacion to our lord. And what
our lord wrought in her in to the tyme y
she passyd out of this world /
¶The thyrde parte shall shewe the pas=
syng out of this world of the same may
de with myracles whiche our lord wrou

a   j

37. De Worde's 'Life of
Saint Katherine'

the *lettre de forme* types instead. What had been occasional type for Caxton became de Worde's principal type. This may be not only because Wynkyn's output was of a more religious nature, but also because his master, who preferred the Flemish handwriting, was no longer there to impose his will on the compositors. For Caxton *lettres de forme* were there for special purposes, such as for ecclesiastical texts and for chapter-headings, and only otherwise for use when the other sets of type were already committed. But this means that this kind of type was used haphazardly and so the dates for its use are less easy to determine. It is for this reason that I suggested earlier that to date the *Royal Book* to 1487 from its type alone is unsatisfactory. Probably when a new *lettre de forme* type was acquired, the old one would have been put to one side; but it does not mean that it would never be used again. Similarly as type of this sort was used only occasionally, it may have been used in an undated printed book two or three years before it is used in a dated one. The dating of the use of the *lettre de forme* type is therefore complicated. I would suggest that type 5 became available about 1484, and was from then on the preferred type for occasional use with the result that type 3 was put aside. Types 7 and 8 became available about 1490, but they did not entirely replace type 5, which continued to be used.

Dating the editions by the use of the *bâtarde* types is less difficult, for these were the types which were in everyday use at the workshop. They were thus worked hard and would ultimately have to be remodelled or replaced as they became worn. Type 2, which was brought back by Caxton from Bruges, was used till about 1479 when it was replaced by type 2*. The last dated text with type 2 is the *Moral Proverbs* printed on 20 February 1478 and the first dated text with type 2* is the English translation of the *Cordial* printed on 24 March 1479. It is reasonable to assume that type 2 was recast as type 2* somewhere between these two dates, and this would mean that all undated texts in type 2 should be placed in the years from 1476 to 1478 and all undated texts in type 2* from 1479 onwards. There is, however, an overlap between type 2* and type 4, the next *bâtarde* script acquired by Caxton. The last dated text in type 2* is *Of Old Age* which was printed on 12 August 1481. The printing of two other books in type 2*, *Reynard the Fox* and *Mirror of the World*, is placed by some bibliographers later than 12 August 1481. But *Reynard the Fox* was certainly printed, and not translated as has been thought, on 6 June 1481 and it seems quite likely that *Mirror of the World*, which was translated on 8 March

1481, was printed immediately before *Reynard the Fox*. But with first dated text to be printed in type 4 is an indulgence with the handwritten date of 31 March 1480, and the first edition of the *Chronicles of England*, also in type 4, appeared on 10 June 1480. In other words Caxton was using both types 2* and 4 in works issued in 1480 and 1481. Type 2* was even used occasionally after 1481, for it is employed in the headings of the second edition of the *Canterbury Tales*, usually dated to 1484 though it may have appeared in 1483. It may be significant that in a book of this importance he decided to revive a *bâtarde* type for his headings instead of using type 3, the *lettre de forme* type which was available and probably in rather better condition. Type 2* was not disposed of after the printing of *Of Old Age* and so it is possible that some undated texts like the second edition of the *Game of Chess* may be later than they are normally dated.

The changeover from type 4 to type 4* is the most unusual of any. The latter was used for the first time in the *Festial*, printed on 30 June 1483, in which it is the only type used. But when *Confessio Amantis* was printed on 2 September of the same year it made use of both types. The compositors started by using type 4. But in gathering 'y', although they used 4 for the outer three folios, the inner folio of this quaternion is in type 4*. In the following gathering the arrangement is even more strange, for one of the leaves, z4^r, has the left-hand column in type 4 and the right-hand one in type 4*. The rest of the book and the prefatory matter, which as we have seen was set up last, is in type 4*. We may notice in passing that the fact that the inner folio of gathering 'y' has type 4* whereas the three outer folios have type 4 confirms the view stated earlier that the compositors broke down the text into passages suitable for individual pages and set up the text by folio rather than consecutively following the text. For the compositors appear to have kept the two types separate even though it is not possible to understand what their reasoning for doing so was. It cannot have been that type 4 was now going to be disposed of, since in the *Knight of the Tower* printed on 31 January 1484 a similar state of affairs exists. But in this case the first part of the book, up to and including gathering 'e', is in type 4, whereas the rest of it is type 4*. But after this book type 4* seems to have become the standard face in the workshop. There is, on the other hand, a much clearer break between the use of type 4* and its successor type 6. The last dated text with type 4* is *Paris and Vienne* from 19 December 1485, though several undated books in this type may have appeared in the following year or two. The first dated text in type 6 is the *Feats of Arms* which appeared only on 14 July 1489, though again several of the undated texts in this type may have preceded it. But there is enough room between these two dates to suggest that the two types were not used simultaneously.

We may conclude therefore that with his *bâtarde* scripts one type does tend to replace another type, though there are periods of overlap when both may be used. So even with types of this kind one cannot use this sort of evidence alone for a definite *terminus post quem* or *ante quem*. But as the periods in which they were in use are shorter than the *lettre de forme* type, they do provide a somewhat better guide to dating. Type should not be used by itself as any certain guide to the dates of Caxton's editions.

VI
THE TEXT AND ITS PRESENTATION

After a text had been chosen for printing, and the reasons behind the choice of such texts to print we will examine later, the supervisor of the workshop prepared the copytext for the compositors. The way in which it was handled depended on its quality. Naturally many of the works produced by the press were Caxton's own translations. No doubt these were written on paper by Caxton and so they could be handled quite roughly by the supervisor, who would not hesitate to make marks over them. The only copytext of a Caxton print that survives is the autograph by Lorenzo Guglielmo Traversagni of his *Nova Rhetorica*, which may be said to fall into the same category as Caxton's own written works since the manuscript was utilitarian. The copytext survives as MS Latin 11441 in the Vatican Library at Rome, and the *Nova Rhetorica* forms folios 1 to 88 of the manuscript. The manuscript shows signs of extensive handling as though it was not treated too gently in the workshop. It also contains marks in the margins which correspond to the pages in Caxton's print. At what is the beginning of each page in Caxton there is a sign in the left-hand margin of the manuscript, and at the end of each Caxton page there is a different sign in the right-hand margin of the manuscript. What is also of interest is that the ends of the pages in Caxton's print correspond with the endings of lines in the manuscript except when a word in the manuscript is split between two lines, in which case the whole word is allocated to one page. These two features have been insufficiently regarded by bibliographers, for they are significant of how the work was prepared for the press. Thus the fact that the beginning of each page is marked as well as the end suggests that the manuscript was divided into potential pages of printed text before the compositor began to set up the type. For if the compositor had been working steadily through the text one mark at the end of each page would surely have been sufficient for his purposes. Similarly that the ends of the pages in Caxton's print correspond with the line-endings in the manuscript indicates that the division into pages was made before the text was set up. There would be no particular reason for a compositor to stop at the end of the line rather than in the middle if he was working right through the text; this would simply create an extra problem for him which would have little point. But for a supervisor going through the text before it was printed it would be natural enough to make the page divisions correspond with the line endings, since he would count the number of lines which he thought would go to make up a page of the printed text. In other words the marks in the manuscript are likely to have been made by a supervisor or even the compositor himself before the text was set up in print and not as the compositor worked on the text. As we saw in the last chapter the ends of the printed pages in Caxton's works are often either crowded or relatively empty; and this is because the compositor had to fit a previously allocated body of text into his page. Indeed the fact that some of Caxton's printed works do not contain the same number of lines on every page may be another indication that the division into pages was made before the text was set up and was not always done too well.

Of course Caxton did not always have the advantage of working from his own or someone else's rough draft. Particularly when he was printing English poets or works already available in English he had to use manuscripts, some of which were very valuable. Clearly he could not allow the pages of luxury manuscripts to be marked in quite the same way as his own rough drafts, for some of them may not even have belonged to him. This may have meant that the compositors worked in a different way with manuscripts of this kind. Unfortunately there is no extant luxury manuscript which can definitely be described as a Caxton copytext. Certainly there is no indication that the manuscript of the Caxton Ovid, now in the Pepys Library, Magdalene College, Cambridge, was used for this purpose. Presumably the manuscript was written from Caxton's rough draft which would also have been used by the compositors. It has, however, been suggested that MS 213 of Magdalen College, Oxford, was the copytext used by Caxton for his edition of Gower's *Confessio Amantis* printed in 1483. This manuscript contains some marks in the margins which correspond with the lines at the top of the columns in Caxton's texts. Unfortunately there are only 37 such marks visible and they fall into two groups: one consists of crosses in a pale brown ink and the other of small circles in a darker ink. Since Caxton's edition consists of over two hundred leaves and since there are two columns of text per page,

versus/actual and mental whiche
he doop ben drawe in me plesably
and ooned wiþ desier of loue. for he
þat areisið hym silf/foldwynge ⁊
pursuynge þe soule/whiche my sone
schewide in þe cros. ¶Furþirmore
my stedfastnes seyde a soþ ⁊ whi
inne it was seyd/I schal drawe
alle þingis to me. if I be areisið
up ¶ þat is to seye/whanne þe
herte of man is drawe. and þe
myȝtis of þe soule be drawe. al
so þise oþe werkis or dedis is schu
len be drawe ¶Also þese wordis.
I schal drawe to me/ben vndur
stonden in anoþir maner/as þus
¶Alle þingis ben maad and
foormed ⁊ into þe seruise of wis/
aⁱⁱ þei ben maad to helpe þe
neede of resonable creaturis/
¶But a resonable creature is
not maad for hem. þat ben not
resonable/ but oonly for me/ þat
he serue me with alle hise affec
cyons and wiþ his herte ¶Also
whanne a man is drawe up ⁊ þou
maist wel parceyue þat alle þin
gis be drawe up ⁊ for alle þin
gis ben maad for hym ¶ Þere
fore it was speedful. þat þat
hool brigge schulde be enhaunsid.
and ȝet it schulde haue in hym
lowdnis. þat ȝe myȝten þe moore
liȝtly passe ouer þe brigge/
¶Thorw þis brigge is wallið
wiþ stoones ⁊ bytokeneþ ver

ry vertues ¶Also up þis brig
ge is a schip ordeyned with me
te ⁊ schal be ȝoue to þe weygo
ers/ ¶ This worþi brigge is
wallið wiþ stoon ⁊ þat greet þei
schulde not lette þe weygoers/
¶ Þese stoones ben soþfaste v
tues/ but þo stoones wereu leid
ne þe was maad to fore my sones
passyon ¶ Þei weren so greet
ly sett to fore þat no man coude
to þe eende ⁊ by what euere wey
of vertues he wente/ Heuene
was not til þat tyme/vndo wiþ
þe keye of his precious blood/
and þe reyn of riȝtwisnes⁊ wol
de suffre no man to passe/
¶But aftir tyme þe stoones
wereu sett/and leyd up þe bo
dy of my holy sone ⁊ he ma
de up þe stoones was of. and
medlid it wiþ chalk. and foor
gide and foormede it up/wiþ
his precious blood/ þat is to
seye / þe blood is medlid
wiþ þe chalk and strenlye
of þe godheed ⁊ and wiþ þe
greet fier of charyte ¶ Þe
stoones of vertues ben sett
up þe brigge by my myȝt ⁊ for
þere is no vertu. But þat it is
preuyd in hym. and vertues
haue liif of hym ¶ Þerfore
no man may haue siche ver
tues ⁊ wiche schulde ȝeue
þe liif of grace/ But þei come

the occurrence of only 37 marks may not be significant. As it is the marks occur in three different groupings in the manuscript. Perhaps they are the jottings of a reader who had a printed text available as well; they may not be printer's marks. On the other hand, their faintness and the care with which they have been made to seem unobtrusive suggest that they have been included so as not to spoil the manuscript, which is a procedure one would expect a supervisor with a valuable manuscript to adopt. Yet it has been recognised that this manuscript, if it was the one Caxton used, was not the only one available to him, since many of the readings in the printed edition differ from Magdalen 213. Even several lines not found in this manuscript but which occur in others are found in Caxton's text. But there is no indication in the manuscript as to when the compositor should look to another text for a different reading or for an insertion. The absence of such indications makes it improbable that Magdalen 213 was Caxton's copytext, for if it were the compositor would have been working from two manuscripts simultaneously without any indication as to when he should use one and when the other. This procedure would have been too time-consuming and cumbersome for the press.

In order to get some idea of how Caxton may have treated his valuable manuscripts we have to go to Wynkyn de Worde, for some of his copytexts have survived and it is likely that he continued the practices of Caxton's workshop. One of the most valuable was the manuscript of the English translation of the *De Proprietatibus Rerum* printed by de Worde about 1495. The manuscript, which is now in the library of Columbia University, New York, was made about 1440 for Sir Thomas Chaworth and it went shortly afterwards to the Willoughby family who lived nearby at Wollaton, Nottinghamshire, in whose possession it remained till 1925. In de Worde's time it belonged to Sir Henry Willoughby, who presumably made it available to be printed. In the manuscript the pages of the book have been marked where they start. Each page is noted and as the book was printed in quaternions there are sixteen pages to each gathering. At the beginning of each gathering a mark like a rather elaborate 'S' followed by a '1' for page one of the gathering is inserted. The other pages of that gathering in the book are simply marked from '2' to '16' in the margin of the manuscript. It is a regular feature of the early copytexts known that each page is marked rather than each folio or even only the first four folios in a quaternion, and different views about this marking are possible. It may be that such marks were made by the supervisor before printing so that the compositors could set up the type by sheets rather than by continuous pages of text; and the cleanness of the text might support this view. Alternatively the markings may have been made by the compositor as he went along setting up the text. The numerals are not uniform throughout: some are in Roman and others in Arabic script. Some are made in pen and ink, others with a fine brush, and yet others have been scratched in with a drypoint. It is usually suggested that these differences reflect the work of different compositors, though I am not convinced that this is a necessary inference. A man might well use one notation on one day and a second on the next; we do not have to assume that everybody is so uniform in his habits. An important feature of the manuscript is that it is very clean and clearly the printers took care not to deface it in any way. An isolated blob may possibly be the impression of the compositor's dirty thumb. But this cleanness does suggest that the compositor touched the manuscript as little as possible. At the same time the printed text does not in its language reflect the manuscript at all accurately in so far as the printed text has a more modernised English. The original old words and inflexions have been replaced by more modern formations so that *iclepid* becomes *namyd* and the old letters like þ are replaced by *th*. In addition numerous small emendations, additions and omissions have been made. But nowhere in the manuscript is there any indication to the compositor that he should change this word or modernise that one. It would appear as though the compositor was given, or took, *carte blanche* in revising the language of the manuscript he was using. Since the corrections were made as the work was being set up in type it is natural enough that they were made haphazardly. In many cases it would seem that the omission of words in the manuscript was made for typographical rather than for linguistic or stylistic reasons. The printed text, like the manuscript, is in double columns and often by omitting a word the compositor was able to make his line of print the desired length. That he may have done this to accommodate a previously allocated body of text is suggested by other omissions in the text. On folio d7^{v} there are several omissions of more than one word, three omissions of a single word, and a number of cases of elision, which are all indicative of an attempt to cram a certain amount of material into one column of type.

A second copytext used by Wynkyn de Worde is in a composite volume in the library of St John's College, Oxford, which contains copies of works printed by Caxton and a manuscript version of Lydgate's *Siege of Thebes*. It was this manuscript which de Worde used when he printed the poem about 1500. In most respects the way in which the printer treated this manuscript is similar to his handling of the *De Proprietatibus Rerum* manuscript. There are printer's marks which indicate the beginning of each page of text in the printed edition. Instead of the flamboyant 'S' figure, the beginning of each gathering is indicated in the margin of the manuscript by the gathering letter of the printed book. So the first page of signature 'b' is indicated in the manuscript as 'b1', the second simply as '2' and so on until '16'. The first number in the manuscript is '3', since the first two pages of signature were left blank in the printed book. This manuscript also contains differences in the marks. Up to signature 'k' the number of the page is linked to the appropriate line of the poem by a small dash, but after that by a small cross. Similarly the marks are made either in ink or with a drypoint. Like the previous manuscript this one was handled very carefully by the printers so that it remained very clean. No indications as to which words should be emended are given in the manuscript. As the language of the printed text exhibits notable differences from that of the manuscript we must again conclude that the compositor was given a free hand in his emendations.

A third manuscript used by Wynkyn de Worde as a copytext has been identified more recently. This is Harley 3432 in the British Library which contains only the *Orchard of Syon*, a translation of *The Dialogues* by St Katherine of Siena. The work was printed by de Worde in 1519 and it is worth while recording how he came to print it. In his prologue he states:

This consyderynge a ryghte worshypfull and devoute gentylman, Mayster Rycharde Sutton Esquyer, Stewarde of the holy monastery of Syon, fyndynge this ghostely tresure, these dyologes and revelacyons of the newe seraphycall spouse of Cryste Seynt Katheryne of Sene, in a corner by itselfe, wyllynge of his greate charyte it sholde come to lyghte that many relygyous and devoute soules myght be releved and have conforte therby, he hathe caused at his greate coste this booke to be prynted trustinge that moche fruyte shall come therof to all that shal rede or here of it, desyrynge none other thinge therfore but onely the rewarde of God and theyr devoute prayers for helthe of his soule.

It would appear as if the manuscript was not considered valuable because it was lying around neglected in Syon Abbey, an important Brigittine house noted for its piety. Presumably Sutton and de Worde considered the text to be of value and so printed the work, and in so doing considered that the manuscript had become superseded and hence worthless in itself. The manuscript is an attractive one with considerable gold leaf decoration, but no pictures. It was, however, not treated by the printers with the care which they normally gave to manuscripts. It contains marks which correspond with the ends of columns and pages in de Worde's print. But these marks are made boldly and disfigure the manuscript even though the ink used is not very dark. They are of two types. Where the end of a page in the printed book coincides with the end of a line in the manuscript, someone has inked in a line underneath the manuscript line—often in a rather nonchalant way. On the other hand, if the end of a page in the printed book falls in the middle of a line in the manuscript, the inked line starts under the manuscript line, then crosses it at the place marking the end of the page and continues above the line. Sometimes of course it will start above the line and finish under it. These lines which have been inked in are often carried right on into the margin of the manuscript. Occasionally when the compositor drew the line in the wrong place he crossed it out and drew a new one in the correct place. But there are no numbers in the manuscript to indicate the pages of the book. These marks are evidently running marks made by the compositor as he set up the manuscript and simply tell him where he had got to. They occur in the titles and chapter-headings of the manu-script and since these were written in red ink the marks made by the compositor produce a discordant note. An interesting indi-cation that this manuscript was used for a printed book is the addition of signatures in the manuscript. The first four pages of each gathering in the manuscript are marked 'ai, aii, aiii, aiiii' and so on throughout the volume. The use of such signatures was confined to printed books and the occurrence of signatures in Harley 3432 indicates that it had been prepared by a com-positor for printing.

The manuscript does contain a few corrections which corre-spond with what appears in the printed edition. Thus at folio 41^r the 'Þei encreessiden' is amended by a different hand to 'Þei dyden encrees'. On folio 54^v 'Þeft' is crossed out and 'a theef' is added in the margin. Often there are paragraph marks added to indicate the beginning of a new section and quotations in the text are noted by 'qo' in the margin. All these corrections and marks appear to be in the same ink as that of the lines marking the ends of the columns and pages. They were probably made by the compositor, although they could have been made by the supervisor. In any event the workshop was prepared to make corrections on the manuscript itself as though it were expendable. However, these few corrections in the manuscript do not include all the changes made by the compositor to his text, for as with all the other prints by de Worde we have looked at so far the language of the printed edition has been modernised. Since this work was printed somewhat later than the other two we have considered, it may be that practice changed in the workshop. But I would suggest that the difference between the Harley manuscript and the St John's and Columbia manuscripts represents a different attitude towards the value of the manuscript in itself. At the same time it may be that a valuable manuscript was marked by a supervisor before the compositors started work in order to preserve its appearance. Where this consideration did not apply the compositor was allowed to make what marks he wanted. While we have no idea whether this state of affairs applied also in Caxton's time, it would not be improbable.

A third type of copy that could be used in Caxton's workshop was his own original print when another edition was called for. We do not know how often the original manuscript was still available when a new edition was issued, but as a general practice the compositors always set up the second edition from the first—a procedure which can be proved from the incorrect readings which the two printed editions share. This method of procedure is quite understandable because the text was already divided into suitable pages and because the printed edition did not have to be handled so circumspectly as the manuscript. Indeed when a text was reprinted it was usual for it to retain the original pagination of the first edition if this was possible. This applies to the first two editions of *Cato*, of *Dicts or Sayings* and of *Quattuor Sermones*, as well as to both editions of *Horse, Sheep and Goose*, *Churl and Bird*, *Chronicles of England* and *Speculum Vitae Christi*. The first two editions of *Quattuor Sermones* provide a good example of what could happen. These two editions are sufficiently alike for it only recently to have been discovered that they form separate editions; most bibliographical lists have them as a single edition. Each page in both editions contains the same amount of text, but the lineation within the pages is not identical. Certain refinements like printed paragraph marks and initial capitals have been introduced into the second edition, and these together with differences in spelling can cause a discrepancy in certain lines. Evidently the com-

ben curatis of this chirch / and for the soules that haue scrupd
in this chirch / Also ye shal pray for the soules of alle cristen
kynges and quenes / and in especial for the soules of them that
haue ben kynges of this royame of englond / and for al tho sow
les that to this chirch haue yeuen boke / belle / chalys or vestement
or ony other thyng by whiche the seruyce of god is better doon / &
holy chirch worshipped / ye shal also pray for your faders soules
for your moders soules / for your godfaders soules / for your god
moders soules / for your brethern & susters soules / and for your
kynnes soules / & for your frendys soules / and for al the sow
les that we ben bounde to prayfor / and for the soules that ben
in the paynes of purgatorye / there abydyng the mercy of our lord
god / and in special for them that haue most nede and leste helpe
that god for his endeles mercy lesse and mynysshe theyr paynes
by the moyen of our prayers / & brynge them / to his euerlastyng
blysse in heuen / And also for the soule of / N / or of them / that
on suche a day this weke we shal haue the annyuersarye / and for
alle cristen soules ye shal deuoutly say a pater noster & an Aue
Psalmus / Deprofundis & cetera with this colecte / Oremus /

Absolue quesumus domine aĩas famulorū tuorū pontificum regũ
sacerdotum parentum parochianorū amicorū benefactorū nostrorū
et omniũ fidelium defuctorum ab omni vinculo delictorum / Vt in
resurrectionis gloria inter sanctos et electos tuos resussitati respi
rent / per xpistum dominum nostrum Amen /

Enprynted by William Caxton at Westmestre /

printed in Anno: 1483:

positor was given a relatively free hand in setting up the page provided he included all the text allocated to it; it is unlikely that there was any attempt to make the editions seem alike for aesthetic or commercial reasons. It may be that the compositors found it easier to work like this, or it is likely that there were at least two compositors at work on the reprint and it would be necessary that their separate parts should link up satisfactorily. Some second editions are separated from the first by several years, and there is no need to assume, as has been done with the second edition of *Quattuor Sermones*, that the second necessarily followed quickly after the first edition.

Naturally it was not always possible to set up a reprint with exactly the same pagination as the original. With different-sized paper or different-sized type it would be possible to accommodate more or less text to a page. Several reprints were issued with woodcuts not found in the first edition and this would also affect the balance of the original pagination. How Caxton used his own editions as copytexts is a problem that has not yet been studied and I can do no more here than give some indication of his methods. The third edition of *Quattuor Sermones* printed about 1491 is in double columns and so differs from the first two editions, which are so similar as to be virtually identical. It is therefore not possible to tell which of these first two editions he used and I have used the first as a basis for comparison. Several features of the third edition are noteworthy. Some pages do not have the same number of lines in each column; thus on d2^v the left-hand column has 33 lines whereas the right-hand one has 34. In fact most columns have 33 lines, which may be considered the number the compositor wanted to produce on each page. The right-hand columns of some pages have an extra word or two, as though the compositor was unable to get all his text in the last line and so was forced to add a few letters on their own. Thus the last line of the right-hand column on a7^v is:

& not onely for drede of payn/ the
se comma

which corresponds in the first edition to the line which reads:

for drede of payn/ These commaundementys and not oonly.

Similarly the last line of the right-hand column of a8^r is

ith he/ therthe shal bring forth his
sede

which corresponds in the first edition to the line which reads:

rayne in tyme sayth he/the erthe shal bryng forth his sede/and.

Finally it is worth noting that the last line of some pages in the third edition is shortened. Thus where the final line of b8^r in the third edition reads '& thinke what sorow might', the first edition has 'what payn and sorowe myght'.

It is difficult to escape the conclusion that these features indicate the text was divided into potential column lengths by the supervisor before being handed over to the compositor. The first and second editions were printed in long lines extending right across the page, whereas the third edition was in double columns. This would mean that a line of the first edition would correspond to two column lines of the third. But as the columns of the third edition normally had 33 lines each, the supervisor would have to indicate where the end of the columns should come alternately in the middle and at the end of the lines of the first edition. It happened often either that he made a mistake and that the compositor had to add an extra line to his column or that the allocated text was too much and so the compositor had to add an extra half-line at the foot of his column. At the same time one must conclude that the division into potential column lines was made rather arbitrarily. So when faced with a line in the first edition which read:

for drede of payn/ These commaundementys and not oonly

which had to be divided in the middle to complete the thirty-third line of the column for the third edition, the supervisor made the division after *comma* without any thought for the look or sense of the text. Unfortunately when the compositor set up the text he was unable to get all this half-line into his final column line and so put *se comma* on a little half-line by itself. It seems most improbable that if a compositor was working through a text, setting it up as he went along, he would go to the trouble of having a separate half-line at the foot of his column, particularly as it meant dividing two words up in an arbitrary manner. We do not have to think that compositors were quite so obtuse. The problem for the compositor was that setting up a text in double columns gave him far less opportunity for juggling with the language of his copytext so that he could lengthen or shorten his line to accommodate all his allocated text, for a column line has fewer words in it which could be adapted in the way the compositors were used to. It is only rarely that he had the good luck of a doublet occurring in his final line, for in these cases he was presented with an easy means of shortening. Thus 'payn and sorowe' became simply 'sorow'.

A comparison of the first and second edition of the *Game of Chess* is less helpful. The difference between the two editions is that the second has a series of woodcuts which meant a re-arrangement of the text to provide room for them. To make life easier it was decided to include woodcuts immediately after the chapter-headings, and the chapter-headings and woodcuts were as a rule included at the top of the page. This meant that the text of many chapters finished in the middle of a page, the rest of which was left blank so that the new chapter with its woodcut could begin the next page. Hence the problems of setting up the text were kept to a minimum, though there was inevitably a certain waste of paper. It was only when a chapter ended after a few lines on a page that it was considered too wasteful to leave the rest of the page blank, and then the chapter-heading and the woodcut were put at the bottom of the page in question. The arrangement shows that some thought was given to the lay-out of the second edition and in itself this suggests that a super-visor may have decided how the new edition was to be set up before it was handed to the compositor. But there are no examples within the actual text which can be used to prove this.

There were many differences between a printed book and its copytext and between two different editions of a book. Generally the changes were confined to spelling and punctuation. As an example of the changes let us consider the same passage in dif-ferent editions. The following passages are from the two editions of Caxton's *Game of Chess*:

The rooks whiche ben vicaires and legats of the kynge ought to be made lyke a knyght vpon an hors and a mantell and hood furryd with meneuyer, holdynge a staf in his hande. & for as moche as a kyng may not be in alle places of his royame therfore the auctorite of hym is gyuen to the rooks whiche represent the kynge. And for as moche as a royame is grete and large and that rebellion or nouelletes might sourdre and aryse in oon partye or other, therfore ther ben two rooks: one on the right side and that other on the lifte syde. [First edition]

The rookes whiche been vycayrs and legates of the kynge ought to be maad a knyght vpon an hors & a mantel and hood furrid with meneuier, holdyng a staf in his hand. & for as moche as a kyng may not be in al places of his royame therfore the auctorite of hym is gyuen to the rookes whiche represente the kyng. & for as moche as a royame is grete and large and that rebellyon or noueltees myght sourde and aryse in one partye or other, therfore ther ben two rookes: one on the right syde and that other on the lift syde. [Second edition]

I have modernised the punctuation, but the spelling of the passages is that found in the originals. The changes are fairly straightforward. Final 'e' is added or omitted arbitrarily; and 'i' and 'y' interchange freely. Consonants, particularly when final, are often doubled; and occasionally the doubled consonant attracts an 'e' as in the pair *al*: *alle*. Instead of indicating vowel length by a final 'e' it can be done by doubling the vowel itself, so that we have the pair *made*: *maad*. Some longer words are spelt differently and abbreviation was a matter for each individual compositor.

In the copytexts we have considered so far there were few indications by the supervisor to the compositor how he should spell or what alterations he should make. The compositor evidently had a free hand in setting up a page. As he worked he would be influenced by both typographical and linguistic considerations. If he was given a fixed amount of text to include on a page of type he would have to make sure he got it all in and would use different spellings or abbreviations to help him in this. The need to justify the lines, that is to have a straight right-hand margin as well as a straight left-hand one on each page, would act as a further constraint on his typesetting. At first Caxton's books had lines of uneven length, but from about 1480 the press started to make all lines in a book a regular length, an improvement which greatly enhanced the page's appearance. To make sure he got his lines even, the compositor could juggle about with the spelling so that the words were expanded or contracted to fill the available space. Thus final 'e' could be omitted or added and a final consonant could be doubled and a final 'e' added or not so that *ship* might appear as *ship*, *shipp* or *shippe*. As for the language the compositor could not but be affected by the natural evolution which takes place in all languages. As it happens the fifteenth century witnessed considerable changes in the English language and these were reflected in how people spelt. For there existed at this time no standard written English to give the language a feeling of tradition and stability. Although spelling conventions did exist, each man could please himself how he spelt. In fact the spellings in early printed books are more uniform than those found in many fifteenth-century manuscripts. But medieval scribes had their own spelling habits and the same no doubt applies to Caxton's compositors as well. If some of his printed books were submitted to a detailed examination, it is possible that we would be able to detect the spelling habits of individual compositors and so decide who set up which pages of text in the same way as has been done for Shakespeare's first folio. There is no standardisation otherwise in the printed books coming from Caxton's workshop and in no way can the language be a true reflection of Caxton's own speech habits.

Several of the works issued by the press were English texts which had been written in the fourteenth century and their language was as a result old-fashioned when it came to be printed. The *Polychronicon* was one of these, for it had been translated into English by John Trevisa in 1387. When Caxton printed it he claimed that he had modernised the language:

therfore I William Caxton, a symple persone, have endevoyred me to wryte fyrst overall the sayd book of *Proloconycon* [sic] and somwhat have chaunged the rude and old Englyssh, that is to wete certayn wordes which in these dayes be neither usyd ne understanden.

The changes made are of the same sort as those in Wynkyn de Worde's print of *De Proprietatibus Rerum* which was discussed earlier. In view of this it is possible that Caxton did not actually go through the text writing in modern forms as he went along, but simply issued a general directive to the workshop to modernise the language. For even if he had not done so, the compositor would have updated the language. In making his claim Caxton was only stating what was standard practice in the workshop, though the way it is phrased makes it sound as though he had done something out of the ordinary. Indeed the compositors not only changed the language, but they also made alterations to the text either to make it more intelligible or often just for stylistic reasons. In Wynkyn de Worde's print of the *Siege of Thebes* the compositor altered the following phrases: 'to shuld' became 'to shelde' and 'hath wasted' became 'hasted'. One line which in the St John's manuscript reads 'Theire tender weping and her wofull sounes' became changed in Wynkyn de Worde's print to 'Theyre tender wepyng and her wofull bale' in order to enable this line to rhyme with *pale* in the next. As there is no indication in the St John's manuscript that the compositor should make any change here, the alterations must have been made on his own initiative. In this he was the true descendant of the medieval scribe. It is interesting to note that the compositors can also show the reverse tendency, to copy the text whether it makes sense or not. There are many instances where Caxton mistranslated his source and produced nonsense, but these are faithfully preserved by the compositors. Even more surprising in fact is that in his translation of *Reynard the Fox*, for example, the compositors should have kept many Dutch spellings which Caxton had taken over from his Dutch original. Spellings such as *ende* ('and') and *laaden* ('load') have not been anglicized by the compositor as one might have expected. But then we must expect that some compositors were less willing to make emendations and others no doubt made changes only haphazardly.

That the compositors were often unconcerned about the quality of the texts they set up is suggested by the second edition of the *Canterbury Tales*. Caxton published his first edition about 1477; his second about 1483. It arose in this way. One of his clients complained that his first edition was textually unsatisfactory because it contained matter not by Chaucer as well as omitting many genuine passages. He said his father owned a manuscript with a more correct text which he would persuade him to lend to the printer if he for his part agreed to produce a second edition. Caxton agreed; the manuscript was procured; and the second edition appeared. One might imagine from this story told us by Caxton that he printed the second edition direct from this manuscript; but this did not happen. It has been proved that he took a copy of his own first edition and emended that against the new manuscript. The changes were haphazardly and irregularly made. The following types of mistake arose. In the first edition a line in 'The Miller's Tale' reads 'A clerk had lowdly biset his whyle', whereas in most manuscripts and in the second manuscript used by Caxton it read 'A clerk had litherly biset his whyle'. But in the second edition the reading of his line is 'Lytherly a clerk had biset his whyle'. The reading arose through Caxton crossing out 'lowdly' and putting the correction for it, 'litherly', in the margin. But the compositor did not understand that 'litherly' was to replace 'lowdly' and simply placed it at the front of the line because it was in the left-hand margin. In other passages there has been conflation. In a line in 'The Pardoner's Tale' the first edition reads 'Thou bel amy John Pardoner, he sayde', whereas most manuscripts read 'Thou beel amy thou pardoner, he, sayde'. One may assume that 'John' was deleted and 'thou' added either above or in the margin. But in this case the compositor included both words so that the line became 'Thou bel amy, thou John Pardoner, he sayde'. The effect is disastrous on the poetry. It is worth noting three things in connexion with these mistakes. The first is that Caxton did not bother to check whether his compositors were producing what he wanted. As soon as he handed over the copy to the workshop he appears to have lost interest in the text. The second is that the compositors seem to have been ignorant of normal scribal practice as far as corrections are concerned. Thus it was usual to delete a word and put its replacement in the margin; but the compositor seems not to have known this convention. It is hardly surprising therefore that there are places in Caxton's books where words and phrases occur in the wrong place. The compositors were equally unconcerned about producing an accurate text and showed little literary feeling. But then they were artisans and not scribes, and they did not have that experience which any proficient scribe would have possessed. The third point reinforces what we have already discovered: whenever possible the printer preferred to work from a printed book instead of from a manuscript. At first glance it seems that he could have saved himself time and trouble to work from a manuscript rather than to write corrections in a printed book. But he did not because he did not want to deface the manuscript and because he could not break it up into three sections so that three compositors could work on it at once. Despite his claims in the epilogue to the second edition of the *Canterbury Tales*, he put the convenience of the workshop before the quality of his text.

The punctuation marks used in the workshop consist principally of the stroke, the stop, and the colon, though not all the founts of type had all three. The stroke appears in a variety of sizes and like the stop it can be placed at any height in the line. There is no evidence that the workshop made any distinction between these marks. The stroke is used more regularly than the stop in poetic texts, where it is placed internally in the line; it is rare to find any punctuation at the end of a line of poetry. In this the early printed books reflect current manuscript practice. But stops are found in the poetry, as in this last stanza of the *Moral Proverbs*:

> Go thou litil quayer/ and recommaund me
> Vnto the good grace/ of my special lorde
> Therle Ryueris. for I haue enprinted the
> At his commandement. folowyng eury worde
> His copye/ as his secretaire can recorde
> At Westmestre. of feuerer the .xx. daye
> And of kyng Edward/ the .xvij. yere vraye

As we see in this example stops were used to mark off figures, but in some books the stroke is also used for this purpose. By and large it is likely that the punctuation in the poetic books reflects that found in the manuscript copy if only because the scope for moving the stroke within the line was so limited. The same does not apply to prose texts, many of which were Caxton's own translations. In these the punctuation was changed quite as readily as the spelling, and there are few principles that one can detect behind the arbitrary use of punctuation marks. In this matter there was no progress in Caxton's printed books throughout his career.

There were occasions, as we have seen, when Caxton's intentions were not carried out by the compositors. This need not mean that there was no system of proof-reading, though there are enough mistakes in most of his books to make it unlikely that there was any rigorous check on what the compositors did. This state of affairs would have applied equally to the work of many fifteenth-century scribes, for it was usually only the larger monastic scriptoria which employed a supervisor to check on what the scribes had written. Only one text mentions proof-reading, the *Sex Epistolae*, printed about 1483. In this epilogue to that work we are told that the letters were 'impresse per Willelmum Caxton et diligenter emendate per Petrum Carmelianum' (printed by William Caxton and carefully corrected by Pietro Carmeliano). If this is not a mere empty formula one must assume that Carmeliano corrected the book in proof to make sure there were no printing mistakes. Caxton himself probably took no part in the correcting, though it should have given him an insight into the possibility, and even the desirability, of proof-reading.

No corrected proof page of a Caxton book is extant, if such things ever existed. All we can do to consider how accurately texts were produced and what concern there was to ensure correctness is to consider the variations in the Caxton books that survive, for individual copies of any given text often show significant differences. These variations fall into several categories. Within an edition individual copies will have letters missing or small changes made. Thus in *Reynard the Fox* on page c6^r some copies have 'the' and the rest 'eth'. It is possible to imagine that the pressman noticed the mistake 'eth' during the printing and stopped the press to have it corrected. Unfortunately, however, there is no way of telling whether 'eth' or 'the' was the original reading. We should remember that some of the equipment used was still relatively primitive and there is evidence to show that lines of type were not always sufficiently securely fastened in the forme. This led to some type falling out of the lines. It is consequently quite possible that 'the' was set up by the compositor and during the printing these sorts fell out, for the type took quite a pounding every time the forme was inked. If so it may be that when 'the' was replaced in the forme the letters were replaced incorrectly, which would not be surprising since the type pieces were small and would then be inky. That letters did fall out is clear from cases where they were not replaced. In the *Knight of the Tower* some copies read *whiche* on page f4ʳ whereas one has only *wh che* because the *i* had fallen out. It would seem that the top and bottom of the pages were liable to suffer from the falling out of type. In addition there are occasions when in some copies the whole or part of a line at the bottom of a page is missing in one copy and not in others. Again it is possible to think that this was a compositorial error corrected as the page was going through the press. But it is equally probable that this was a 'bite', the obscuring of part or the whole of a line of type by the frisket which was used to keep the sheet of paper in place while it was printed.

Some minor variations may be the result of nineteenth-century touching up or forgery and some of these are so cleverly executed that they are difficult to detect. Mrs Offord has shown that one of the copies of the *Knight of the Tower* in the British Library has variants which have been inked in during the nineteenth century. What seems to have happened in this case is that the page was washed to clean it up and so increase its value. Then the restorer inked in the letters again following the faint traces that were left. At times when the washing had been so well done that he could not see what the text should read, he guessed and so produced a variant. On other occasions whole pages were reproduced in facsimile from extant pages in order to make good a defective copy. The John Rylands copy of *Reynard the Fox* has a facsimile page of the half-sheet π which is extremely well done. But it too has slight variations which have led to its detection.

An interesting example of a correction was discovered by Dr Bühler in the *Cordial*, printed on 24 March 1479. On folio 61 (h5ᵛ) the last two lines read:

> partie of the foure last thingis/ whiche be forto come
> And here beginneth the prologue vppon the fourth

The two lines were clearly reversed through some oversight on the part of the compositor. They were not corrected as the book was printed, but the mistake was noticed at some stage. In order to rectify the mistake a lower-case 'b' was written in before 'partie' and a lower-case 'a' before 'And', a regular way in manuscripts of indicating that two lines should be reversed. Since the 'a' and 'b' occur in most, but not all, the extant copies the correction was almost certainly made in the workshop. At the same time it should be emphasised that the page was not reset. A handwritten correction was felt to be sufficient, for the concept of a clean and accurate book had not yet percolated through to England. On the other hand, in this same text there is an example when a reversal of lines has been corrected. On folio 26 [d2^4] the copy in The Hague has two lines printed as follows:

> that our Lorde hath geuen vs to vse for the proufite
> and Reckenyng. Therfore our body is as a Mare

In the Rylands copy they are printed in the reverse order, which is indeed the correct one. This may be an example of correction during printing, though the editor of this text felt that this change signified that more than one edition had been printed.

It is useful to keep these examples in mind when considering other cases where there are significant differences between copies of a particular edition. The *Cordial* again provides an interesting example. The third folio of this volume [a3] contains important divergences in different copies. There are two copies of this folio in the copy now at The Hague, but both are slightly different. Some words, though spelt alike, have different letter forms, so that what is 'present' in one occurs as 'pzesent' (with the z-shaped 'r') in the other. There are differences in lineation: line 2 ends with 'other sin-' in one, but with 'other' in the other, for 'sin-' has been placed on the next line. There are also differences in spelling: *ther, thre*; *Iugemnt, Iugement*; *blilsful, blisful*; *be, he*. Unfortunately the correct forms are not all on the same leaf, so that if these are corrections the compositor made new errors in correcting the old ones. The differences are sufficient to suggest that the page was broken down and set up again. The question is why? Three reasons can be suggested. One is that one of the pages represents a different edition which has otherwise not survived. The second is that the pressman noticed some errors and stopped the press to have them corrected, though in fact other errors crept in during the correction. The third is that for some reason insufficient copies of the sheet were pulled the first time and the page was broken down as normal. When the shortage of pages was discovered, the sheet had to be set up again so that the desired number of copies could be produced.

Of these possible reasons the second is the least convincing.

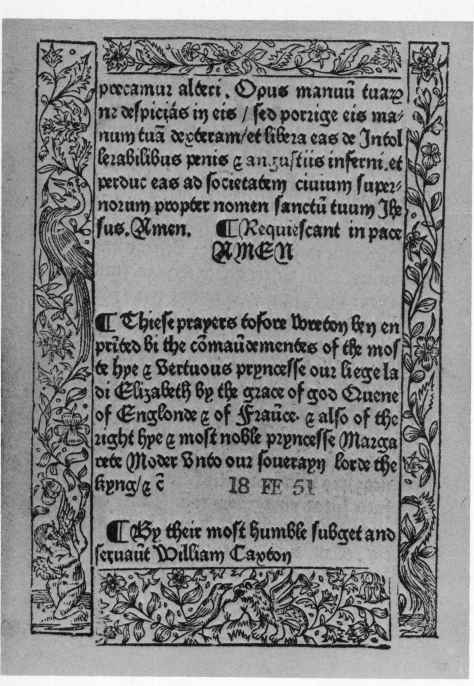

precamur alteri . Opus manuū tuaꝝ
ne despicias in eis / sed porrige eis ma﹣
num tuā dexteram/et libera eas de Intol
lerabilibus penis ꝗ angustiis inferni.et
perduc eas ad societatem ciuium super﹣
norum propter nomen sanctū tuum Ihe
sus.Amen.   ℂRequiescant in pace
AMEN

ℂ Thiese prayers tofore wreton ben en
prited bi the cōmaūdementes of the mos
te hye ꝗ vertuous pryncesse our liege la
di Elizabeth by the grace of god Quene
of Englonde ꝗ of Frāuce. ꝗ also of the
right hye ꝗ most noble pryncesse Marga
rete Moder vnto our souerayn lorde the
kyng/ꝗ c̄   18 FE 51

ℂ By their most humble subget and
seruaūt William Caxton

40. *A colophon*

If he would not break down a page to replace two lines when reversed, it is hardly likely that he would do so to make what were relatively minor corrections. The first is possible but presents certain difficulties. If there were two editions one would imagine that they were separated by at least a year and that all copies of the first edition were disposed of before the second edition was contemplated. If this was so, how did the same sheet from two different editions come to be bound together in one volume? Strange things do happen with early printed books so we cannot exclude the possibility of another edition, but at present it would seem that the third reason is most probable. In view of the many mistakes that were made in the workshop it would be surprising if the pressmen did not sometimes pull the wrong number of sheets or even that some sheets got damaged after they had been printed. Quite apart from that it is known that copies of a given edition can vary. The best example is the first edition of the *Dicts or Sayings,* for the Rylands copy of that has a colophon lacking in all the other extant copies, although they are otherwise identical. This case is slightly different from the *Cordial* page, but it does show that we must accept some differences in copies of texts, though the reasons for such changes remain obscure. All one can say at the moment is that proof-reading is perhaps the least likely reason for such changes being made, but until all texts published by Caxton are produced in modern editions it will not be possible to come to a final verdict.

With reference to the handwritten corrections in the *Cordial* it may be worth recording that several texts have handwritten alterations. Caxton had a Missal of the Sarum Use printed for him in Paris by Guillaume Maynyal in 1487. But the English portions of the marriage service were written in by hand, presumably when the edition arrived in England. Similarly when the *Mirror of the World* was printed it contained many woodcuts. Some of these needed words included to make the illustrations clear. These words were added by hand in the illustrations. But these two are special cases in that it would be known before printing that additions would have to be made and they do not prove that the text was gone through to look for omissions.

Early printed books resemble manuscripts in that they did not at first have title-pages; there was only a haphazard system of providing the reader with information about the contents of the book or where, when and by whom it was produced. The first title-page in a Continental book appeared in 1476 and the use of title-pages soon became common, particularly in books

oz like som leef of a tree woten/that were wel/Thenne ap;
perceyue they wel and byleue that it is no sterre,ffoz the
sterres may not falle , but they muste alle in their cercle
meue ozdynatly ⁊ contynuelly nyght ⁊ day egally/

Of the pure Ayer and how the seuen planetes ben sette/
capitulo   xxxj°

The pure ayer is aboue the fyre, Whiche purpriseth
and taketh his place vnto the heuen/ In this ayer
is no obscurte ne derknes, ffor it was made of clene purete
it resplendissheth ⁊ shyneth so clerly that it may to nothing
be compared/in this ayer ben vij sterres Whiche make their
cours al aboute therthe, the Whiche be moche clene ⁊ clere ⁊
be named ý vij planetes/of Whome that one is sette aboue

that other/and in
suche Wyse oz dy;
ned that ther is
moze space fro that
one to that other/
than ther is fro
the erthe to the
mone / Whiche is
ferther fyften ty;
mes than al .the
the erthe is grete/
⁊ euerich renneth
by myracle on the
firmament and

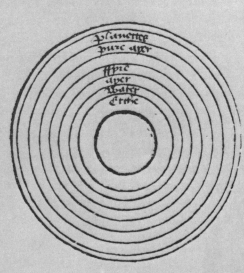

41. The Celestial
    regions

produced in Italy where many elaborate and decorative pages were produced. In England a title-page was used for the first time in Machlinia's third edition of the *Treatise on the Pestilence* by Bengt Knutsson (Canutus), Bishop of Västerås in Sweden, which appeared about or slightly before 1490. Caxton never adopted the practice of a title-page and even Wynkyn de Worde seems not to have included a title-page before his edition of *The Chastising of God's Children*. After 1500, however, the title-page quickly gained currency and soon became an established feature of printed books, thus helping to give them a character significantly different from manuscripts. Until the title-page became standard, the use of titles for individual works was sporadic and somewhat abitrary. Some works printed by Caxton have no title of any sort, whereas others are referred to by several. Thus the first edition of the *Canterbury Tales* opens without any heading or title with the familiar line 'Whan that Apprill with his shouris sote' and concludes with Chaucer's Retraction. On the other hand, his edition of *Siege of Jerusalem* is referred to by a variety of names. After the table of contents it is said to be entitled 'The Siege and Conqueste of Jherusalem by Cristen Men'; but at the beginning of the work we find 'Here begynneth the boke intituled Eracles and also Godfrey of Boloyne'. In the epilogue we find the title 'The Laste Siege and Conquest of Jherusalem'.

❡ The prouffetable boke for mañes soule/ And right comfor⸗ table to the body/ and specyally in aduerfitee gtrybulacyon/ Whiche boke is called The Chaftyfing of goddes Chyldern

42. *An early title-page: The 'Chastising of God's Children'*

A modern title-page tells the reader the name of the book and its author as well as who published it and when and where it was published. It is rare to find the author mentioned in titles at this time and as a rule the plain title of the work is found only in Caxton books printed from English manuscripts, probably because they also occurred in the manuscript, whereas a prologue or colophon is included in works he translated or edited or which had been translated only shortly before being printed. The first book printed in English, *History of Troy*, contains the following preface printed in red ink. The use of a different ink and the placing of the preface on its own page gives this preface very much the feeling of a title-page, and it is surprising that he did not employ this practice more often in other books he issued.

Here begynneth the volume intituled and named the *Recuyell of the Historyes of Troye*, composed and drawen out of dyverce bookes of Latyn into Frensshe by the ryght venerable persone and worshipfull man, Raoul Lefevre, preest and chapelayn unto the ryght noble, gloryous and myghty prynce in his tyme, Phelip Duc of Bourgoyne, of Braband et cetera, in the yere of the incarnacion of Our Lord God a thousand, foure honderd, sixty and foure; and translated and drawen out of Frenshe into Englisshe by Willyam Caxton, mercer of the cyte of London, at the comaundement of the right hye, myghty and vertuouse pryncesse, hys redoubtyd lady, Margarete by the grace of God Duchesse of Bourgoyne, of Lotryk, of Braband et cetera. Whiche sayd translacion and werke was begonne in Brugis in the countee of Flaundres the fyrst day of Marche, the yere of the incarnacion of our said Lord God a thousand, foure honderd, sixty and eyghte, and ended and fynysshid in the holy cyte of Colen the xix day of Septembre the yere of our sayd Lord God a thousand foure honderd, sixty and enleven et cetera.
And on that other side of this leef foloweth the prologe.

In fact this preface is modelled on a similar one in the French text used by Caxton for his translation, though he expanded it considerably. In the French copy the preface is not made to seem so important, for it is not in a different ink or on a separate page. The French reads simply:

Icy commence le volume intitulé *Le Recueil des Histoires de Troyes* composé par venerable homme Raoul Lefevre, prestre chappellain de mon tres redoubté seigneur. Monseigneur le Duc Phelippe de Bourgoingne, en l'an de grace mil cccclxiiii.

The correspondence between the two versions is interesting to note because Caxton was clearly influenced by the manuscript as to what he thought should be included. Thus he gives the name of the book, of the translator from Latin to French and of the translator from French to English, and the date of the translations. But he does not mention that the book is printed and he therefore says nothing about who printed it, where it was printed, or even when it was printed, all features that one would take for granted in a modern book. It is true that in the epilogue which he composed for this volume he does include the information that the book was printed, but this is included more because of the expense involved than because the printer wished to give any information about the book's printing.

The next book in English printed by Caxton is very similar. The *Game of Chess* has a prologue he wrote in which he refers at great length to its dedication to George, Duke of Clarence, and the fact that he had translated the book from French. Once again we can see that the patron and the translator were more important information in the printer's eyes than any details of the book's printing. The only difference in this book is that the epilogue concludes 'Fynysshid the last day of Marche the yer of Our Lord God a thousand, foure honderd and lxxiiii'. As we have seen in a previous chapter this date probably refers to the printing, and, if so, it provides us with the first example of a dated printed book. But there is still no name of the printer or place of publication. The four other books printed by Caxton in Bruges were French texts and they were all printed direct from the manuscripts without any additions by the printer. They were no doubt intended for the Burgundian market, rather than the English one, and they were not issued under patronage. As Caxton found it unnecessary to add any details of these works, he would probably not even consider adding anything about their printing. With his return to England there was a change in his habits for there are relatively complete details about the printing of the first edition of the *Dicts or Sayings*, which appeared in 1477, the year after his return. It is likely that this book is later than his edition of *Jason* which like the *History of Troy* simply mentions details of the book, its patron, and its translator without any information about the printing. But *Dicts or Sayings* was translated by Anthony, Earl Rivers, and Caxton's contribution was to print the volume. He added in an epilogue:

Here endeth the book named the *Dictes or Sayengis of the Philosophres*, enprynted by me William Caxton at Westmestre the yere of Our Lord mcccclxxvii. Whiche book is late translated out of Frenshe into Englyssh by the noble and puissant lord, Lord Antone Erle of Ryvyers, Lord of Scales and of the Ile of Wyght, defendour and directour of the siege apostolique for our holy fader the pope in this royame of Englond, and governour of my Lord Prynce of Wales.

Here we have for the first time the name of the printer and the place and date of publication. Caxton included his epilogue because he wanted to add a section of the French original which Earl Rivers had overlooked. However, since he was not the translator of the book but merely its printer, the only thing he could refer to on his own behalf was the printing. So it is quite probable that the name of the printer and the date and place of publication were added not because people might be interested in these details, but because Caxton wanted to emphasise the part he had played in the volume's appearance. In fact some copies of this edition have after the epilogue a colophon which states that the printing was finished on 17 November 1477. It is likely that the epilogue had been written before the manuscript was handed to the compositor and that the colophon was written after the book was in type. But for some reason not all the sheets pulled had the colophon included. It might have been imagined that once he had started for whatever reasons to introduce details of his books' publication he would continue to do so; but this is not the case. The other editions of *Dicts or Sayings* illustrate this point. The second edition reprinted all the details which applied to the first edition, even though it was not printed till about 1479. In the third edition, which appeared about 1489, Caxton still included the details of printing found in the epilogue, though he did revise the colophon. Yet instead of inserting the date or details of the new edition, he abandoned the colophon and inserted the words 'Caxton me fieri fecit'. Although I have written 'he' in the previous sentence, it may in fact have been the compositor or the supervisor who made this change, for it is a formula which appears in several of the later books and may have been added as part of the house style.

It is significant that until the middle of 1480 the only books to include details of printing are the translations by Earl Rivers: *Moral Proverbs* printed at Westminster by Caxton on 20 February 1478 and the *Cordial* printed by him on 24 March 1479. The place of printing is not included in the *Cordial* and this omission shows that no firm formula had emerged. The information provided was rather of an impromptu nature to advertise Caxton's part in the appearance of the volume. His wish to draw attention to his own contribution to these volumes was motivated by the importance in his eyes of the translator and his desire to be associated closely with him. For in other volumes Caxton did not make any reference to himself. Even his advertisement gives no indication that the printer of the *Ordinale* is Caxton; it merely invites customers to come to the shop at the sign of the Red Pale. As we have seen, his first edition of the *Canterbury Tales* was issued without any mention of his own part as printer or publisher or indeed with little reference to Chaucer. Although Chaucer is highly praised in some of Caxton's volumes it would seem that in general he preferred his name to be associated with living patrons rather than with dead poets, however illustrious, for even in the volumes where Chaucer is praised it is usually in a sponsored edition. Indeed most of the Chaucerian poems printed by Caxton in his early years appear without title or incipit, though some of them have an explicit. The most likely explanation for this is that such texts were printed exactly as the compositor found them in the manuscripts. Only Boethius was issued with a title. This title, *Boecius de Consolacione Philosophie,* and the chapter-headings are printed in a different type from the body of the text, a refinement of a technique he had used in Bruges. The *History of Troy* had its preface in red ink, and another Bruges text, the French version of the *Cordial,* has its title and also its chapter-headings in red ink, though in this case the red ink is superimposed on the black. This method was cumbersome and time-consuming, but it did highlight the title. The same effect could, however, be achieved by using different type. As with several other developments it did not immediately become adopted as standard practice even though for the rest of his career Caxton always had more than one set of type available. Nevertheless, the majority of his books are printed in only one type.

Of other books printed in the early years the Lydgate poems always have an explicit and many have titles as well. In this connexion it is worth noting that the two editions of *Horse, Sheep and Goose* differ. The first edition has no title, but it has an explicit 'Thus endeth the horse, the ghoos and the sheep'. The second edition, on the other hand, has the title 'The hors, the shepe and the ghoos' as well as the same explicit as the first edition. Since the second edition was reprinted from the first, it may be that the title was considered an added refinement and was thus included, though a title was not regularly adopted in Caxton books from now on. As was the case with the insertion of 'Caxton me fieri fecit' in the third edition of the *Dicts or Sayings,* so also in this case it is possible that the title was added on the initiative of the compositor or supervisor. It was done a little carelessly since the form of the title is different from that of the explicit.

After the publication in his early years of the poems by Lydgate Caxton appears to have given up the use of a simple title to introduce a work. Even a poem like the *Court of Sapience* which was attributed to Lydgate by many at that time and which appeared about 1480 has no title; the poem begins immediately without any form of introduction, though there is an explicit at the end. Only the *House of Fame* by Chaucer is introduced by a title in the second lot of Chaucerian poems published by Caxton about the year 1484; and this appeared under the title 'The Book of Fame made by Gefferey Chaucer'. This is the one occasion when a simple title includes the name of the author. *Troilus and Criseyde,* on the other hand, has no title at all or any other form of introduction. Those books with a table of contents or an index usually have some kind of introduction to lead into the table, and a formula such as one finds in *Reynard the Fox* ('This is the table of the Historye of Reynart the Foxe') occurs frequently in one form or another. Apart from such indications of a book's name, some volumes do also have a prologue at the front which may have been set up in type after the rest of the work. In view of this it is surprising that all information about date, place of publication, and the name of the printer should be given in a colophon or epilogue at the back of the book. Let us consider the case of Gower's *Confessio Amantis* which Caxton printed in 1483. We know that Caxton included the first few pages after the rest of the book was in print since their signatures are dislocated and since they contain an index referring to the page numbers of the work which presupposes that the pages were already numbered. But the colophon with the date of printing occurs on the last page of the book following the end of the poem:

Enprynted at Westmestre by me Willyam Caxton and fynysshed the ii day of Septembre the fyrst yere of the regne of Kyng Richard the Thyrd, the yere of Our Lord a thousand ccccxxxiii.

Are we to assume that the compositor finished the main body of the text on 2 September and that he had not yet tackled the prefatory matter? Or are we to assume that after finishing the main text he set up the introductory matter in type and only then returned to the last page to add the colophon with the date of printing? The example of the colophon in *Dicts or Sayings* which is not found in all copies suggests the second alternative, but my own view would be to accept the first, since the prefatory matter could possibly have been completed on the same day or only a day or two afterwards. If so, it does mean that the date Caxton gives for the printing of his texts need not be absolutely accurate.

An exception to the principle that all colophons indicating the place and date of printing and the printer's name come at the end of their respective volumes is the volume containing *Of Old Age*, since the colophon comes after that work, which is then followed in the volume by *Of Friendship* and the *Declamation of Noblesse*, which have no colophon. But *Of Old Age* has one set of signatures and the other two works have a separate set. Previously I thought that this difference in signatures indicated that Caxton intended to print *Of Friendship* and the *Declamation of Noblesse* as one volume and when it was almost ready he acquired *Of Old Age* which he decided to issue with them.

But this is not possible since in his prologue and epilogue to *Of Friendship* he refers back to *Of Old Age* in such a way that makes it clear he already had *Of Old Age* before he wrote his own additions to go with *Of Friendship*. Thus in the epilogue to *Of Friendship* he wrote:

Thenne whan I had enprynted the *Book of Olde Age*, whiche the said Tullyus made, me semed it acordying that this said *Booke of Frendship* shold folowe bycause ther cannot be annexed to olde age a bettir thynge than good and very frendship.

As the prologue and epilogue to *Of Friendship* cannot have been added after the rest of the book since there is no break in the signatures, *Of Old Age* was evidently acquired 'with grete instaunce, labour and coste' before the other two works were in type. Why then did Caxton add the date of printing and the name of the printer after *Of Old Age* instead of at the end of the volume? The colophon reads:

Thus endeth the *Boke of Tulle of Olde Age*, translated out of Latyn into Frenshe by Laurence de Primo Facto at the comaundement of the noble prynce Lowys Duc of Burbon, and enprynted by me, symple person, William Caxton, into Englysshe at the playsir, solace and reverence of men growyng into olde age the xii day of August the yere of Our Lord mcccclxxxi.

It may be that Caxton added the details of the book's printing here because there was already an embryo colophon formed by the information of the book's translation in French by Laurence Premierfait. Furthermore that there are two sets of signatures indicates that there were two compositors at work on the volume, for *Of Old Age* is about the same length as both the other texts put together. If so, it may be fortuitous that the date of printing comes at the end of what became the first part of a composite volume rather than the second. The explanation may be simply that the compositor who was setting up *Of Old Age* finished his section of the text after the compositor who was working on *Of Friendship* and the *Declamation of Noblesse*, and hence the colophon was included there.

Only two volumes give dates in their prologues and these are the *Mirror of the World* (first edition) and *Aesop*. The dates refer only to the translation. The occurrence of a date in *Mirror of the World* is understandable since it is introduced immediately after the date when the original French manuscript was made in Bruges. No doubt this date encouraged Caxton to include the date of his own translation. In *Aesop* Caxton informs us in his incipit when he made the translation:

Here begynneth the book of the subtyl historyes and fables of Esope, whiche were translated out of Frensshe into Englysshe by Wylliam Caxton at Westmynstre in the yere of Oure Lorde mccccslxxxiii.

His incipits in general give either the name of the book or that and the name of the translator. In this isolated case he has gone a stage further to include the year of the translation as well. This example again shows the lack of regularity in the preparation of volumes for publication. The date of the printing is given as usual in the epilogue.

We have already noted that the first texts with dates and other information about their printing are all translations by Earl Rivers. The first text to appear with this information which is not a translation by the Earl is the first edition of the *Chronicles of England* printed in 1480. It is hardly likely to be significant that this text is the first to appear with these details; we can assume that what he had regarded as important for a Rivers volume was gradually accepted as being important in itself and so extended to other volumes. From now on the inclusion of this kind of detail is common, though it never became regular. There are, however, few books produced at the end of Caxton's career without any indication as to the printer included. For a habit which increases in frequency in these later years is the addition of a formula incorporating Caxton's name to conclude a volume. In many of his early works he had copied the words *Explicit* (with or without the title of the book) or *Et sic est finis* from his manuscript source to conclude his print. What happened now was that Caxton added his own name to such phrases to produce a formula like *Explicit per Caxton* and then to vary this formula. The first example of this particular form occurs in the volume *Of Old Age*. The colophon in that volume is found after the work *Of Old Age* itself, but the 'Explicit per Caxton' occurs after the *Declamation of Noblesse* right at the end of the volume. It may be that the compositor of this section simply added this formula at the end of his piece without knowing that a colophon was to be included after *Of Old Age*. The same formula occurs about this time also in the second edition of the *Game of Chess*. The first edition had ended with 'Fynysshid the last day of Marche the yer of Our Lord God a thousand, foure honderd and lxxiiii', and the 'Explicit per Caxton' of the second edition may have been designed to replace that. At all events either this formula or a variant occurs frequently in later books. The variations include 'Fynysshed per Caxton' (*Polychronicon*), 'Enprynted by

Wylliam Caxton at Westmestre' (*Quattuor Sermones*), 'By me Wyllyam Caxton' (*Golden Legend*), 'By Wylliam Caxton' (*Canterbury Tales*, second edition), 'Emprynted by Wylliam Caxton' (*House of Fame*), 'Caxton' (*Curial*), 'Caxton me fieri fecit' (*King Arthur*), 'Explicit et hic est finis per Caxton etc' (*Book of Good Manners*), 'Per Caxton' (*Feats of Arms*), 'By their most humble subget and servaunt William Caxton' (*Fifteen Oes*), and 'Emprynted at Westmestre by desiring of certeyn worshipfull persones' (*Horologium Sapientiae*). Apart from the last volume the invariable feature is Caxton's own name, though some texts contain an extra detail such as the place of printing. None of them includes a date. In some reprints, like the second editions of the *Mirror of the World* and *Festial,* the formula has been included in place of information given about the printing of the first edition; and it is likely that in these cases the formula was added by the compositor in lieu of the details of the first edition. The apparent exception of the *Horologium Sapientiae* is partly accounted for by the fact that this is a composite volume containing three works, each with its own set of signatures. Caxton included his own name at the end of the first work, though in a rather unusual way. He wrote 'Emprynted at Westmynstre. Qui legit, emendet; pressorem non reprehendat, Wyllelmum Caxton, cui Deus alta tradat'. Once again we see that in composite volumes the habits of the workshop were not always carried through regularly. When it does appear, the formula is printed on its own line right at the end of the volume and so it is thrown into prominence; Caxton's name was thus made quite conspicuous. It thus played the same sort of role as his mark which he introduced into many volumes. And the introduction of this formula may be accepted as an indication of who the printer or publisher was; it was not meant to signify the translator. So in the *Curial* the poem which precedes the formula need not be regarded as a translation by Caxton simply because it is followed by the formula 'Caxton'. Although at the beginning of his career he was not too concerned to publicise himself, as we saw in his *Advertisement,* he evidently learned that the introduction of a distinctive feature or mark would set his volumes apart and perhaps guarantee a certain standard. He never adopted this as a regular habit, but we can see some development towards a more consistent means of making sure his customers knew which volume was a Caxton, and this in its turn was a move towards the production of books as we know them today.

The poems printed by Caxton usually appeared without a table of contents or an index. Even when he published a composite volume containing several poems there is nothing to inform the reader what he can find in it. The first poem may well have its own title to introduce it, but a reader would have had to thumb through the leaves of the book to discover what other poems might be there. Even Chaucer's translation of Boethius, a prose work, was not given a table of contents, for it was not normally provided with one in the manuscripts of the time. Otherwise prose works, particularly those which originated on the Continent, often had a table of contents which was taken over from the manuscript used as the source. These tables come at the beginning of the works and give a list of chapter-headings with the relevant chapter number, but they do not provide the numbers of the pages on which the chapters begin. Generally the occurrence of a list of this kind in a Caxton print does not imply any editorial initiative on the part of the printer. Often indeed the translation was not perfect, so that confusion could arise. When Caxton translated the table of contents for *Reynard the Fox* he omitted the heading for the penultimate chapter, chapter 43, and so he gave the final chapter in the table the number 43. But there were 44 chapters in the work and when he came to chapter 43 in the text he translated the heading and gave it the appropriate number. This meant that the last chapter should have been 44, though it was numbered 43 in the table of contents. To get over this difficulty he numbered this chapter '43' as well, so that there were two chapters with this number in the body of the text. It seems not to have entered his mind to enquire how this had arisen or what he might do about it.

Sometimes he was more venturesome and attempted to give a more accurate indication of where material was to be found. The earliest example is found in the *Polychronicon* printed on 2 July 1482. This work was printed from Trevisa's translation into English of the original Latin text by Ranulph Higden to which Caxton had added a final book to bring the historical account down to Edward IV's reign. To complete his editorial activities he added a table of contents which is nearer in scope to an index. The contents of the whole work were grouped alphabetically rather than chronologically, though there were two departures from a strict alphabetical system. In the first place all references beginning with 'a', for example, are grouped haphazardly under 'a' in the index; they were not arranged alphabetically within the letter 'a'. In the second place the items referring to the last book added by Caxton were placed after the items referring to the other seven books. The folios of the book were numbered and the appropriate folio references have been added to the index which, with the prologue, were printed after the rest of the book. While not perfect, it is the first index to make its appearance in an English printed book.

Unfortunately it was not a practice that he continued to use with any frequency. A similar index occurs in the *Golden Legend* from 1483; which is likewise included at the beginning after the prologue. It is certain that this index was compiled by Caxton since it includes the various items which he added to the volume, but the idea may well have come from the manuscripts he used since it was not unusual to find an index of saints in manuscript versions of the *Golden Legend*. An index is also provided in *Confessio Amantis*. This deserves some comment because Caxton added it and it is the only poetic text he issued which has an index or table of contents. It is not quite clear why he thought one necessary for this text, though he claimed it was for the following reasons:

And bycause there been comprysed therin dyvers hystoryes and fables towchyng every matere, I have ordeyned a table here folowyng of al suche hystoryes and fables where and in what book and leef they stande in, as hereafter foloweth.

It is possible that as he included indices in other books around this time he thought of the idea for an index in *Confessio Amantis*. It is a long poem and contains many stories which people may have wanted to read separately as illustrations of particular sins. But the principal reason for its inclusion was probably that the job of making an index was already half done for him. Most manuscripts of the *Confessio Amantis*, and this is certainly true of the one Caxton used, divide the poem into sections, each of which was introduced by a brief statement in Latin as to the contents of that section. All Caxton had to do was to translate these Latin headings, collect them at the front of his work, and add the appropriate folio numbers.

Two books produced in 1484 deserve mention since they show that Caxton had not fully mastered the idea of pagination and index-making. The first of these is *Caton*, which he finished translating on 23 December 1483. After his prologue there is a résumé of the divisions and subdivisions of the book's contents. Since the original manuscript has not yet been identified it is not known whether this résumé was added by Caxton or not, though probably it was. After it he added this passage:

But to th'ende that th'ystoryes and examples that ben conteyned in this lytel book may be lygh[t]ly founden and also for to knowe upon what commaundementes they ben adjousted and alledged, they shalle be sette and entytled by maner of rubrysshe in commaundement upon whiche eche shalle be conteyned and alledged. And they shalle be signed as that, folowed of the nombre of leves where they shalle be wreton.

There follows the table of contents with the appropriate references to the various folios on which the individual commandments could be found. As the prologue and table of contents are printed on a gathering with a separate signature from the rest of the book, no doubt they were printed after the rest of the text so that the correct folio-numbering could be added to the table. The surprising thing is that the folios in the text are without any numbering, though the page numbers in the table are correct as though the folios were numbered. It may be that some copies which have not survived had the foliation added in by hand after printing, but as this proved a cumbersome process it was abandoned. Whatever the reason, it shows that there was faulty preparation in the editing of this volume. What looks like the opposite fault is found in the other work, *Aesop.* This was also translated in 1483; it was printed with folio numbers as though it had been intended to provide an index. Possibly when the printing was finished, the index was overlooked. Since the signatures in this work are regular, nothing was added at the beginning after the rest of the work was in type.

    The only other work provided with a table of contents by Caxton is *King Arthur,* his printing of Malory's *Le Morte D'Arthur.* This work exists now in only one manuscript at Winchester School, and that is not complete. The manuscript has a number of sections, some of which contain excipits. The manuscript that Caxton used was probably similar. But he completely revised the whole appearance of the work by dividing it up into twenty-one books, each of which had many chapters. As he wrote in his prologue, 'And for to understonde bryefly the contente of thys volume I have devyded it into xxi bookes, and every book chapytred as hereafter shal by Goddes grace folowe.' He did not number the pages and so could not provide an index. But after his prologue he included first a list of the contents of each book and then a table of contents of the various chapters in each book, of which there were in all 507, as he himself proudly stated. The prologue and the tables occur at the beginning of the printed book and as they have separate signatures they must have been added after the rest of the book was in type. It may be that the table of contents was compiled by the compositor simply by going through the printed pages and printing each heading as it occurred. Although there is no index, the provision of books and chapters did mean that a reasonable system of reference was included in what was after all a very long book. It made the work much easier to handle than it had been in manuscript form.

Between 1482 and 1485 Caxton took his editorial duties sufficiently seriously to provide forms of reference for some of the books published then. However, in later books there were few alterations made to help the reader find out what the volume contained. If there was a table of contents in his original it was translated; if not, none was provided. In only one book did he provide some indication of the book's contents and that was in the composite volume *Horologium Sapientiae*. This contains three treatises and in order to make this clear Caxton added a note at the end to inform his readers what they were:

Thus endeth this present boke composed of diverse fruytfull ghostly maters of whiche the forseyde names folowen to th'entent that weldisposed persones that dersiren to here or rede ghostly informacions maye the sooner knowe by this lityll intytelyng th'effectis of this sayd lytyll volume, in as moche as the hole content of this lityll boke is not of one mater oonly as hereafter ye maye knowe.

The three treatises which make up the volume are then briefly listed. The passage as a whole occurs right at the end of the volume immediately before the note concerning its printing. This is the only time that a list of contents occurs at the end of a book, and perhaps Caxton thought of this as a comprehensive explicit rather than a table of contents, for some of the treatises do in fact have their own tables of contents at their beginning. It is interesting to note in reference to this volume that the other composite volume issued by Caxton, *Of Old Age*, does not contain any indication either at the beginning or at the end of what works are contained in it.

VII
DECORATION AND
ORNAMENT

As Caxton paid scant attention to the textual quality of the works he produced, it might be thought he would make the products of his press aesthetically satisfying. Nothing could be further from the truth, for a glance at Continental books or at later English ones will show how primitive and utilitarian his are. Since he was familiar with the luxury manuscripts produced in Flanders, for he had been a partner of Colard Mansion, a well-known Bruges scrivener, and since he had manuscript copies of some of his translations (like the Caxton Ovid) made in an elegant format, it is surprising that he did not take more trouble with the appearance of his printed books. When all is said and done they are neither textually accurate nor aesthetically appealing.

One reason for this was the lack of control exercised over the compositors, who felt it their duty simply to set up a text in type, not to make it look attractive. Their treatment of the colophon is a good example of their lack of concern. In later books it was quite usual to space out the colophon so that the words formed a pattern on the page and occupied all the available space; in some books the final page is often a little work of art on its own. But Caxton's compositors go on setting up type until the text is exhausted and then they finish; they make no attempt to space the type out agreeably. For example, *Paris and Vienne* is printed in double columns. The text with the colophon finishes on e5^r about halfway down the left-hand column. The rest of that column and the right-hand one are left blank. The compositor has made no concession to how the page looks; he has not even attempted to divide the available text into two short columns so that both sides of the top of the page are filled. Other texts finish just as abruptly. The same lack of concern for appearance is exhibited at the beginning of the books, where because there is no title-page the text usually starts right away. Even within the text there is little attempt to set out the material attractively. Chapter-headings are not placed at the head of a page; if there is room for it it goes at the bottom of the page after the end of the preceding chapter. In *Reynard the Fox* the first page of text, a3^v, contains the first chapter, and then at its foot the heading for the second one is given; and this sort of thing occurs frequently. The heading for chapter four is divided between folios a5^r and a5^v. Naturally there are occasions when the chapter-heading does come at the top of the page, but these are usually fortuitous. It is only when special circumstances intervene such as the need to accommodate woodcuts, as in the second edition of the *Game of Chess*, that chapter-headings are regularly at the top of a page. As a rule the text was divided into pages of type quite arbitrarily and without any concessions to the reader; it is this arbitrary quality which suggests that the division was made before the text was set up. Within the page all kinds of gaps are present. In some copies these gaps have been filled with handwritten paragraph marks, though some texts contain so many gaps that this could not be the main reason for their inclusion. The spaces themselves occur haphazardly within the line, at the beginning, middle or end; no attempt was made to organise them into any pattern and clearly it was not considered necessary to begin a paragraph with a new line. The compositor used the gaps to fill in his page, not to beautify it. Indeed the only time the compositor made an attempt at decoration was after a heading or colophon, when occasionally he produced a little pattern with the punctuation marks.

One way in which a book's appearance could be enhanced was by the addition of a printer's device. But in this as in so much else Caxton's work is uninspired. His device consists of the initials 'WC' separated by a symbol which some commentators have interpreted as '74' set within a decorated border. But the execution of the device is primitive. Even if we compare his device with the one used by the Printer of St Albans, who was working in the 1480s, the difference in standards is considerable. The St Albans device has a simple elegance modelled on the better Continental models. The closest affiliation of Caxton's device is with merchant marks and his is equally utilitarian. It is doubtful in fact whether the symbol occurring within the 'WC' monogram can be interpreted as '74' and even less likely that the symbol has any significance for the history of Caxton's press. He nowhere gives any information as to the date he started printing and there is no evidence that he attached any importance to that date. It is most unlikely that he would have referred to it so obliquely in his device, if he considered it important. It is more probable that the device he used was modelled on, if not actually a copy of, the mark he used on his wares when he traded in other forms of merchandise. Indeed several Continental printers used similar symbols within their devices, a detail which in itself strengthens the views that the symbol in his device is not a date and that printers' devices were imitations of merchants' marks which were the only trademarks with wide European currency.

Caxton used his device for the first time in the Missal after the Sarum Use printed for him by Guillaume Maynyal in Paris in 1487. It seems certain that the device was added to the books in England before they were distributed. As such one might more properly refer to it as a publisher's device rather than a printer's device. But the Missal had a colophon stating that it was printed by Maynyal for Caxton: 'Exaratum Parisius impensa optimi viri Guillermi Caxton arte vero et industria Magistri Guillermi

43. Caxton's device

Maynyal anno Domini mcccclxxxvii iiii Decembris.' What Caxton's device was meant to add to this is uncertain. After all, as it is the first time in which it occurs in one of his books he could not expect that his customers would recognise it and realise that this was a Caxton book. We can hardly assume that his initials were as yet so well known, and in his *Advertisement* he had referred only to the shop at the Red Pale without including his own name. But that he went to all the trouble of inserting his device in the book suggests that he wished to claim some credit for the edition. It is not known whether the device was made specifically for this edition, but it is not improbable. For Maynyal also printed a Legend after the Sarum Use, of which only fragments survive, for Caxton at about this time, and Caxton may have thought it sufficiently worth while to have a device made for these imported volumes. The device itself was made in England, and although the idea of a device was no doubt imported from the Continent the design is almost certainly native, for few other devices contain the rather heavy stylised decoration above and below the mark itself.

The device is included at the end of the Missal on the final blank leaf of the edition, and this may be said to be its normal position in Caxton's works. It follows and emphasises the colophon. It was incorporated in most of Caxton's books issued after the Missal. It occurs on the final blank in the second edition of *Speculum Vitae Christi*, the *Doctrinal of Sapience*, the second edition of *Mirror of the World*, the second edition of the *Festial*, the third edition of *Quattuor Sermones*, and *Eneydos*. However, it is found at the beginning of the second edition of *Reynard the Fox*, where it occurs on the opening leaf with the heading 'This is the table of the historye of Reynart the foxe' below it. The contents follow on the verso of this leaf. The end of this edition is not extant and so it is not possible to tell why the device was included at the beginning, though the occurrence of the heading under the device would indicate that the device was not included as an afterthought. It also occurs at the beginning of the third edition of *Dicts or Sayings*, and in this case the device occurs on a leaf by itself. As there are blank leaves at the end of this edition, one can only assume that its inclusion at the beginning was another example of that lack of regularity in the workshop which we have noted many times already. In the second edition of the *Directorium Sacerdotum* the device is found on folio a8^v. But there are two gatherings in this volume with signature 'a' and it seems likely that the first quaternion with the first signature 'a' was printed last. In other words the device may have been printed last even though when the book was assembled it came after the prefatory matter. As it happens this edition contains no blank leaves and so the device fills the only space available for it. In the composite volume which contains the *Horologium Sapientiae*, the *Twelve Profits of Tribulation* and the *Rule of St Benedict* the device is included after the second work. The three texts have separate signatures and may have been printed independently. If we take our cue from the example in the *Directorium Sacerdotum*, it may be that the *Twelve Profits of Tribulation* was the last of the three works to be printed. On the other hand, it is the only work which contains blank pages suitable for the device. So it may be that when the texts were divided up into pages of type the supervisor realised that the only place to put the device was after the *Twelve Profits of Tribulation* and put it there accordingly. It is preceded by a woodcut of the mocking of Christ, which is the only other illustration in the book.

Of other texts printed towards the end of Caxton's career two, *Blanchardin and Eglantine* and *Four Sons of Aymon,* are defective at the end in the extant copies and so we cannot tell whether they had the device or not. Four works are without it. The *Fifteen Oes* is a highly decorated text. It has a blank for the first leaf, but as its verso is occupied by a flamboyant woodcut it would be nice to think that the press decided it would be too much to add the device as well. The *Governal of Health* has no available blanks at beginning or end, and so the device is not found. The device was not so essential that steps were taken to leave suitable space for it when the text was set up. The *Feats of Arms* and the *Statutes* both contain blank pages at the end which could have accommodated the device. Its omission indicates that the device was not yet included as a regular feature. Although meant to indicate the publisher or printer, it was still in some ways a decoration which could be added or omitted as circumstances allowed.

The device passed after Caxton's death with the rest of his printing materials into the hands of Wynkyn de Worde, who used it in several books such as the *Lives of the Fathers,* printed about 1495. A second device which is very similar to, but much smaller than, the first was used by de Worde in some of his earliest books such as the *Book of Courtesy,* printed about 1492. It consists of Caxton's mark with floriated decoration above and below. It may indeed have been ordered by Caxton before his

death, though he is not known to have used it. Wynkyn de Worde appropriated the initials 'WC' and Caxton's symbol as his own and his later devices all include them. But he does add his own name to his later devices and one also includes a sun, for when he moved to Fleet Street he had a shop at the Sign of the Sun. Other English printers, however, tended to look to the Continent for their models and the style of Caxton's device did not inspire any imitators.

Fifteenth-century English books are notable for their overall poverty of decoration. Continental books were more ornate and included floriated initials, borders and endpieces as regular features. It may be because the art of book decoration had been insufficiently developed by 1471–72 when Caxton learned the art of printing in Cologne that he himself failed to introduce much decoration in his books. But he maintained regular contacts with Continental producers and he imported foreign books, so he can hardly have been unaware of developments there. The reasons for his failure to keep abreast of Continental advances were the absence of competition in England and his own conservative nature. When printing started the printer took over the role of the scribe. But the scribe had been only one of the craftsmen involved in manuscript production. The rubricator drew in the capital letters and the signs for paragraphs, and the illuminator added the illustrations and the decorated borders. Printed books were produced in the same way. The printer produced the text and the leaves were then handed over to the rubricator for the decoration, such as the capitals, to be added by hand. The history of printing shows that the printers gradually took over the roles of the rubricator and the illuminator by using wood blocks, so that eventually a whole page could be produced by one pull of the printing press.

The process can be seen with paragraph marks and initial capitals. The earliest books printed by Caxton had spaces throughout the text. In some copies these spaces have been filled in with hand-painted paragraph marks in either red or blue. However, individual copies vary as to where the paragraph marks are inserted and some have no marks at all. If the workshop had its own rubricator he clearly did not have any plan to follow to indicate where he should include a mark. He took each copy as it came along and inserted whatever marks seemed appropriate to him. But the absence of marks in many copies may indicate that the press sold off the printed sheets without decoration so that customers could take them to the rubricator of their choice to have them decorated to their own taste. The diversity that can arise among the copies of a particular edition will be appreciated by considering some of the copies of the first edition of *Reynard the Fox*, printed in 1481. The John Rylands Library copy has a wide range of paragraph marks and capitals painted in red or blue, usually alternately. One of the British Library copies has no painted initials or paragraph marks at all, but the other has them painted in red only, though the rubricator has not painted in as many in his copy as are found in the Rylands copy. The Eton College copy has initials and paragraph marks painted only as far as folio b1^r in red, gold and blue, though it is possible that these were added after the fifteenth century. The Pierpont Morgan Library copy contains no painted marks of any sort.

The change from painted to printed paragraph marks took place in 1484, for the first dated text to contain printed ones is *Aesop*, printed on 26 March of that year. The second edition of *Quattuor Sermones* also contains printed paragraph marks, but this text is undated and it may be wiser to date its appearance after the *Aesop* volume. *Caton*, which like *Aesop* was translated in 1483, also contains printed paragraph marks, but its date of printing is unknown. It cannot, however, have appeared till 1484, since the translation was finished only on 23 December 1483. The *Knight of the Tower* appeared on 31 January 1484; as it contains no printed paragraph marks, it seems likely that Caxton acquired the requisite type-sorts while the *Knight of the Tower* was at press and used them immediately afterwards in *Aesop* and *Caton*, though which came first is uncertain. If we can date the acquisition of the sorts for paragraph marks to about January 1484 two points of interest emerge. The first is that type 4 had been introduced in 1480 and type 4* in 1483. So the introduction of the paragraph mark did not occur at the same time as a new type was introduced, for *Aesop*, *Caton*, and the second edition of *Quattuor Sermones* are all in type 4*. The second is that a number of undated texts, particularly Chaucerian poems, have been allocated to 1484. These texts contain no printed paragraph marks, even though the marks otherwise became a regular feature of his books from then on. Two solutions are possible. Either the marks were used only haphazardly at first or else the undated poems should be allocated to 1483 rather than to 1484. If the redating was thought the better solution, this in its turn would mean that the first edition of the *Canterbury Tales* would have to be redated. Though neither edition is dated, Caxton stated he published the second edition six years after the first. So if the

45. Some woodcut
initials

second edition was dated to 1483, the first would have to be put in 1477, which would make it one of the earliest texts to be issued by the press at Westminster.

A consideration of the initial capitals may help us to come nearer to a solution. All types used by Caxton had capitals, but they were only one line high and were meant for use within the body of the text. But chapters and paragraphs were introduced in manuscripts by capitals which extended over several lines and the early printers imitated this layout. The compositors left spaces for these initials when they were setting up the text, and the space varied usually from two to five lines, with three being the normal gap. When a space was left for a large initial capital, the second letter would be printed in ordinary upper-case capitals, and it was only from the third letter that lower case was used. In order to help the rubricator the compositor included a guide letter or director in the space where the capital should be so that he knew which letter he had to paint. The guide letter was painted over when the capital was made. Because of the use of guide letters, mistakes as to which letter to paint in are rarely made, though they do occur.

As with printed paragraph marks, printed initials make their first appearance in a dated text in 1484. Once again it is *Aesop* which is the first dated book with printed initials. They are printed from wood blocks which are three lines deep except for a very floriated 'A' which extends over eight lines. The woodcuts are quite pleasantly made and no doubt were acquired from the Continent. Indeed they may have arrived together with the paragraph marks early in 1484. But the use of these capitals is less straightforward than that of the paragraph marks. *Caton,* which was probably printed in 1484, has printed paragraph marks but no initial capitals. The second edition of *Quattuor Sermones,* which may also date from 1484, uses some printed paragraph marks and also a few capitals. But the printed capitals occur towards the end of the volume in a relatively inconspicuous part, whereas the first page is without a printed capital and has the space with guide-letter for the capital to be painted in by hand. *Saint Winifred,* usually dated to 1485, again has printed paragraph marks but no printed capitals. All the poetic texts attributed to 1484 and which lack paragraph marks are likewise without printed capitals. However, after 1485 all texts printed by Caxton, excluding *Saint Winifred,* contain both printed capitals as well as paragraph marks. So in the case of the printed initials it would seem as though at first their use was somewhat irregular and it was only after they had been in the workshop for about eighteen months that they became adopted as a part of the standard make-up of a book.

The printed capitals used by Caxton are not uniform and do not belong to one series. The large floriated 'A' is quite different from all the other capitals and seems to exist in isolation. Apart from its use in *Aesop* it was used only once again, in the *Order of Chivalry.* This text, which was addressed to Richard II and so appeared between 1483 and 1485, also contains printed paragraph marks and capitals in addition to the 'A'. The use of this

'A' would put it close to *Aesop* in time, and it may in fact have followed *Aesop* in the workshop. The large 'A' was not used again and may have been disposed of. The series of capitals used in *Aesop* occupy three-line spaces. But already by 1485 Caxton had a larger series, for *King Arthur* has capitals filling both three-line and five-line spaces. And some later books like the *Doctrinal of Sapience* have woodcut capitals designed for a two-line space. One of the later books to exhibit a wide range of Caxton's initials is the *Fifteen Oes,* printed about 1491. This contains the elaborate five-line initials as well as the simpler two-line and three-line models. Some of the capitals are varied by having white lines drawn through the wide black descenders and the larger ones also have floral patterns attached to them. Few of them, however, can be said to possess much elegance and their use in printed books probably arose more from the wish to print as much of the book as possible than from any aesthetic sensibility.

In addition to paragraph marks and capitals the only other form of decoration associated directly with the text is the sign of a Maltese Cross. Crosses of this type arose probably in the fourteenth century and were used to decorate Books of Hours. Caxton used a Maltese cross only in association with his type 6, of which it may be said to form a sort. But the cross was not included in all books printed in type 6; it was confined for the most part to books of a more technical nature. Its use in such books was purely decorative; it had no functional purpose.

Like most other ornaments decorated borders arrived late in England. The edition of *Expositio super libros Aristotelis de anima* by Alexander of Hales printed by Theodoric Rood at Oxford on 11 October 1481 has borders around three of the pages in some copies of the book. It has been suggested that either the work was issued twice or the borders were added by the printer as an afterthought. But as Lathbury's *Liber moralium super threnis Ieremiae* issued at Oxford on 31 July 1482 has the same borders in only some of the copies, it may be that it was Rood's policy to issue decorated and undecorated copies of the same edition. At any event he has the honour of being the first printer in England to use borders. But the foreigner, William de Machlinia, was the second printer to have borders in one of his books. His Book of Hours after the Sarum Use, printed about 1485, has borders for the pages which begin each section, or so it would seem for the book survives only in a fragmentary state. The cuts fall into two sections: one is used round the text and the other round the woodcuts. In the most complete copy that survives the borders have been lightly coloured in by hand. The borders are simpler than those used by Rood and were probably imported from France.

Caxton himself did not make use of borders till the very end of his life. The *Fifteen Oes*, which appeared about 1491, has a border round every page of text as well as on the page with a woodcut of the Crucifixion. The borders form a frame within which the text is presented and so give this volume a florid appear-

46. *The initial 'A'*

ance quite unlike anything else produced by him. The borders consist of four oblong woodcuts: two long and thin pieces for the sides of the page, of which the one for the outer margin is wider than that for the inner one; and two shorter pieces for the top and bottom pieces were designed to fit inside the side pieces so that it would have been possible to make a tight-fitting and continuous frame. But it must be admitted that the borders were very carelessly assembled. There are gaps between many of the pieces and some of the woodcuts have been put in upside-down or the wrong way round. Each page consists of four wood-cut borders of different size and each piece has a different design on it. There were eight separate cuts for each border, so that the possibilities of variation were numerous. The designs are basically floral, though they are enlivened on some blocks by birds or grotesque animal representations. The blocks probably came from France, for similar designs were used by Jean du Pré in Paris. Whether Caxton went out of his way to get hold of them or whether their acquisition was largely accidental we can-not tell. But we should remember that the English printers main-tained close contacts with their Continental counterparts and the trade in printing materials was lively. However, that he waited till the end of his life before using borders suggests that Caxton did not think too highly of their value and so made little attempt to acquire them. The borders passed into Wynkyn de Worde's hands after his master's death and he used them in several of his editions. He also acquired another set of borders from the Low Countries shortly after taking control of the business, though in this case it was as part of a consignment of type.

In general English printers in the fifteenth century used borders sparingly. It will be noted that they used them to decorate the whole book rather than a particular part of it. In the sixteenth century borders were used much more for title-pages, for devices and for colophons. The fifteenth-century printers had not reached this stage of specialisation and so naturally preferred to decorate their books with woodcut illuminations rather than with borders. The fifteenth-century printers did not bother with endpieces for chapters and books and kept their non-representational decora-tion to a minimum.

The first Caxton book with an illustration is his *History of Troy*, the first book he printed. But as only one copy, now in the Huntington Library, California, has the illustration in it, it is uncertain whether the book was issued with it or whether it was added later. If it was designed to go with the volume it is surprising that Caxton made no reference to the illustration in the various prologues and epilogues which he added to the edition. The picture is in fact a copper-plate engraving, a form of illustration otherwise unknown in his books. It represents a scene in a noble lady's parlour in which a kneeling figure is presenting a book to a lady. An elegantly dressed man is looking at the scene from a half-open door on the left, while various other ladies, gentlemen and pages are grouped around the room. On the canopy over the fireplace are the initials 'C' and 'M' linked by an intertwined thong and an inscription, *bien en auiengne*. The initials, standing for Charles of Burgundy and his wife, Margaret, and the motto are sufficient to identify the lady receiving the book as Margaret of Burgundy, Caxton's patron of the *History of Troy*. The style of the engraving is similar to that found in illuminations executed in Flanders for Margaret by an artist who is today known as the Master of Mary of Burgundy; and the engraving can be dated with reasonable accuracy to the 1470s—the same time as the *History of Troy* was printed. There is, however, no indication that the kneeling figure is meant to be Caxton or even that the engraving was designed for this book. Margaret was a considerable patron of letters and many manuscripts were made for her, so that such presentation scenes must have been a familiar feature of her life.

However, one further piece of evidence might be taken into account. The copy in which the illustration is found apparently belonged to Elizabeth Woodville, the wife of Edward IV, for there is a manuscript inscription on the paper lining of the vellum covering of the book which reads 'This boke is mine, Quene Elizabet, late wiffe vnto the moste noble King Edwarde the Forthe, off whos bothe sooles Y beseche almyghty Gode take to his onfinyght mercy above. Per me Thomam Shukburghe juniorem.' Margaret of Burgundy was the sister-in-law of Elizabeth Woodville and it is possible that a copy of the edition belonging to the Queen of England had a special picture representing the patron of the volume, her sister-in-law, which was not included in the other copies. This is speculation. All we can say is that the illustration is of the same age as the edition and as it is found in a copy of that edition it is possible that it was meant to be attached to it. Otherwise we would have to accept that someone who realised the picture was of Margaret of Burgundy thought it would make a suitable frontispiece for the *History of Troy* which she had patronised. Nevertheless, if we could tentatively accept that the illustration was meant for this edition,

47. *The presentation of a book to*
   Margaret, Duchess of Burgundy

it would still leave the interpretation of the other figures as a matter of doubt. Should one of them be thought of as Caxton? If so, should it be the kneeling figure or the person looking in at the door seeing how the gift was accepted? The point is perhaps academic, for it is unlikely in any case that the portrayal would be lifelike, partly because of the tendency towards idealism in such subjects and partly because the artist would have drawn the figures from his imagination rather than from nature. So in view of the many problems surrounding this illustration it is best not to attach too much significance to it. One should not look for a true representation of Caxton in it and one should not forget what an isolated position it occupies in illustrations within his books.

Apart from this picture all other illustrations in Caxton books are from woodblocks. Although he may have used a rubricator for painting in paragraph marks and initials, he did not use the services of an illuminator to paint pictures in his books. There is only one place where this might be considered a possibility. In his edition of Gower's *Confessio Amantis* from 1483 the folio with the signature 1 2 has at the top of the page the heading *Prologus* and the number of the leaf *Folio 2*. Otherwise the top half of the leaf is blank and the prologue occupies the second half of the page only. As the book was printed in double columns, the gap at the top of the page was left free deliberately and it is natural to think it was designed for an illustration. If so, it may have been meant for a hand-painted one. But as Caxton had started to use woodblock illustrations by this time, it is just as likely that the space was left for a woodblock picture which was not yet ready and which in fact was never completed.

Scholars are divided as to which book was the first to be issued with woodcuts, the two contenders being the third edition of *Cato* and the first edition of the *Mirror of the World.* Neither is dated, though both appeared about 1481. The translation of the *Mirror of the World* was completed on 8 March 1481 and was no doubt printed not long afterwards; *Cato* appeared about the same time. *Cato* contains two woodcuts, one of a schoolmaster in a chair holding a birch in his hand with four scholars in front of him and the other of a schoolmaster seated at a lectern containing an open book with five scholars in front of him, which both occur in a larger series of cuts included in the *Mirror of the World*. They form numbers five and six of that series. The woodcuts in the *Mirror of the World*, including the two also found in *Cato*, form a coherent group which was evidently prepared by one

¶After this foloweth the Recapitulacion of the thinges
aforsaid capitulo ¶ .vviij.
¶Hier endeth the table of the Rubrices of this
present book.

¶Prologue declaryng to whom this book apperteyneth

Consideryng
that wordes ben
perisshyng / vayne / &
forgeteful / And wri-
tynges duelle & abi-
de permanēt / as I rede
Voy audita perit / lit-
tera scripta manet /
Thise thinges haue
caused that the faites
and dedes of Auncyent men / ben sette by declaracion in
fair and Aourned volumes / to thende that science and
Artes lerned and founden of thinges passed myght be
had in perpetuel memorye and remembraunce / ffor the
hertes of nobles in eschewyng of ydelnes at suche tyme
as they haue none other vertuouse ocupacōn on hāde ought
to excersise them in redyng / studyng / & visytyng the noble
faytes and dedes of the sage and wysemen somtyme tra-
uaillyng in prouffytable vertues / of whom it happeth ofte
that somen ben enclyned to visyte the bookes treatyng
of sciences particuler / And other to rede & visyte bookes
spekyng of faytes of armes / of loue / or of other merueails

a4

48. *The master and
scholars woodcut*

prologue declar
ant a qui ce vo
lume appartient

Onsiderant
que polices sont
le demeurex baines
et escriptures p
mainteres ont
les fais des anci
ens este mis par
declaracon en

braulp e aouvrex volumes Affin que
des sciences acquises e chose passees fust
pretuelle memoire pour les cuers des
nobles eceruser en lisat e estudiant
les fais des sages Jadiz traueillant en
bertz proussitables Dont il aduient q
les vngs sont enclins a visiter les liure
traitans de sciences pticulieres Et les
aultres a visiter les liures parlans
de fais darmes e damours ou aultre
ment Et est ce put volume appelle
lymage du monde Et su translate de
latin en franchois p le comandement

ymage du monde
translate de latin en
francois.

49. The master and
    scholars
    manuscript
    illustration

artist, for the style is uniform. Hence some scholars have argued that the whole series was cut for the *Mirror of the World* and two of them were taken out of the group and re-used by Caxton in *Cato*. Others, however, feel that the two *Cato* woodcuts were made first and subsequently added to the series designed for the *Mirror of the World*. The latter seems the more likely hypothesis. These two are slightly smaller than the rest of the cuts in *Mirror of the World*. If the whole of the series was available when *Cato* was printed, it is not clear why these two cuts alone were used in it. Furthermore the woodcuts for the *Mirror of the World* were modelled on illustrations found in MS Royal 19 A ix of the British Library of the French *Image du Monde*, a manuscript which Caxton used as the basis of his own translation and which must have been in the workshop. But the two cuts used in *Cato* are not copies of any pictures in Royal 19 A ix, for the relevant chapters in the French manuscript are without illustration. So it seems likely that Caxton employed an artist to make blocks for *Cato* and *Mirror of the World* and that those for the former were made immediately before those for the latter book. Indeed it is quite likely that the artist was familiar with the illustrations in Royal 19 A ix before he started on the *Cato* cuts, since they have a stylistic and thematic similarity with one of the blocks modelled on a manuscript illumination. This would mean that *Cato* was printed early in 1481 and *Mirror of the World* shortly after 8 March.

That Caxton should have used the cuts for *Cato* in the *Mirror of the World* need cause us no surprise, for although a printer had blocks cut for a particular book, when they had been used for that book they passed into his general stock and were used in books of different subject matter. As it happens the two cuts from *Cato* were included in the chapters on grammar and logic in the *Mirror of the World* and so may be said to fit quite as suitably in the second book as in the first. Other examples are less happy. The most famous example of the re-use of a woodblock is the cut of the twenty-four pilgrims made for Caxton's second edition of the *Canterbury Tales* which was used by Wynkyn de Worde to depict the assembly of gods in his edition of Lydgate's poem of that name printed about 1498. This re-use of material was naturally much easier with religious scenes, which formed a large part of most printers' stock anyway. It was this kind of cut which was mainly used a second and third time by Caxton, possibly because many of them were not acquired for a specific book in the first instance. Some of the cuts found in the first

edition of the *Speculum Vitae Christi*, for example, were used
in the *Royal Book*, the *Doctrinal of Sapience*, the *Commemoratio*,
and the second edition of the *Mirror of the World*. Since Caxton
acquired or had made several sets of woodcuts he was not forced
to re-use his pictures too frequently. It was Wynkyn de Worde
with his larger output and with the increased demand for
illustration who was forced to use some cuts excessively. Caxton's
cut of the Crucifixion which appeared for the first time in the
Fifteen Oes was used by Wynkyn de Worde in more than twenty
of his editions.

The re-use of these blocks is of course a useful aid in dating
the various editions, for through use they became cracked round
the edges or generally split or worn. Since Caxton did not re-use
his blocks frequently their state is less useful in dating his output.
But the Crucifixion scene used for the first time in the first edition
of the *Speculum Vitae Christi* was used again in the second edition
and in the *Doctrinal of Sapience*, both undated as to their printing.
To judge from the woodcuts the block was more worn when
used for the *Doctrinal of Sapience* than it had been for the second
edition of the *Speculum Vitae Christi*. It would therefore be reasonable to date the latter before the *Doctrinal of Sapience*.

By no means did all books printed by Caxton after 1481 have
woodcuts in them. The following is a list of his books which
do contain them together with their dates of printing; hypothetical dates are in brackets. Some of these dates are disputed and
will be discussed later.

(1481) *Cato*.
(1481) *Mirror of the World*, first edition (re-using two *Cato* cuts).
(1483) *Game of Chess*, second edition.
(1483) *Canterbury Tales*, second edition.
20 November 1483 (?)   *Golden Legend*, first edition.
26 March 1484   *Aesop*.
(1484/5) *Royal Book* (re-using one cut from *Aesop* and using six
          from *Speculum Vitae Christi*).
(1486) *Speculum Vitae Christi*, first edition.
(1487) *Golden Legend*, second edition (re-using cuts of first
        edition).
(1487) *Image of Pity*, first edition.
(1490) *Doctrinal of Sapience* (re-using two cuts from *Speculum
        Vitae Christi*).
(1490) *Horae*, third edition.
(1490) *Commemoratio* (re-using one cut from *Speculum Vitae
        Christi*).

(1490)   *Image of Pity*, second edition.
(1491)   *Fifteen Oes.*
(1491)   *Horologium Sapientiae.*
(1491)   *Festum Transfigurationis.*

These books add up to less than half of the editions issued by Caxton from 1481 onwards. The omission of woodcuts in some of his editions is at first sight surprising. Thus *Aesop* contains

Liber Tercius

His enſample/ne to take hym for to be adāmaged/as thou maiſt ſee by this prꝛeſente fable/ ffor men ought not to gyue the ſtaf/ by which they may be beten with

¶ The xviij fable is of the wulf and of the dogge ǀ

The ffables of Auian

It is not wel arayed/ nor wel apꝛopynted/ which is clothed luxury oꝛ ſo goldne / ne alſo it is not honeſte to make large tyo..̄ꝛ of other mennes text

¶ The v fable is of the frogge and of the foxe

One ought to auaunce hym ſelf to doo that which he can not doo/ As hit apperieth of a frogge / which ſomtyme yſſued oꝛ came oute of a dych/ the which pꝛeſumed to haue kepte vpon a hyghe montayne/And when ſhe was vpon the montayne/ſhe ſayd to other beſtes / I am a maiſtreſſe in medecyn/ and canne gyue remedy to al maner of ſekenes by myn arte/ and ſubtylyte /and ſhalle rendre and brynge you vp ageyne in good helthe/ wherof ſomme byleued her/ And thenne the foxe which perceyued the folyſſhe byleue of the beſtes/began to laughe/and ſayd to them/ poure beſtes/ſow may this folile and venemous beſt which is ſeke and pale of colour rendre and gyue to you helthe/ ffor the ſeek which wylle hele ſomme other / ought fyrſte to hele hym

an extensive series of cuts, but *Reynard the Fox* has none though the subject matter is just as suitable and later printers were to illustrate the story. Similarly the second edition of the *Canterbury Tales* has a series of cuts made specially for it, but neither *Troilus and Criseyde* nor the *House of Fame,* both of which were printed about the same time, has any. Malory's *Le Morte D'Arthur,* a very suitable book for illustration, has no pictures, and all the chronicles and history books issued by Caxton were without illustrations. One reason for the discrepancy between books with and those without illustration lies in the manuscripts and printed books Caxton used as his sources and his own response to the manuscript tradition. The *Mirror of the World* and *Āesop* had woodcuts because the sources he used, in one case a manuscript and in the other a printed book, had illustrations. The Dutch edition of *Reynard the Fox* which Caxton used to make his translation was without woodcuts and so he clearly felt no need to include them in his own edition. It is presumably because most manuscripts of the *Canterbury Tales* have illustrations, and we may assume that this was true of the manuscript loaned him

51. *Two woodcuts from 'Aesop'*

52. *The woodcut of a different artist in 'Aesop'*

by his customer for the second edition, that he decided to include woodcuts in this edition; the first had appeared before he had started to introduce them. But manuscripts of *Troilus and Criseyde* and the *House of Fame* are found without illustration, and it may be that Chaucer responded by not including them. The only extant manuscript of Malory's *Le Morte D'Arthur*, now at Winchester School, has no illustrations, and although it is not the one Caxton used it is very close to it. Once again we may assume that Caxton's source was unillustrated. In other words Caxton was prompted to use woodcuts only if this was suggested to him by his source, for he and his artists were clearly not prepared to design cuts from their own imagination or literary response to the works. They were only prepared to copy accepted illustrations. While this principle that only those books were illustrated which were copied from illustrated manuscripts or books is sound, it should not be pushed too far. When blocks were re-used, it was not necessarily in response to illustrations in the source. And there may have been occasions when illustrated manuscripts used by Caxton were not produced as illustrated books simply because an artist was not available to make the woodcuts.

The cuts were made by twelve different artists and form nine series with three miscellaneous illustrations. Of the twelve artists, six were English; the work of the other six was imported. The six native workers executed the following cuts. One did the cuts for *Cato* and *Mirror of the World*, amounting to eleven in all. A second, who may be regarded as Caxton's principal artist, did all sixteen cuts for the second edition of the *Game of Chess*, the twenty-three for the second edition of the *Canterbury Tales*, and the bulk of the cuts for both *Aesop* and *Golden Legend*. In all, this second man was responsible for about three hundred woodcuts. A third artist finished the cuts needed for the *Golden Legend* and a fourth and fifth completed the series for *Aesop*. In addition there is the isolated cut of the transfiguration in *Festum Transfigurationis* executed by a sixth. If we assume as a result of the reasoning above that *Cato* and *Mirror of the World* were printed early in 1481, then Caxton started to think of woodcuts by English artists in late 1480 or early 1481. Apart from the isolated cut in *Festum Transfigurationis* printed about 1491, he dispensed with the work of English artists in 1484. Only *Aesop* of the other four books with cuts is dated and that appeared on 26 March 1484; if it was not the last book with English woodcuts issued by Caxton, it cannot have been far removed from the one that was. Indeed as *Aesop* and the *Golden Legend* have the majority of

¶ Octauo Id? Augusti. siat seruie / de tñssigu
racõe Jhũ xpi dñi nostri / Ad pmas vs Añ /

Asumpsit ihũs
discipľos & al
cendit i montẽ & tñs
figurat? est ãte eos .
ps / Laudate pueri
Añ / Dum tñsfigu
rarctur ihũs / moy=
ses & helyas cũ dño
loquẽtes discipulis
apparuerũt . ¶ au
date dũm oẽs .5.ñ/

Tunc petr? dixit ad Jhm . dñe si vis faciam?
hic tria tabnacula. tibi vnũ Moysi vnũ et helpe
vnũ. ps. Lauda aĩa mea / añ / Ad huc co loquẽ
te ecce nubes lucida obũbrauit eos .5. Laudate
dũm q°. Añ De qua voz isonuit hic e filí? me?
dilect? in quo michi cõplacui ipm audite / ps

Lauda iherusalem dũm / ¶ Capm
Aluatozẽ expectam? dũm nostrũ Jhm
xpm qui reformabit corp? humilitatis
nře gfiguratũ corpori claritatis sue. scdm opera
cõnẽ qua possit et subicere sibi oia. B. Assumẽs

the cuts in their respective series executed by the same man, it seems likely that he was working on them about the same time. Since both series were finished by different workers, it is possible that this second artist ran some kind of illuminators' workshop and that he allowed his apprentices or helpers to finish his work when he was hard pressed. But as yet neither the artists nor their places of work can be identified.

The woodcuts in *Cato* were modelled on one of the pictures of a schoolmaster in the *Mirror of the World*, in which the cuts were in their turn modelled on the illustrations in MS Royal 19 A ix. The scenes portrayed in this work vary from portrayals of Christ, the creation of Eve, and schoolteachers to geometric designs to illustrate celestial computations. The cut of Jesus is not found in the 1490 reprint and may have become detached from the main series to be used individually in some other work no longer extant. These cuts are quite small and extend only to half the width of the page. Those in the second edition of the *Game of Chess* are larger and fill half a folio side. There are sixteen cuts in this series, though some have been used twice so that there are twenty-four illustrations in all. It follows of course that some of the cuts are hardly appropriate to the second occasion of their use. The series was probably modelled on cuts found in some Continental printed book or manuscript, for copies of this work were common in the fifteenth century. The outstanding cut of the *Aesop* series is the frontispiece depicting the hunchback Aesop surrounded by various emblems representing his fables. The name ESOPVS is cut into the top and shows that the picture was originally intended for a Latin version. In fact the series was copied from the French edition used by Caxton for his translation, which had in its turn borrowed from the Latin edition produced by Johan Zainer at Ulm. This large frontispiece is the nearest that Caxton ever came to producing a title-page, but it is improbable that he had this object in mind. The artist simply reproduced what was in his original. Otherwise the cuts generally fill half of a folio page and illustrate the fables. Like those in the *Game of Chess,* they come immediately after the chapter-heading of the fables they represent. After Caxton's death this series came into the hands of Richard Pynson, who used them for his 1497 edition of *Aesop*. Pynson may have been one of Caxton's apprentices and may have maintained links with his successor, Wynkyn de Worde, though it is not known how he acquired this series. Although the series for the second edition of the *Canterbury Tales* owes its inspiration to pictures of the

Here begynneth the squyers tale

At surry in the lond of Tartarye
There dwellyd a kynge that warryd russhy
Thorow whyche there dyde many a doughty man
Thys nobyl kynge was clepyd Cambuscan
Whyche in hys tyme was of so gret renoun
That ther was nowhere in no regioun
So excellent a lord in alle thynge
He lackid nought that longed to a kynge
As of the secte of whyche he was born
He kepte hys lay to whyche he was sworn
And therto he was hardy wyse and ryche
Pytous juste and alwey y lyche
Soth of hys word benygne and honourable
Of hys corage as ony center stabyl

So hote he louedz that by nyghter tale
He slepte nomore than a nyghtyngale
Curteys he was lowly andz seruysabyl
He carf beforn hys fader at the tabyl

A Yeman hadde he andz seruauntis nomo
At that tyme for he lyst to ryde so
Andz he was cladz in cote & hoodz of grene
A sheef of pecok arowes bryght andz shene
Onder hys belt he bare ful thryftyly
Wel coude he dresse hys takyl yomanly
Hys arowes droupedz not wyth fetherys lowe
Andz in hys hondz he baar a myghty bowe
A not hedz he hadz with a broun Vysage
Of wodemannes craft coude he al the Vsage
Op on hys arme he bare a gay bracer
Andz by hys syde a swerdz andz a bokeler
Andz on that other syde a gay daggar
Harneysedz wel andz sharpe as poynt of spere

55. *The yeoman*

pilgrims found in fifteenth-century manuscripts of the poem, there is no extant manuscript which can have been the direct source. But as the manuscript which Caxton borrowed for the second edition has not been identified, this state of affairs is hardly surprising. Twenty-two of the cuts portray individual pilgrims and the other one depicts twenty-four pilgrims at dinner. The cuts of the individual pilgrims were used several times within the book, for although they were designed to illustrate the descriptions of the pilgrims in the General Prologue, they were also included at the head of the tales. The cut of the Merchant, for example, is used in the General Prologue of the Merchant, the Franklin, and the Summoner, but it is found only at the head of the tales by the Merchant and the Summoner. The cut used to introduce the Franklin's Tale is the one used to illustrate the Manciple in the General Prologue. It is not clear whether this reuse of woodcuts in the *Game of Chess* and the *Canterbury Tales* is the result of insufficient time by the artist to complete the series or of economy on the part of the printer who did not order sufficient woodcuts. The cuts themselves are quite simple and schematised; the artist has not attempted to follow the descriptions found in the poem. Indeed it might be argued whether the cut illustrating the Merchant, the Franklin, and the Summoner was designed originally for the Merchant, as is generally thought, or for one of the other two. The cut of the twenty-four pilgrims at dinner, which was positioned in the General Prologue before the passage describing how well the host entertained the pilgrims, shows them seated at a round table with various dishes in front of them. A model for this cut is not known. This cut together with the first four in the series, those of the Knight, the Squire, the Yeoman and the Prioress, are slightly deeper but less wide than the rest, though it is uncertain whether any significance could be attached to this discrepancy in size. The series passed with the rest of Caxton's stock into the hands of Wynkyn de Worde who used it for his edition of the tales from 1498. Many of them also reappear in the 1532 edition attributed to T. Godfrey.

The series for the *Golden Legend* is the most diverse and in some ways the most interesting. It contains the largest cut used by Caxton, which is of the saints in glory grouped under a representation of the Trinity flanked by angels. This cut occurs as the frontispiece of the volume, though it does not occupy the whole page by itself. For the pages in the *Golden Legend* were very large, and if it had filled the whole page it would have

been impossible to re-use it. Even so it measures 223 × 168 mm.
At the end of the author's prologue there is another large cut.
This depicts the arms of the Earl of Arundel, the patron of this
edition. It is the only occasion Caxton honoured one of his patrons
in this way. The reason for its inclusion cannot be decided definitely. It may be simply because there was room for it. For it
is found in the introductory unsigned ternion which was added
after the rest of the book was printed. Apart from the two woodcuts and the prologues of author and translator the ternion contains the index. As it is, the ternion has several blank sides and
without the large woodcuts it would have seemed empty indeed.
On the other hand, Caxton may have wanted to honour the
Earl, for the book was a large one and Arundel had promised
to take a certain number off his hands. Indeed it is even possible
that the idea of the arms was suggested to Caxton by the Earl
or his servant, John Stanney, for the model to copy would most
probably have been provided by one or the other.

Part of the fascination of the woodcuts lies in speculating
whether they can provide any clue as to the date of the printing
of the *Golden Legend*. As we saw in a previous chapter the book
was 'finished' on 20 November 1483 and this date may refer
to either the translation or the printing. In his prologue Caxton
stated that he had been on the point of abandoning the translation
because of the labour involved and that it was only at the insis-
tence of the Earl of Arundel that he had decided to complete
it. The story probably has a grain of truth in it, but not much
more, for the political conditions of the time were so confused
that he might well have hesitated for that reason alone. In fact
Arundel's name is mentioned only in the colophon and in the
prologue in the introductory ternion, which was printed last.
So as far as that evidence is concerned the book could easily
have been already at press before he became associated with it.
The cut of the Arundel arms by itself cannot help us to get any
closer to the date of the book's printing. But the artist who made
the bulk of the cuts in the *Golden Legend* also made those in
the *Game of Chess*, the *Canterbury Tales*, and *Aesop*, and as *Aesop*
and the *Golden Legend* have series completed by others they may
have been prepared at about the same time. *Aesop* is the only
dated work (26 March 1484), and of the others the *Game of
Chess* is thought by bibliographers to have appeared in 1483 and
the *Canterbury Tales* and the *Golden Legend* in 1484. But as we
saw earlier the absence of paragraph marks in the *Canterbury
Tales* would make it feasible to date its appearance in 1483 rather

than in 1484. And the fact that the artist managed to complete all the cuts for that text and the *Game of Chess* reinforces the impression that these texts appeared before the other two. It would be natural to go on to more ambitious projects, such as the extensive series in *Aesop* and the *Golden Legend,* after smaller projects involving considerable duplication had been tried. It is also relevant to consider the type used in these four books, for though not a reliable guide it may help to provide confirmatory evidence. The *Game of Chess* was printed in type 2* only and is almost certainly therefore the earliest of these four books. *Canterbury Tales* appeared in type 4* with type 2* used only for headings. *Aesop* and the *Golden Legend* are alike in that both use type 4* with headings in type 3. The use of type ⸗* in headings when the main text is in type 4* is found also in *Caton,* which was translated on 23 December 1483 and probably printed in 1484 before *Aesop.* This text was probably not too distant in time from the *Canterbury Tales,* though as it has paragraph marks but no initial capitals it may well have been later. The *Golden Legend* is like *Aesop* in having types 4* and 3, but it differs in that it has no printed paragraph marks or initial capitals. The absence of these features suggests that, although close in time to *Aesop,* it preceded it. In that case the 'finished' on 20 November 1483 which Caxton uses could refer to the printing. In other words the four texts could have been printed in the following order: *Game of Chess* in 1483 or even 1482, the *Canterbury Tales* in 1483, the *Golden Legend* on 20 November 1483, and *Aesop* on 26 March 1484. *Aesop* would then be the last dated text with English woodcuts and the first dated text with initial capitals; perhaps the two details are not entirely unconnected.

In addition to the two cuts already mentioned the *Golden Legend* has another 84. These fall into two types: one portraying scenes in the life of Christ and the Virgin Mary is bigger, for it extends over two columns of type, whereas the other illustrating individual saints extends over one column of type only. The exceptions to the second category are cuts illustrating the slaying of Holofernes, the martyrdom of St Thomas of Canterbury, and the festival of All Saints. One of the larger series of cuts, that representing the Nativity, may be part of a series of cuts made for the Oxford press of Rood and Hunte. A similar connexion between the Oxford and Westminster presses has been suggested for the cuts of St Andrew appearing in Caxton's *Horae.* It is not known, however, what the relationship between the two presses was, for this is the only evidence we have that there may have been some association. The exact sources of Caxton's woodcuts are not known, though the larger series was modelled on the source also used in the Oxford cuts. It may be that one of the manuscripts Caxton used to make his edition also served as a model for the artist. The series of saints shows little originality. The cuts are meant to identify the saints by their symbols and are designed to enable the reader to recall the saint and his story from the picture, but some saints' emblems were sufficiently ambiguous for the cuts to be used more than once.

Of the woodcuts imported by Caxton the set which was used principally in both editions of the *Speculum Vitae Christi* is of some importance because individual cuts were employed in other books. The series was probably acquired from Flanders, for the artist has Flemish associations, and it was already worn by the time it came into Caxton's hands. Various cuts which appear in both editions of the *Speculum Vitae Christi* were used again in the *Royal Book*, the *Doctrinal of Sapience*, and the second edition of *Mirror of the World*. But three cuts which were not used in the *Speculum* nevertheless seem to belong to the series and to have been cut by the same hand. One of these appears in Caxton's *Horologium Sapientiae* and the other two in books printed by Wynkyn de Worde. Presumably Caxton got hold of the whole series at the same time and for one reason or another he decided not to use them all in the *Speculum*. This naturally raises the question whether he used individual cuts before he used the series in the *Speculum*, which is perhaps another way of asking whether he bought them as a form of speculation and possibly decided afterwards to print the *Speculum* because he had some suitable woodcuts. At the moment the assumption that he used the cuts first of all in the *Speculum* and only then in other works is one of the reasons for putting the printing of the *Royal Book* in 1487, even though the translation was finished on 13 September 1484. As we have seen, the use of type 5 for this book is not in itself a satisfactory reason for placing the printing of the book back to 1487. Indeed the *Speculum* is also in type 5, and if we can date the *Royal Book* to late 1484 or early 1485, we may also wonder whether the printing of the *Speculum* should be brought forward to a time closer to that of the *Royal Book*. In other words the printing of the *Speculum* ought perhaps to be adjusted to that of the *Royal Book* rather than vice versa. But it is not in fact necessary to assume the two books were printed close in time, since the use of type 5 and of this series of woodcuts was spread over several years. However, if we can make the assump-

of hys zele brennynge within forth for the worſhyppynge of
hys fader ſpecyally in that place. where he owed moſt to be wor
ſhypped ſhewed hym ſo dredeful in hys face wythoutforth that
they weren wonderfully adred and diſcomfited. and hadden
no power to wythſtonde hym: Thys proceſſe after the expoſici
on of ſaynt Gregory and other doctours is ful dredeful to alle
criſten men. but namely to prelates and curates / & other men
of holy chyrche & ſpecyally we relygyous that ben ſette in gods
des temple for to ſerue hym contynuelly in deuoute prayer and
other ghoſtly exercyſes. yf we yeue vs to coucytyſe and vany
tees and medle vs ouer nede wyth worldly occupacyons and
chaffarynges as they dyden / we maye ſkylfully drede the In
dygnacyon of Jheſu and hys caſtynge out fro grace in thys lyf
and after departynge of hys blyſſe euerlaſtyng / ❡wherfore
thou that wylt not drede the indygnacyon of Jheſu. loke that in
no maner thou putte the wylfully nor medle the to thy power
wyth worldly occupacyon . ❡But for thys matere is fully
and plentyouſly treted in the expoſicion of thys goſpel in ma

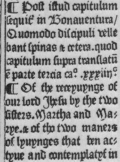

ny places. therfore we pal
ſen ouer thus ſhortly at
thys tyme.
❡Poſt iſtud capitulum
ſequiſ in Bonauentura /
Quomodo diſcipuli velle
bant ſpinas & cetera. quod
capitulum ſupra tranſlatũ
e parte tercia cao .xxxiiio
❡Of the receyuynge of
our lord Jheſu by the two
ſiſters. Martha and Ma
rye. & of the two maners
of lyuynges that ben ac
tyue and contemplatyf in

*57. 'Horae' woodcuts
from 'Speculum
Vitae Christi'*

tion that Caxton used individual cuts in a series before using the series as a whole, we could think that he acquired the *Speculum* series in 1484. This would mean that *Aesop*, the last dated text with English woodcuts, appeared early in the same year that he started to use imported woodcuts. The proximity of these two important points in his use of woodcuts may be significant. All his Continental cuts make their appearance after 1484 and it may be the facility with which he could acquire foreign cuts which caused him to abandon English ones. Though the imported ones are more artistic to our eyes, we cannot necessarily assume that Caxton thought so and that this was the reason for his abandoning English ones. The result of this change was that English books could now hardly be decorated, particularly if they were concerned with chivalry and knighthood, for all the imported

cuts were of religious scenes, since these would naturally be the most flexible if bought without a particular book in mind.

The woodcuts used by Caxton for the *Horae* fall into two groups, one dealing with the life of Christ and the Virgin Mary and the other depicting various saints. They are quite small, for most *Horae* were printed in quarto. These cuts were also imported

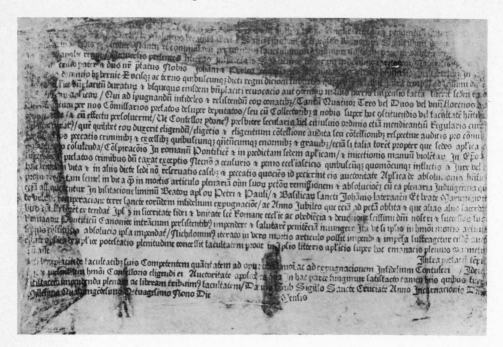

59. An indulgence

from Flanders. The finest series of imported woodcuts is the one known as the *Fifteen Oes* series, though only one of the cuts was used in that work. The others occur in some of Wynkyn de Worde's editions. Again we may assume that Caxton acquired the whole series, but chose to use only one cut at first. Indeed this book answers our query raised in the last paragraph: whether he would use an individual cut before he used the whole series. This example would also suggest that he bought the whole set without knowing what he was going to use it for and then used parts of it as opportunity arose. The borders which surround the pages in the *Fifteen Oes* were probably cut by the same artist. We have noticed that the imported woodcuts are of religious scenes. If the woodcuts were purchased without regard to what was going to be printed in the immediate future, one could think that the large number of religious works in Caxton's later career was the result not so much of any religious feeling on his part, but simply of the availability of woodcuts with religious subjects. Three different cuts of the *Image of Pity* are known from Caxton's output. One is found with the *Horae* series and is without an indulgence. The other two are in single sheets and were designed principally for indulgences. The pictures represent Christ in glory surrounded by the various emblems of the passion. Beneath the picture is a box in which the indulgence would be presented. All are of Continental origin.

As a final word it should be said that all Caxton's woodcuts are black and white; there is no attempt at colouring, even though printing by coloured block was used at the press in St Albans and touching up by hand is found in the books issued by other printers.

VIII
THE EARLY BOOK TRADE, PUBLISHING AND PATRONAGE

As manuscripts were produced individually by hand it might be thought that before the introduction of printing there would be no need for a book trade, since all a man needed to do to acquire a copy of a book was to employ a scribe to write it out for him. This would presuppose that not only was the material to be copied readily available, but also the services of the other artisans needed to complete the book, such as the illuminator and bookbinder, were obtainable. These skills are specialised and it was only the richer monasteries which had scriptoria able to provide all the books required for their own needs. It is true that a nobleman, particularly in the later Middle Ages, could get his clerk or any scribe to produce a manuscript for him as Sir John Fastolf did, for he employed William Worcester in a kind of general secretarial capacity which included writing manuscripts. But manuscripts produced in this way were utilitarian and unattractive in appearance. While there are of course manuscripts of all levels of richness from the plainly practical to the sumptuously elegant, it is simplest to divide them into these two categories: the working manuscript and the luxury one. The latter type were written in magnificent scripts, illuminated with pictures and other forms of decoration, and bound expensively. The cost of producing manuscripts like this was high and they were therefore valued possessions to be bought and sold, bequeathed or taken as booty in times of war. Often it may well appear that the contents of such manuscripts were regarded as their least valuable part, though it is naturally possible to spend time and money on works considered important in their own right.

In the early Middle Ages the provision of manuscripts was to all intents and purposes a monastic monopoly. St Benedict had underlined the importance of learning in his rule and Benedictine monasteries usually made provision for the reproduction of manuscripts in their scriptoria. When in the ninth century Alfred decided to send a copy of his translation of Gregory's *Cura Pastoralis* to every bishopric in the land, he must have turned to a monastic scriptorium to provide the necessary copies. Similarly the *Anglo-Saxon Chronicle* was kept in various monasteries. Even the manuscripts containing the extant Old English poems were probably written and preserved within monasteries. In England this tradition continued until the dissolution of the monasteries in the sixteenth century, and Westminster Abbey and St Albans both had well-known scriptoria in the late Middle Ages. The regularity of the language found, for example, in the manuscripts produced at Winchester in the tenth century and in those of the *Ancrene Wisse* in the early thirteenth indicates that the monks took their duties seriously and conscientiously. Some orders attached more importance to the provision of manuscripts and had active scriptoria in their houses, though in many cases there was a tendency for periods of activity to be followed by others of greatly reduced industry. The majority of books produced by the monasteries were of a liturgical or theological nature. But, particularly in the later Middle Ages, individual monks and religious houses were quite willing to copy works of a more secular nature. John Gower had an association with St Mary Overeys Priory in Southwark where he spent the last years of his life. Not only did he make use of its library, but also some of the presentation copies of his *Confessio Amantis* seem to have been copied there, for they were clearly made under his supervision. Indeed it would be strange if monasteries had refused to copy manuscripts of a secular type since monks themselves wrote works of this nature. Lydgate is the prime example. A monk of Bury St Edmunds, he wrote poems for aristocratic and merchant patrons and many of them may well have been copied in his house's scriptorium. After all, the monastery might expect a share in the patron's favour by copying the work in a luxurious and elaborate manuscript.

The monastic scriptoria produced new copies of works, and where more than one copy is involved they may be thought of as publishers. As early as Bede's time it seems as though copies of his *Ecclesiastical History* were made with a view to circulating the work to various people. However, there could hardly be said to be any trade in books at this time, though it may be that second-hand books were bought and sold at some medieval fairs. A step towards booksellers as we understand them today was taken in the thirteenth century when universities started to license stationers. The *stationarii* or *librarii* were closely supervised by the universities. The problem facing a university then, as now, was how to provide reliable textbooks at a price the students could afford, and naturally in the days before printing this was a serious problem. Each stationer was licensed by the university to make master-copies of the textbooks in use and each master-copy was inspected to make sure it contained no errors. The copies were broken down into fascicules or *peciae*, to use the technical word, and members of the university could hire each *pecia* from the stationer at a price fixed by the authorities so that they could make their own copies. For the limited number of textbooks used in medieval universities the system was adequate. Several master-copies survive today and they were utilitarian; they are naturally in Latin and deal with subjects of academic interest. The stationer was thus not essentially a seller of books, though it seems probable that in many towns he also supplemented his earnings as a university stationer by acting as a bookseller. The name itself gave us the title of the Company of Stationers, founded in London in the fourteenth century, and indeed our modern stationer's shop. When printing arrived many of them took to printing and publishing as a matter of course. It is hardly surprising that an early printing press should have been established at Oxford. Though the printer, Theodoric Rood, was a German, the other partner, Thomas Hunte, was a local stationer and bookseller. Whatever the actual extent of their interests may have been, the importance of the stationers lies in the impetus they gave to the provision of multiple copies of books in a non-monastic environment.

It was not long before England saw the rise of bookshops to provide material for a secular market. No tangible proof for the existence of such bookshops in the fourteenth century has been found; their presence can only be inferred from certain manuscripts. Of these the most interesting is the so-called Auchinleck manuscript, now at Edinburgh, since it has been argued that it was produced in a London bookshop about 1340. The manuscript contains many religious pieces as well as more than a dozen romances in rhyming couplets which have been translated from French. It seems likely that the translations were for the most part made for this manuscript by the scribes who worked in the bookshop. The manuscript is large and even by fourteenth-century standards it cannot have been cheap. What is so fascinating about it is that if the theory of the bookshop can be accepted we have a record for the first time of a selection of literary material being produced speculatively in England. No one asked for these particular translations to be made or that just those pieces should be brought together in one manuscript. Presumably an entrepreneur or his scribes made a selection of material which they hoped would sell and then produced a manuscript volume which was offered for sale. There must by this time have existed a buying public that was prepared to spend money on manuscripts and to buy a selection of literary material in which they had had no choice. Indeed noblemen about this time were beginning to take more interest in books and to patronise works of literature; in this they may have been aping their counterparts in France, for they had become more familiar with French ways through the Hundred Years War. Similar bookshops may have existed in the fifteenth century as well, though again their presence can only be inferred; some English translations of French romances like *Partonope of Blois* exhibit many of the same features of hack translation as are found in the Auchinleck manuscript, and thus possibly indicate that they originated in the same way.

There were, however, few compulsive collectors of books in the fourteenth century. The only one known to us is Richard de Bury, Bishop of Durham (1281–1345). He had a host of scribes at his disposal who copied the manuscripts he could not acquire outright. Many of his religious friends searched through Continental monastic libraries for copies of the books he wanted and Richard himself was not slow in visiting monasteries to see what he could pick up. Unfortunately his library was dispersed at the Dissolution and its catalogue has not survived, though some record of his passion for books survives in his *Philobiblon*. Ironically it would seem that just as the merchants and aristocrats were learning to value books, the monasteries were ceasing to pay attention to the many manuscripts in their care which were often plundered by the monks themselves for their parchment. Boccaccio tells us of a visit to the monastery of Monte Cassino which left him dismayed at the appalling conditions in which the books were kept and the disdain with which they were treated by the monks. Secular humanists soon outstripped medieval churchmen in their love for books.

The growth of a secular book-buying public encouraged the creation and dissemination of secular literature, and the work of Chaucer and Gower is in part a response to this new audience. It was natural that in England London should become a centre of this type of literature because of the patronage of the court and because it was the only town large enough to provide secular jobs for poets who were unable to support themselves by their writings alone. In the provinces the nobles tended to rely still on clerics of one type or another, people like John Trevisa, Osbern

Bokenham, and even no doubt the author of *Sir Gawain and the Green Knight*. In France writers in secular life attached to different courts had been a familiar feature for some time. In the fourteenth century Froissart, a typical court poet, came to England to see what patronage he could acquire here. Although well known previously to Edward III's wife, Philippa of Hainault, he came to England when Richard II was on the throne and presented him with a book of his poems. Richard's reactions are recorded in Froissart's *Chronicle*, here quoted from the translation by Earl Berners.

Whanne the kynge opened it, it pleased hym well, for it was fayre enlumyned and written, and covered with crymson velvet, with ten botons of sylver and gylte, and roses of golde in the myddes, with two great claspes gylte, rychely wrought. Than the kyng demaunded me whereof it treated, and I shewed hym howe it treated of maters of love; wherof the kynge was gladde and loked in it, and reed in many places, for he could speke and rede Frenche very well; and he tooke it to a knyght of hys chambre, named syr Rycharde Creadon, to beare it into his secrete chambre.

One of the interesting points of this story is of course that the 'maters of love' were not written for Richard II or specifically for an English audience. A writer, having composed certain works, looked around for someone who would support him and increase the distribution of his work. We may assume that Richard II read Froissart's poems, but naturally his first reaction was pleasure at the richness of the manuscript and its ornamentation. Literature by itself was not a sufficient gift for kings; it had to be presented in a suitable framework.

The lives of Chaucer, Gower, and Hoccleve reveal the new class of authors arising at this time. Chaucer was born of a family of wine-merchants. As a young man he was sent to the household of Elizabeth, Countess of Ulster and wife of Prince Lionel, where he would have served as a page learning court ways. Later he served in the wars in France and was ransomed, when captured, by Edward III. About 1366 he married Philippa, daughter of Sir Payne Roet and sister of Katherine Swynford, John of Gaunt's third wife. During the latter part of Edward's reign and the beginning of Richard's, Chaucer made several trips to the Continent, at least some of which were for diplomatic ends. In 1374 he became the Controller of Customs and Subsidy of Wools, Skin, and Hides in the port of London, which carried with it a regular stipend, augmented by various pensions and sinecures from the crown. In 1389 he was made Clerk of the King's Works. In

other words his career was on the surface that of a successful   *60. Chaucer*
civil servant, for whom writing was a leisure pursuit. The ancestry
of John Gower, on the other hand, is less certain; he may have
come from the lesser gentry. When we can trace him first he
is a lawyer in London dealing in land and property. Often these
deals seemed to have involved sharp practice and two at least
of them ended in legal proceedings. Whatever the exact nature
of his business, he had made enough money by his late forties
to retire from active business life and to settle down to literary

pursuits. Both Chaucer and Gower belonged to the prosperous middle class; their contemporary Thomas Hoccleve was less fortunate. Born in Bedfordshire about 1368 and destined for the Church, he nevertheless became a clerk in the office of the Privy Seal, where he spent his whole life. He was supposed to receive a salary for his job, but the money was paid only infrequently so that Hoccleve often found himself short of cash, a subject which forms a constant theme in his work. The lives of these authors show that writers could support themselves in a secular occupation; but in a feudal environment the need to attract the attention of the nobility must have been constant.

Some of the works of these authors may have been commissioned. Gower tells in the prologue to *Confessio Amantis* how he met Richard II sailing on the Thames, who requested him to write a poem on some new topic. Hoccleve translated the *Regement of Princes* for Henry V. Other works by these authors are occasional pieces. Hoccleve's *œuvre* includes numerous welcoming poems and panegyrics. Chaucer's *Book of the Duchess* may be an elegy written on the death of Blanche, wife of John of Gaunt, and his *Parliament of Fowls* may have been written to commemorate a particular St Valentine's Day. But except where a translation was involved, the patron can at most have suggested the general subject to be treated. By and large the poet was left to his own devices as to what he should do and how he should tackle it. It was becoming more common for authors to write a work which they thought would appeal to their contemporaries and then try to get a patron to accept and support it. While this meant more freedom for the poets, that freedom was restricted by the need not to go too far beyond what their public would like and approve.

Translation has always been a feature of English literary life, but the great rise in the number of translations in the fourteenth and fifteenth centuries is significant. It shows that there was a growing public for literary work which could not be satisfied by the output achieved by the native authors. It indicates a growing interest in secular works since, though many religious pieces were also translated, the bulk of the translations were of a chivalric or educational nature. It suggests the growing interest in patronage by the rich and influential, for they could more readily find a translator than an author to support and they could more readily exercise control over the finished result if they chose the work to be translated. While poetic translations may largely have been carried out in bookshops similar to the one which prepared the

Auchinleck manuscript, those prepared by scribes for individual patrons were more often than not in prose. This may be the result of the greater frequency of prose works in French in the fifteenth century, and also possibly of the lack of facility in translation that such provincial scribes would suffer under.

It is time now to consider the growth of patronage in England in greater detail. We should remember that even today most writers, apart from the exceptional ones, are forced to rely on some form of patronage or to have some secondary employment. The difference in the position of patronage in the Middle Ages is that then the patron not only provided material support for the author but also helped to make his work accepted and read. When writers were monks or members of a religious order, patronage was less necessary, since the monastery would provide a home for the author and the means for the circulation of his works. But when writing ceased to be confined to religious houses, the need for patronage became more pressing. Monarchs on the one hand and noblemen and merchants on the other responded to this need. The early Norman kings seem to have taken an interest in letters from the time of the Conquest, though their patronage was extended to either French or Latin writings. The three Edwards, however, seem to have taken little interest in this side of the royal duties, though the wife of Edward III, Philippa of Hainault, had supported several writers including Froissart. It is with Richard II that we can trace a change in the royal attitude towards patronage. As we have seen, Richard received Froissart's poems, encouraged Gower to write his *Confessio Amantis*, and paid a pension to Chaucer. The public reading of poetry as illustrated in some Chaucer manuscripts may have been a feature of court life under Richard. Whether Henry IV was also a patron of Gower, for the dedication in later versions of *Confessio Amantis* was changed to him, or simply his political hero is difficult to decide, but his son, Henry V, extended his patronage to many authors. For him Lydgate wrote his *Troy Book,* and Hoccleve his *Regement of Princes,* and Jean de Gallopes dedicated his French translation of Bonaventura's *Pilgrimage of the Soul* to him. Though the literary talent may not always have been of the highest, it was certainly encouraged. From now on it became accepted that kings could be approached to act as patrons of literary works, though the involvement of individual monarchs depended on their own taste and the political conditions in which they found themselves.

In the provinces patronage likewise comes into prominence

in the fourteenth century. Modern studies have illuminated two
areas, the West Midlands and East Anglia, in which it flourished,
but it should not be thought that it was confined to them. In
the West Midlands we can see the courts of the nobility gradually
becoming centres of literature, no doubt in imitation of the royal
court at Westminster rather than, as was once suggested, in opposition to it. There is little to suggest that noblemen there were
interested in literature in the thirteenth century, but as soon as
the next century starts we hear of the gift of books by Guy Beauchamp, Earl of Warwick, to Bordesley Abbey. Here we have
evidence of a private library which contained secular epics as
well as religious and didactic pieces; and presumably the Earl
had taken some trouble in the acquisition of his library. About
1351 Humphrey Bohun, Duke of Hereford, commissioned the
adaptation of *William of Palerne,* the first poem in the so-called
Alliterative Revival. Thomas, Lord Berkeley, was the patron of
Trevisa's translations of Higden's *Polychronicon* and Bartholomaeus Anglicus' *De Proprietatibus Rerum.* No doubt the author
of *Sir Gawain and the Green Knight* was a clerk in some nobleman's
household in the North West, and it may have been one belonging
to John of Gaunt. It has been suggested that Tutbury, where
performances by minstrels and other chivalric ceremonies are
known to have figured, would have been a suitable locale for
the creation of the poem. In East Anglia, on the other hand,
patronage was extended to authors by merchants and the lesser
nobility as well as by the great nobles. Here, though there are
records of literary activity from the beginning of the Middle
English period, the great age of patronage was the fifteenth, rather
than the fourteenth, century. Here people like Sit John Fastolf
and the Pastons figure prominently, but there were ecclesiastics
like Thomas Burgh, a member of a house of friars at Cambridge,
and ladies like Katherine Denton, wife of the coroner of the
county of Suffolk, and Katherine Howard, wife of the future
Duke of Norfolk, who commissioned various writings. There
is, however, a noticeable difference in the patronage in East Anglia
in the fifteenth century as compared with that in the West
Midlands in the previous century. This difference is one of time
rather than one of place. For by the fifteenth century it had
become accepted that writers should address their works to
patrons who were named and glorified in the works in question;
the whole attitude to patronage thus took on a different colour.
Whereas nobles in the fourteenth century simply got a member
of their household to produce a poem or translation for them,

in the fifteenth century one tried to engage the services of the poets who were best known even if they were not local. Famous authors like Lydgate were swamped with commissions—perhaps to the detriment of their verse. Because of Chaucer's reputation English authors were becoming known as individuals who each had their own reputation; people were no longer satisfied with any translation or poem, it had to be by someone famous. The days of anonymity and of provincial writing were therefore numbered.

On the Continent patronage of letters and book-collecting flourished. Booksellers, such as Regnaut du Montet, were sufficiently affluent and astute to have luxury manuscripts made and then to sell them to their wealthy clients. Regnaut sold various volumes to Jean, Duc de Berry, including in 1402 a sumptuous manuscript of the Arthurian story which cost the duke three hundred gold crowns. Regnaut has his interest for England as well since he sold a copy of the prose *Tristan* to Richard Courtenay, Bishop of Norwich, who was ambassador to France from 1414. Englishmen were beginning to acquire Continental habits in that they purchased expensive manuscripts and went to well-known booksellers for them. Individual booksellers built up their own clientele, which was not a national one by any means. The library of the Duc de Berry was extensive and in 1416 when an inventory was made at his death it included 297 volumes, of which fifty may be said to have been of a secular, literary character. But the royal library kept at La Tour du Louvre was perhaps more famous and certainly much larger, since the inventory of 1424 shows that it then contained 1,239 volumes. As in the Duc de Berry's collection the principal weight was given to theological, patristic, and liturgical works, though there were romances and epics as well as some collections of lyrics. For our purposes perhaps the most important Continental collection was that belonging to the Dukes of Burgundy, for they had acquired Brabant and Flanders through dynastic marriages and were thus in close touch with England because of the contact arising from the wool trade between England and the Low Countries. Although started in the fourteenth century when it was kept at Dijon, the library was expanded considerably in the fifteenth century under Dukes Philip the Good and Charles the Bold, and a high proportion of the books were then kept in Flanders where indeed many of them had been made. After the death of each of these two dukes, inventories of their possessions were made, and both have survived. They give an invaluable insight into the library's composition. An important characteristic is that it contained few works in Latin apart from some service and liturgical volumes. The dukes employed several secretaries, one of whose duties included the making of French translations of Latin works considered suitable for the library. Jean Mielot and Raoul Lefèvre are among those whose work can be traced in the library's holdings. The collection was therefore essentially a vernacular one, an important point in respect of Caxton since it shows that the vernacular was considered by some famous men as a suitable medium for the books in their libraries. When the inventory of 1467 was drawn up on the death of Philip the Good it was divided into the following sections: 'Etiques

61. Philip the Good,
Duke of Burgundy

62. *Charles the Bold,*
   Duke of Burgundy

et Politiques; Chapelle; Librarie meslée; Livres de gestes; Livres de Ballades et d'Amours; Croniques de France; Oultre-Mer; Medécine et Astrologie; Livres non parfaits.' The last category refers to books which were incomplete at the time of the inventory. The books in the chapel were the liturgical and service books which were kept separate and hardly formed a section of the library as such. The other sections suggest an interest in courtly and secular affairs with a sprinkling of works of a moral and didactic nature. The books that Caxton produced could be grouped under similar headings. Many of the manuscripts in the dukes' library have survived and a large number are to be found today in the Royal Library at Brussels. We can see from them that the dukes patronised the Flanders bookshops and so gave a boost to the local production of luxury manuscripts.

We have seen that in England the use of the *pecia* system and the growth of the London bookshops helped the spread of manuscripts in a non-monastic environment. That the multiplication of manuscripts was becoming commonplace is suggested by the Wycliffite writings. Although such writings were proscribed, they were copied regularly and circulated widely. The Wycliffite Bible, a lengthy work, must have been copied many times if the extant manuscripts are any guide. Another indication of the growth of interest in manuscripts is the number of Chaucer manuscripts that survive. None of the extant ones was written in Chaucer's own lifetime, but a good guide to the date and provenance of those that do survive is provided by the illuminations which decorate so many of them. Most decades in the fifteenth century saw the production of some Chaucer manuscripts. It cannot be proved that any of them were made for a particular recipient. The majority of them fall into small groups of four or five manuscripts which were all made at the same bookshop. In other words it would seem as though there was a Chaucer industry with bookshops turning out luxury manuscripts of the *Canterbury Tales* on a speculative basis. That the production of these manuscripts carried on through the fifteenth century is sufficient proof that the business was profitable and that people wanted to possess copies of such works as the *Canterbury Tales*. For there is no indication that any one decade of the fifteenth century witnessed the production of a larger number of the manuscripts, and most styles of art associated with that century are to be found in the Chaucer manuscripts. The only one which is absent is the Flemish (Bruges) style introduced in the reign of Edward IV.

The work of John Shirley provides further evidence that the works of such authors as Chaucer, Gower, and Lydgate were read in the fifteenth century. A member of the retinue of Richard Beauchamp, 14th Earl of Warwick, he appears to have established himself in London in the early fifteenth century. Here in St Bartholomew's he rented a house and four shops from at least 1444, and possibly from 1429, until his death in 1456. It seems probable that in his shops he ran some kind of book business, for several manuscripts have survived which are connected with him. The two most important of these are British Library MS Additional 16165 and Trinity College Cambridge MS R. 3. 20. Like all his manuscripts they were written on paper without illumination but with carefully traced initials. The contents of these manuscripts were varied but consist for the most part of fashionable literature. Thus Additional 16165 contains Chaucer's *Anelida and Arcite* and his translation of Boethius, Trevisa's translation of Nicodemus's *De Passione Christi*, the Duke of York's *Master of Game*, four works by Lydgate, and a poem by the Earl of Warwick as well as some shorter poems. This manuscript and the others contain indications of Shirley's ownership, of which the following stanza is a good example:

> Yee that desyre in herte and have pleasaunce
> Olde stories in bokis for to rede,
> Gode matieres putt hem in remembraunce
> And of the other take yee none hede,
> Bysechyng yowe of youre godely hede
> Whanne yee this boke have over-redde and seyne
> To Johan Shirley restore yee hit ageyne.

From the evidence of stanzas like this it has been proposed that Shirley ran what might be called a lending library. This might account for the rather plain, workaday nature of the manuscripts, which were intended to be read rather than to be treasured as valuable artifacts. Similarly it might account for his residence at St Bartholomew's, since it was suitably placed for the acquisition of writing materials and favourably located for the lending of manuscripts to wealthy merchants and others. This theory, which has much to recommend it, would of course imply that there was quite an extensive reading public in and around London by the middle of the fifteenth century.

This conclusion is itself supported by the growth of the book trade in London. The Company of Stationers was incorporated in 1404 and its headquarters were established at Stationers' Hall.

From the beginning of the fifteenth century we find ever-increasing references to booksellers in London and we may assume that the majority were employed in the provision of secular manuscripts for their clients. Manuscripts were imported from the Continent, as were printed books after the invention of printing.

Finally as humanism spread from Southern Europe we find that there were Englishmen who responded to the new interest in the past and that yet another impetus was given to the spread of books and literary matters. Prominent among the English humanists were Humphrey, Duke of Gloucester, and John Tiptoft, Earl of Worcester. Humphrey was the brother of Henry V and may have acquired his humanist tastes through contacts with Italy. He acquired a large number of manuscripts from Italy and he employed various scholars and humanists in literary occupations. His manuscripts were bequeathed to the University of Oxford on his death, and as the collection was much admired at the time it must have been one of the finest libraries in the country. Naturally as befits a collection of this kind classical works abounded, though the duke had many volumes of medieval learning. John Tiptoft was equally influenced by the new humanist spirit emanating from Italy. Though an indifferent scholar himself, he also was anxious to have Italian humanists attached to his household and he encouraged the translation of Greek works into Latin. He himself tried his hand at translating, and Caxton printed two of his translations from French: Cicero's *Of Friendship* and Buonaccorsso's *Declamation of Noblesse*. It is no longer possible to discover what Tiptoft's library contained, but there is no reason to doubt that ancient and modern authors as well as important medieval ones were well represented.

From the evidence presented in this chapter we can see that England was not unaffected by the renewed interest in books characteristic of the fifteenth century in Europe. Manuscripts were produced in great numbers, patronage of authors was established as a familiar occurrence, and even the new humanism left its mark. At the same time we should not forget that many religious works were produced within the Church. There were several active orders intent on the teaching of their members and this necessitated the provision of suitable books for them. New houses like Sheen and Syon were founded and proved to be important centres of spirituality and writing. There are many strands in the skein of fifteenth-century literacy and culture, and printing came at an advantageous time to draw them together.

IX
CAXTON AND DE WORDE
AS PUBLISHERS

So far in this book I have concentrated on Caxton himself, but in this chapter I would like to consider his publishing policy in relation to de Worde's. Since de Worde inherited the printing presses and the business, it might be supposed that the policy of the house would be maintained. But whereas printing is a technical matter in which there is little scope for individual preferences, publishing has always been, and still is, a very personal profession in which the output of a particular house reflects the taste, education, and outlook of the proprietor. By comparing Caxton with de Worde we can see how unusual Caxton was as an early English printer; in several ways he reminds one of some of the greater Continental publishers.

Let us first consider his character and attainments. He was a merchant who had moved on the periphery of aristocratic society in the years before becoming a publisher. He was familiar with the tastes of the upper echelons of late fifteenth-century society since he had a hand in supplying them with the manuscripts they wanted. He was familiar therefore with the book-buying tastes of a secular audience, though with his religious inclinations it would be surprising if he were not also acquainted with current religious ideals and writings. As a result of his Bruges experience he knew French and Flemish and may well have learned Latin as a boy, for he knew enough to make a translation from it.

The first book he printed, the *History of Troy*, gives us a good idea of the way in which he was to work. Two important points to notice are that it is a translation from French and that he made the translation himself. The significance of the first point lies not only in that he did not print an English book, but also in that the translation was from French and not from either of the two other languages he knew. Why should he have gone to all the trouble to translate a French book when as yet no English work had been printed? The answer to this question is to be found partly in his own career and partly in his assessment of the cultural fashions at the end of the fifteenth century. After all when he started to translate the *History of Troy* in 1469 he was in Bruges, where French manuscripts were more accessible than English ones. This cannot have been the whole reason, since even after his return to England he continued to make translations from French and sometimes had to go out of his way to find the originals to translate. One consideration that weighed with him was the pre-eminent position of the Burgundian court in literary and cultural matters at this time. The dukes maintained a court where art and literature flourished and where considerable attention was given to the preservation and even the recreation of chivalric ideals and methods of behaviour. In his prologue to *Jason* Caxton refers not only to the Order of the Golden Fleece established by Duke Philip the Good, but also to the castle at Hesdin which Philip had had decorated with the history of Jason, Medea, and the Golden Fleece. The hall decorated in this way was fitted out with some mechanical contrivance which enabled the duke to make it seem as though there was lightning, thunder, rain, or snow in the hall. No doubt this was used as a stage effect in pageants recreating the story of Jason, though Caxton does not say so. He does, however, give the impression that he was overawed by the ingenuity of the machinery and the magnificence of a court that could provide a spectacle of this nature. The implication is clear: this is not the sort of thing one would expect to find in England and that therefore Englishmen should admire anything that came out of the Burgundian court. And the *History of Troy* was of course a work closely associated with that court. For the French version used by Caxton had been made by 'Raoul Lefevre, preest and chapelayn unto the ryght noble, gloryous and myghty prynce in his tyme, Phelip Duc of Bourgoyne, of Braband, et cetera, in the yere of the incarnacion of Our Lord God a thousand, foure honderd, sixty and foure'. Caxton is quick to point out to the reader in the preface to his translation what the noble affiliations of the book were. Because the book had been made for Philip of Burgundy it was naturally aristocratic reading matter and suitable for any of Caxton's clients.

As it happens his contemporaries were not slow in their admiration of the Burgundians. The dukes tried to maintain an independent political position *vis-à-vis* the kings of France, who were technically their feudal superiors. Consequently there was a great deal of political manœuvring from England, Burgundy, and France, and the first two were often in alliance against the French. For the Low Countries were England's best customers for wool, then the most important English export and the major source of the crown's revenue. Hence many Englishmen made their way to Flanders on diplomatic missions of one sort or another. One of these occasions was the conferment of the Order of the Garter on the Duke of Burgundy, and the Latin oration delivered by John Russell, Bishop of Lincoln, on that occasion was printed by Caxton shortly after his return to England. Another, and even more significant, occasion was the marriage of Margaret of York, Edward IV's sister, to Duke Charles. Englishmen who became familiar with Burgundian habits through these journeys started to follow their example in cultural matters. Many manuscripts from the Flemish workshops were shipped across the Channel and some are still to be found in English collections such as the Royal Library, which now forms part of the British Library. The chivalric ideals of the Burgundians were aped in England, and tournaments like the famous one between Anthony, Earl Rivers, and the Bastard of Burgundy were no doubt modelled on those held across the Channel.

As we have seen, the Burgundian ducal library was largely a vernacular one; but in this connexion vernacular means French rather than Flemish. For French was the language of the most influential literature in Europe and in the fifteenth century of the Burgundian court. Although he translated one text from Dutch and one from Latin, Caxton's choice of texts to translate was determined by the fact that they should preferably be in French. This decision naturally put a lot of medieval writings and many humanistic texts beyond his choice, for most of them were simply not available in French versions. Special reasons were responsible for his choice of the texts translated from Dutch and Latin. It is his preference for a text to be in prose rather than in verse which seems to lie behind the choice of *Reynard the Fox,* the text he translated from Dutch. This Dutch version was itself ultimately based on the French poem, the *Roman de Renart,* but there was no French prose version of this poem available in the fifteenth century. Whether Caxton knew of the French *Roman de Renart,* we cannot tell, but it is quite possible since manuscripts of it were in the Burgundian ducal library and the text may well have been known about in Flanders at this time. However, it may not have been his knowledge of the French *Roman de Renart* but his familiarity with Chaucer's use of the story in his Nun's Priest's Tale which encouraged him to make a translation of it. In his desire for a prose text Caxton was to some extent following the tendency of the fifteenth century, but it may also be that he did not consider himself sufficiently expert to translate from French poetry into English poetry. So the choice of a Dutch text in this case suggests that he may have been prepared to use a less courtly language in order to have a prose original to translate. The text translated from Latin was the life of St Winifred. As we have seen, this life is associated with the *Golden Legend*, which Caxton had printed a couple of years previously. In this case we may assume that he was prepared to use Latin, partly because it was a rhetorical language and partly because the text he wanted to translate was an addendum to a work he had already published.

The other important point about his edition of the *History of Troy* is that he made the translation himself. This is somewhat unusual in many ways. The nobility got their secretaries, chaplains, or famous poets to make translations for them. But as we saw in the last chapter there was a tendency in the fifteenth century for this type of work to go increasingly to people with established reputations. Caxton may well have felt that if he employed any scribe to make his translations they might then have been less acceptable to his noble clientele because they would be by unknown authors, even though the resulting translation may have been as good as or even better than his own. For there was a certain snobbery attached to style at this time and it is a subject to which Caxton alluded frequently in his prologues and epilogues. No doubt there was a feeling that you could trust the style of a man you knew or whose origins were acceptable. Despite the many conventional disclaimers about his own style, Caxton wanted his customers to feel that they were obtaining the best literature in the most suitable English. It is for this reason that he makes so much play with the comments on his style by the Duchess of Burgundy, the patron of this his first printed book. Caxton informs us that he had translated five or six quires of the work and then gave it up in despair for a time. However, he happened to mention what he had done to the duchess, who asked to see the relevant quires. 'And whan she had seen hem, anone she fonde a defaute in myn Englissh whiche sche comanded me to amende and moreover comanded me straytli to contynue and make an ende of the resydue than not translated.' Nowhere does he say that she saw and approved the finished version, which would in any case have been difficult since it was finished in Cologne, but the implication is that the style had been adapted to suit her tastes and therefore must be elegant and acceptable to any other reader. By making his own translations Caxton was able in this way to capitalise on his contacts with the nobility and turn them to commercial advantage. To have got others to do the work would have made the translations less saleable in his eyes. This does not necessarily mean that he did not enjoy translating and that he found it a chore, but there seems little reason to doubt that he was very much aware of the need to make the style of his books acceptable to his customers. After all he was the first English printer and was trying to build up a secure market. It is significant in this respect that he acknowledged printing translations by members of the aristocracy or by writers with known reputations. Thus he was quite happy to print the translations by Earl Rivers and by John Tiptoft, Earl of Worcester, on the one hand, or by Chaucer and Lydgate on the other. The rest of the translations he printed had to be made to seem respectable. Thus *Of Old Age* 'was translated and th'ystoryes openly declared by the ordenaunce and desyre of the noble auncyent knyght, Syr Johan Fastolf of the countee of Norfolk banerette'. Nothing is said of the translator himself, for the patronage of Fastolf was more important in the book's pedigree than the name of some otherwise little-known translator. Trevisa's translation of Higden's *Polychonicon*, however, had to be modernised in order to make it respectable. Trevisa's other translations, including that of the Bible, are mentioned so that customers can rest assured of the translator's skill. Although Caxton modernised Malory's *Le Morte D'Arthur* he made no reference to any change in the language in his prologue or epilogue, presumably because he felt the name of 'Syr Thomas Malory, knyght' was sufficient to guarantee the acceptance of any book by his customers; indeed one of them had lent him the copy from which he printed his own version.

It is perhaps understandable that as the *History of Troy* was his first translation he should stress Margaret's involvement in it, even if that involvement was in practice rather more limited than he suggests. At every opportunity he refers to her commandment that the book should be completed: it was made at her commandment (preface), she ordered him to complete it (prologue), she was the cause of the translation (conclusion to book II), and it was done at her commandment (epilogue to book II). That the book was also presented to her is made little of, though it is mentioned in connexion with the rewards which she bestowed on the printer. In this his first book he wants to make the patron play as large a part as possible, and with the attitude towards patronage which had developed in the fifteenth century he could hardly do otherwise. Patronage had in fact altered from being a means of winning acceptance for a work to including the material support for an author. With printing the position should have been different and it is interesting to speculate whether the material reward was as necessary as the seal of aristocratic approval. Caxton does in fact refer frequently to the payments he had received or to those which he had anticipated and had not yet received. Yet he was presumably fairly wealthy when he started his publishing business and he would have sold his books at a sufficiently economic price to enable him to make a profit on each work. No doubt any material gift was always a welcome extra, but it can never have been as important a consideration to him as it was to authors for whom such gifts were the only financial return they could expect from their writings. In Caxton's case such gifts and the references he makes to them are the result of the tradition which had grown up round the patronage bestowed on authors, and they figure much less in the work of later printers such as de Worde. A dedication was always desirable in a book since it helped to guarantee safety from attack and respectability, but the printer would get his own reward from the sale of his wares.

An indication that this was the way things were going is provided by Caxton's second book in English to be printed, the *Game of Chess*. This, like the *History of Troy*, was printed in Bruges, but it was dedicated to the Duke of Clarence: 'Whiche booke, right puyssant and redoubtid Lord, I have made in the name and under the shadewe of your noble protection not presumyng to correcte or enpoigne onythynge ayenst your noblesse.' Caxton was not at this time acquainted with the Duke of Clarence and probably never met him. He was not looking for any personal reward as an author might, he was hoping that the duke's name would help the distribution of his edition in England. Authors often wished to present their works in person to their patron (as many illuminations witness), for this was the safest way of guaranteeing that the patron gave them something for their pains. On the other hand printers were satisfied simply to have an important name linked with their editions, since that was enough to sell the books from which they hoped to make their money. When at a later date Caxton dealt with Rivers and the Earl of Arundel, the negotiations may have been through their respective secretaries, since in these cases as well Caxton was interested in the name rather than the financial reward. It was for him an important consideration presumably that the Earl of Arundel agreed to dispose of some copies of the *Golden Legend*. But the name associated with the book had to have weight and influence. When the Duke of Clarence fell from grace and was executed for treason, Caxton was forced to omit his name from the second edition. In the same way he is prepared to refer to several patrons in the troubled days of 1483–85 without actually naming any of them. Thus the *Knight of the Tower* was translated at the request of a 'noble lady' who is otherwise unnamed, but who is to be identified with Elizabeth Woodville, now the widow of the late Edward IV. Because she was then in the political wilderness he could not refer to her directly, but it was important to him to let his customers know that the book had been requested by a member of the nobility. In this way he was able to combine political expedience with his own commercial interest.

One aspect of patronage worth emphasising as it developed in the fourteenth and fifteenth centuries was that patrons usually belonged to the secular nobility. Though the subjects of books may be religious and though some authors were in orders, the patrons were secular, for the system developed not to support monks and other religious but to give help to authors who had to support themselves. Caxton followed fifteenth-century practice in this. Although he knew many ecclesiastics (in his prologues he refers to such differing ones as the Abbot of Westminster and the High Canon of Waterford), he did not include any among his patrons; these were either merchants or members of the secular nobility. Even texts with a religious bias such as the *Golden Legend*, which was printed on such a large folio that it was suitable only for reading on a lectern, were dedicated to secular people. The *Golden Legend* is a good example of this refusal to think in terms of a clerical patron. It was published in that difficult period 1483–85 when Caxton was forced to look for new patrons among those now in power. It would have been safer for him perhaps to have looked for some ecclesiastic to act as patron for the book, but he did not. Instead the Earl of Arundel became the patron of the book. Caxton may well have thought that as a book of saints' lives it would appeal in its own right to clerics of all kinds who would not therefore need to be assured of the virtues of its style by the quality of its patron. At the same time he no doubt felt that to have an ecclesiastical patron would not give the book sufficient appeal for secular readers. It was the secular readers who had to be wooed; clerics would buy the books they needed anyway. Hence it was not necessary for him, just as it was unnecessary in manuscripts, to have a patron for works of a technical religious nature.

It may also be remarked that his patrons are all English and, apart from Margaret of Burgundy, they are all associated with the court or the City of London; and even Margaret was the sister of Edward IV. Despite the general admiration for things Burgundian, Caxton felt that it was the English style which was an important constituent of his books. The style could be made acceptable only by having an English patron. The Continental affiliations of the books could be, and were, mentioned in the prologues and epilogues so that his customers could rest assured that they belonged to the fashionable class of literature. Hence Caxton is happy enough to refer to the secretaries of the Dukes of Burgundy or to Poggio Bracciolini who had a magnificent library in Florence and yet considered *Caton* the best book in it. But Caxton never dedicated a book to the Pope, to any Continental aristocrat, or to anyone outside the rather closed London circle. The books were sold from the Westminster shop and the names Caxton used would have carried the most weight there.

When looking for a text to print Caxton thought in terms of what could be patronised by a member of the nobility or a richer merchant. These people were of course also acting as patrons of authors whose writings were still appearing in manuscript form and so it was necessary for him to strike out in a slightly different direction while yet adhering to the tastes of his time. It was for this reason that he relied so much on translation, since it meant he could offer a new version of a text, and that he chose French texts to translate, since this was part of the current taste. In his publishing policy Caxton differs from all printers who had operated up till this time, for they had catered for monastic, humanistic, or academic audiences by printing works in Latin of a theological or learned nature. But Caxton's policy was to issue texts in the vernacular and to provide reading matter which was up-to-date. In this way he managed to achieve a monopoly in England, though naturally he could not sell his books abroad where there would be no sale for fashionable reading matter in English. Though limited, his audience could buy books like that only from him. As he imported many books and manuscripts from the Continent which he sold through his shop at Westminster, he was aware of what was being written and published abroad. And he still maintained close contacts with his fellow mercers who were engaged in the cross-Channel trade and so were in a good position to advise him on new fashions and trends. Indeed William Pratt and Hugh Bryce had a hand in the promotion of some of the editions issued by the press and so they may have had a financial stake in them.

It is not possible to prove that all the works Caxton translated or printed had a direct connexion with Burgundy, and this is not necessary. All his customers would be interested in was the fashionable quality of his matter, and an association with Burgundy was one of the easiest ways of doing this; but it was not the only way. However, many of the editions do have affiliations with Burgundy. Both the *History of Troy* and *Jason* were written by Raoul Lefèvre for Philip, Duke of Burgundy. French versions of these two texts were printed by Caxton in Bruges and so may be assumed to have had appeal for readers there. *Feats of Arms* was written by Christine de Pisan, an extremely popular author at the court of Burgundy, and many of her works had been dedicated to the dukes. Two others of Caxton's translations, *Art of Dieing* and Ovid's *Metamorphoses,* are textually very close to the French versions printed by Colard Mansion, his former partner, in Bruges after Caxton's return to England. Some of the manuscripts used by Caxton came from the Flemish workshops. The most important in this connexion is the original French manuscript of the *Mirror of the World,* which, as Caxton says, 'was engrossed and in alle poyntes ordeyned by chapitres and figures in Frenhsshe in the toun of Bruggis, the yere of th'yncarnacion of Our Lord mcccclxiiii in the moneth of Juyn'. This manuscript is now British Library MS 19 A ix.

It was not only Caxton's own translations but also those by others he printed that show some connexion with Burgundy. Earl Rivers translated the *Moral Proverbs,* another work by Christine de Pisan; and his translation of the *Cordial* was from the French version made by Jean Mielot, a secretary to Philip of Burgundy, and it was this version which was printed in Bruges by Caxton before he came back to England. To this same Jean is attributed the French version of the *Declamation of Noblesse,* the English translation of which was made by John Tiptoft. There was little to separate Caxton's own leanings towards this type of literature from those of his contemporaries, and arguments as to whether he led or followed public taste are rather meaningless. In general he followed the tastes current in the fifteenth century, but he modified and developed them in his own way. But it is not correct to think that he had a policy which led him to seek particular texts to publish; he was normally quite satisfied if the texts were within a certain type. The choice of individual books within those categories was quite arbitrary and depended for the most part on what he had in stock when he was looking for another book to translate.

The translations he printed, whether his own or by his contemporaries, may be divided into two broad categories: works of chivalry and works of a moral religious nature, though the distinction should not be pushed too far since the works in each category partake of many characteristics of those in the other. The difference is most easily expressed in formal structural terms in that works of chivalry concern the deeds of a hero told within a narrative framework, whereas those of a moral religious nature are episodic, consisting of a variety of short stories, *exempla*, and moral exhortations. The heroes of chivalry are drawn from all ages and places: they include classical, mythical, fictitious, and historical heroes. But whatever their origin they are all given the ideals and modes of thought of the fifteenth-century chivalric code. A concept to which Caxton recurs often and which may have had some influence with him in choosing his editions is that of the Nine Worthies. It probably arose in the fourteenth century, but its age of greatest popularity and extent is the fifteenth, when it occurs not only in literary works but also in works of art like the famous tapestry now at the Cloisters, New York. As a concept it survived until the seventeenth century, where the name used was more frequently the Nine Nobles. The Nine Worthies consist of three heroes from Biblical times, Joshua, David and Judas Maccabeus, three from pagan times, Hector, Alexander and Julius Caesar, and three from Christian times, Arthur, Charlemagne and Godfrey of Bouillon. The latter was one of the leaders of the first Crusade, who became the first Latin king of Jerusalem. Caxton printed the exploits of the three Christian worthies; the life of Arthur was his version of Malory's *Le Morte D'Arthur*, and the lives of Charlemagne and Godfrey were translated from French versions. Typical of his remarks about the Nine Worthies and of his interest in them is this passage from the prologue to *King Arthur*:

For it is notoyrly knowen thorugh the unyversal world that there been ix worthy and the best that ever were: that is to wete thre paynyms, thre Jewes and thre Crysten men. As for the paynyms they were tofore the incarnacyon of Cryst, whiche were named: the fyrst, Hector of Troye of whome th'ystorye is comen bothe in balade and in prose; the second, Alysaunder the grete; and the thyrd, Julyus Cezar, Emperour of Rome, of whome th'ystoryes ben wel kno and had. And as for the thre Jewes, whyche also were tofore th'yncarnacyon of Our Lord, of whome the fyrst was Duc Josue whyche brought the chyldren of Israhel into the londe of byheste; the second, Davyd Kyng of Jherusalem; and the thyrd, Judas Machabeus. Of these thre the Byble reherceth al theyr noble hystoryes and actes. And sythe the sayd incarnacyon have ben thre noble Crysten men stalled and admytted thorugh the unyversal world into the nombre of the ix beste and worthy. Of whome was fyrst the noble Arthur, whos noble actes I purpose to wryte in thys present book here folowyng. The second was Charlemayn or Charles the Grete, of whome th'ystorye is had in many places bothe in Frensshe and Englysshe. And the thyrd and last was Godefray of Boloyn, of whos actes and lyf I made a book unto th'excellent prynce and kyng of noble memorye, Kyng Edward the Fourth.

While he did not print the lives of the other heroes as separate works, he did make a translation of some Old Testament books in his *Golden Legend* and that translation includes the biblical accounts of the Jewish worthies. Similarly the *History of Troy* contains an account of some of Hector's deeds, and those stories of classical heroes he does print are not very different in tone and approach from those of the worthies themselves, which is why Gavin Douglas attacked him so sharply for his translation of the *Aeneid*. As part of this general coverage of chivalry we may take his translations of the *Feats of Arms* and the *Order of Chivalry* which are based on the ideals of knighthood found in the fifteenth century, though the works treat chivalry within an allegorical and Christian framework.

The translations in the moral Christian category are more diverse in their approach. A tradition of using stories to provide guidelines for moral behaviour was of course well known from classical times, as 'The Fables of Aesop' make clear. The use of works like these fables and 'The Distichs of Cato' as school texts made them popular and familiar to a wide audience. Many of course already existed in English translations and it is an indication of the pull of French style and the kudos it had that Caxton was prepared to make new translations. The books he printed vary from versions of classical works like *Aesop* to works expounding the basic tenets of Christian belief such as the *Royal Book* and to allegorical works like the *Game of Chess*. In choosing works of this sort Caxton was working within an established tradition, the only originality he showed being in the choice of individual titles.

The one translation which fits into neither category is *Reynard the Fox*. This started as a parody of chivalric attitudes and of the hypocrisy of clerics, though humour rather than satire is uppermost because of the use of the animal figures. There was an attempt by adaptors of this tale to moralise it by suggesting that we should learn from the various episodes how we ought not to behave. As Caxton puts it in his own translation:

And this booke is maad for nede and prouffyte of alle god folke as fer as they in redynge or heeryng of it shal mowe understande and fele the forsayd subtyl deceytes that dayly ben used in the worlde, not to th'entente that men shold use them but that every man shold eschew and kepe hym from the subtyl false shrewis that they be not deceyvyd.

It is, however, interesting to note that Caxton did not take any steps to make this object clearer within the text or indeed within the second edition. Thus although he was offended by the style of Malory's *Le Morte D'Arthur* and was prepared to amend it, or that of Trevisa's *Polychronicon* and modernise it, he was not so interested in the moral of his stories that he had to change them. As a translation, though from Dutch, he felt that its style would be acceptable and so did not bother to make any alterations of importance. This is one more indication that he was very conscious of style in his works. Provided the matter was in general suitable, the thing that concerned him most was style.

Of the works which were not translations by Caxton or his contemporaries the two major categories were works of fashionable poetry and those of a technical religious nature. Fashionable poetry consisted of the works of Chaucer, Gower, and Lydgate and of those who wrote in the same way as they did. This meant for the most part basing one's work on French models, using an elaborate vocabulary within rhyming stanzas, and relying upon rhetorical and allegorical techniques. It excluded works in the alliterative style, like *Piers Plowman* or *Sir Gawain and the Green Knight,* and in general those which could be considered provincial, old-fashioned, uncourtly, or even simple. As we have seen, there were many manuscripts of Chaucer's *Canterbury Tales* produced in the fifteenth century and here Caxton may have met some competition. But he printed the majority of Chaucer's works and so could offer a wider range of the poet's works than was usually found in individual manuscripts. Whether it was his intention or not to offer a series of Chaucerian works as a unit is uncertain, though his editions fall into two groups, those printed about 1477 and those about 1483. But these two periods are the ones in which he printed other English poetry as well and it may be that he wanted to produce not a series of Chaucerian poems

so much as a series of English poetry in the Chaucerian manner. As with the translations the important thing was the style
in which the work was written. By and large the names of the
authors and their established popularity guaranteed this style and
so patronage was unnecessary for these volumes. Even though
Chaucer's translation of Boethius and Lydgate's of the *Pilgrimage
of the Soul* are in prose they can be thought of as fitting into
this category, for they carried the same prestige as the poetic
works. Although old, they were still fashionable. The same may
apply to such prose works as Trevisa's translation of the *Polychronicon*, when suitably modernised, and such works as the
Chronicles of England, for these stand in the same relation to
Chaucer's prose translation as the Chaucerian poetic imitations
stand in relation to his poems.

The technical religious works are again something of a mixed
bunch. Some are in Latin and are meant for use in services or
to help clerics conduct the Church's liturgy. Others are in English
and explain various aspects of Christian belief or contain works
of Christian encouragement and moral edification. As such they
are by their nature not very dissimilar from the translations in
the moral religious category; the main difference is more one
of time, for the former had existed in English versions for some
time already and had a known popularity in their English forms.
Even so the audience to which these works appealed could well
have varied, for the English translation of *Speculum Vitae Christi*
was found particularly within monastic and aristocratic houses,
whereas Mirk's *Festial* was more popular with parish priests.

Finally there is a group of miscellaneous pieces which might
perhaps be called occasional works since most were asked for,
and no doubt paid for, by clients. The indulgences, for example,
were clearly prepared to order. The humanist works in Latin
like the *Nova Rhetorica* and the *Sex Epistolae* were commissioned
by Italian humanists and seen through the press by them. The
Propositio may similarly have been printed at the request of John
Russell, who wrote it. Other occasional pieces like the *Donatus*
and the *Vocabulary* are more in the nature of educational texts,
which as far as we can tell were not commissioned and may
have been printed simply to give the pressmen something to
keep them occupied. For although Caxton preferred to print translations, it should be remembered that the press could print a
work far more quickly than he could translate it. So unless he
could acquire translations by fashionable or aristocratic authors,
he was forced to issue texts of a more pedestrian nature. School

texts would fall into this category, since there would be a steady, if unspectacular, sale for them. What is surprising is that he did not print more of them, since they were really much less trouble; that he did not shows that he had a policy to which he tried to adhere unless circumstances prevented it. We should probably interpret the printing of the *Infantia Salvatoris* in the same way, for it is unusual in that although not a work of a technical religious nature it is nevertheless in Latin. It is more in the nature of a meditational or instructive text, and these were in general in English. We should not expect absolute rigidity in Caxton's output, for there was after all a certain amount of opportunism there. And the real reasons behind the printing of some of these texts remain uncertain. He included prologues and epilogues only in those works which wanted some form of introduction for his clients, those works which though fashionable were new in the sense that they had been translated from French. Other works which had an established audience needed no such introduction and so Caxton tells us nothing about his reasons for printing them, which can only be inferred from the rest of his output.

One important aspect of Caxton's publishing policy which has not received much attention is the reprints he issued of his own texts. We cannot tell how many copies of any first edition were printed, but we must assume that he thought they would be sufficient to satisfy the expected demand. Reprints would only have been necessary when an underestimate of this demand was made. It is interesting to note that the only translations he re-issued were the *Dicts or Sayings*, reprinted twice, *Game of Chess, Mirror of the World*, and *Reynard the Fox*. The *Golden Legend* exists in different versions, but whether the second version was a full reprint or not has not yet been decided and so it is best to leave this text out of consideration. What is immediately apparent is that none of the chivalric translations, whether by himself or by others, was reprinted. It is worth making two points about this. The first is that the printing of such works may have been rather risky, since the market was limited and so easily satisfied. The second is that, despite this consideration, Caxton nevertheless went on printing works of this sort, which meant that he had to keep on translating in order to satisfy the market with something new. The translations which were reprinted are works of a moral religious nature except *Reynard the Fox*, which as we saw is a text which stands slightly apart from the rest of the translations. Whether the *Game of Chess* was reprinted because of the woodcuts we cannot tell, but it seems quite probable, and an important consideration with the reprinting of *Dicts or Sayings* may well have been that it was a translation by Earl Rivers. The *Mirror of the World* has woodcuts, which would make it an attractive text to reprint. Of the English poetry only the *Canterbury Tales* of Chaucer's works was reprinted, a fact which may well lead us to reconsider how highly Caxton or his contemporaries valued Chaucer. For several of the shorter poems by Lydgate and *Cato* by Benedict Burgh were reprinted; indeed the latter appeared in three editions. However, as the third edition of *Cato* and the second of the *Canterbury Tales* appeared with woodcuts, it does seem likely that the provision of woodcuts was an important consideration in the decision to issue a reprint, whether of a translation or of an English poem. Reprints of works of a technical religious nature occur more frequently. There were four editions of the *Horae*, three of *Quattuor Sermones*, and two each of *Directorium Sacerdotum*, the *Festial*, the *Speculum Vitae Christi* and the *Image of Pity*. This is not surprising since these works were issued to keep the presses busy, and provided the market was not yet satisfied it would be reasonable to issue new editions. What is interesting is that there were no second editions of works I have put in the miscellaneous category, works issued by request as occasional pieces, since this would seem to confirm that they were done at the request of, and at the expense of, others.

There are many areas of literature which Caxton did not touch, though three deserve special mention. He printed no classical work in its original language simply because his policy was to publish books in the vernacular. Likewise he printed few humanist texts. Those he did issue were printed at the request of Italian scholars, and the reason that he printed none on his own initiative is again that his policy was one of printing books in English. However, within English literature he printed none of the great fourteenth-century mystical and religious writers. The only book within this area is the *Speculum Vitae Christi*, which may have been issued because of the available woodcuts. The absence of these books is partly dictated by his attempt to satisfy a secular audience and partly by his desire to provide that audience with books that were novel and this was best done by providing translations of works hitherto unavailable in English. For the three bases on which Caxton built his list were novelty, fashionable literature, and courtly style.

It is time now to turn to a consideration of the publishing policy of Wynkyn de Worde. We know very little about him

Lyke as this boke hath shewed to you expresse

And many an other wonderful conceyte
Shewyth Bartholowe de proprietatibus
Whyche helped hymself to take the swete recepte
Of hollow cunnynge his tyme dyspendynge thus
Geuynge example of vertue gloryous
Bokes to cheryssh and make in sondry wyse
Vertue to folowe and Idelnesse to dispyse

For in this worlde to rekon euery thynge
Plesure to man there is none comparable
As is to rede and vnderstondynge
In bokes of wysdom they ben so dilectable
Whiche sowne to vertue and ben profytable
And all that loue suche vertue ben full glade
Bokes to renewe and caule theym to be made

And also of your charyte call to remembraunce
The soule of William Caxton first prynter of this
In laten tonge at Coleyn hymself to auaunce (boke
That euery well dysposyd man may theron loke
And John Tate the yonger Joye mote he broke
Whiche late hathe in Englond doo make this pa
That now in our englyssh this boke   (per thynne
                                    (is prynted Inne
That yong and olde thrugh plente maye reioyse
To gyue theym self to good occupacion
And ben experte as shewyth the comyn voyce
To voyde alle vyce and defamacion
For Idylnesse alle vertue put adowne
Than rede and studie in bokes vertuouse
So shall thy name in heuen be gloriouse

For yf one thyng myght laste a.M.yere
Full sone compth aege that frettyth all away
But lyke as Phebus wyth his bemes clere
The mone repeyreth as bryght as ony day
Whan she is wastyd ryght so may we say
This bokes old and blynde whan we renewe
By goodly prynntyng they ben bryght of hewe

except that he was born in Wörth in Alsace and was probably recruited by Caxton in Cologne in 1471–72. He cannot have been very old at that time for he lived on till 1535. Although there is no proof for it, the usual view is that he accompanied Caxton to Bruges in 1472–73, and remained with him there till 1476 when he accompanied him to England at the time Caxton established his press at Westminster. Caxton makes no reference to him in his prologues and epilogues, for it was his policy to mention only those whose names would help to sell his books, and in his eyes de Worde did not fall into that category. Presumably de Worde was the foreman in Caxton's workshop and attended to the running of the presses and the supervision of the compositors. It would be for this occupation that Caxton had recruited him in 1471–72, since Caxton himself was not concerned with the day-to-day printing. When Caxton died in 1491–92 de Worde inherited the business. We should remark immediately what a different background de Worde had from Caxton. The latter was a member of a powerful guild and had mixed with the aristocracy during a distinguished career. The former had no mercantile experience and no entrée into society and may well have spent the major part of his life till 1491 within the printing shop. Very probably it was a greater change for de Worde to become a publisher than it had been for Caxton. No doubt he gained some financial expertise through working with Caxton, though he could not have the same insight into or contact with the financial world that his master had. All credit is due to him then that he managed to run a successful business for forty years. We cannot be certain what languages he knew, but we may accept that he was familiar with his native tongue of Low German as well as with English and Latin. There is no evidence that he knew any French. If this is so, it meant that certain avenues of Caxton's publishing policy would be closed to him. He could not translate French works into English because he did not know French, and even if he did as a foreigner he would have found it difficult to persuade his clients of the virtues of his style. It is unlikely that his command of Latin was extensive and this may have prevented him from making translations from that language. That he did know some Latin is suggested by the occurrence of colophons in Latin in his earliest books. As the words used there vary, it is probable that de Worde wrote them. But his command may have been insufficient even to contemplate printing works in Latin without someone else to see such works through the press. It is notable that he did not even attempt to translate books from German, presumably because that was a language which carried little literary respect.

What opportunities then were open to de Worde? He could naturally issue reprints of Caxton's translations or editions. Here one is struck immediately by the absence of reprints of chivalric works. Apart from reprinting *King Arthur,* most of the reprints are of religious or moral writings. Thus before 1500 he had produced reprints of the *Festial, Quattuor Sermones,* the *Golden Legend,* the *Speculum Vitae Christi* and two of the *Horae.* He did not confine his attention to reprinting works issued by Caxton. By the time he inherited the business several other printers had established themselves in England, and as there was no copyright law de Worde was able to avail himself of their works too. He made particular use of several editions by Richard Pynson, who may conceivably have had some kind of business association with him; but once again the works reprinted were those of an educational or moral nature, except possibly for *Mandeville's Travels* which may be considered more courtly.

Another possibility open to de Worde was to imitate Caxton by producing editions of courtly English poems. He did follow his master in this, but once again he made significant departures. Thus he reprinted many poems like the *Canterbury Tales* which Caxton had been the first to publish, but he also issued poems by Chaucer and Lydgate like the *Siege of Thebes* which Caxton had not printed. He interpreted what was acceptable as English poetry much more generously than his master had done. He printed several romances which had been translated from French or modelled on French originals and which were popular in the fifteenth century. Similarly he was prepared to issue poems in the alliterative tradition, such as the *Quatrefoil of Love,* even though he did modify their language and style before publishing them. They thus appeared in a more London-based dialect, even though there was still as much alliteration. Likewise he was prepared to print the work of living poets. He issued Skelton's *Bowge of Court* almost immediately after it was written, and though Skelton had a reputation by this time it seems as though de Worde was prepared to print something on a man's reputation rather than on the work's proven popularity. In this he looks forward to modern publishing practice.

Just as de Worde extended Caxton's range of publishing by choosing a wider variety of English poetry, so he departed from his former master's habits by printing English prose works, particularly those which belonged to the great tradition of English

mysticism. In 1494 he printed Hilton's *Scale of Perfection*. Prior
to that he issued the *Treatise of Love*, an adaptation of part of
the *Ancrene Wisse*, and the *Chastising of God's Children*, and English
translation of one of Ruysbroeck's works, and shortly afterwards
he printed the *Meditations of St Bernard*. It may be that the shortage of material forced him to look for religious material, which
was the most readily available work in English at this time, but
there is no reason to doubt that he was a man of strong religious
convictions who wanted to publish works of this sort. Thus when
he printed an abridged version of the *Book of Margery Kempe*,
there is every reason to suppose that he himself made the abridgement. The patrons of some of his early books included people
from the same classes as those which Caxton had tapped. Margaret
Beaufort, the mother of Henry VII, for whom Caxton had printed
Blanchardin and Eglantine and the *Fifteen Oes*, was the patron
of de Worde's *Scale of Perfection*. Roger Thorney, a prominent
mercer, asked for the re-issue of Caxton's edition of Trevisa's
translation of Higden's *Polychronicon* and for the publication of
the translation of Bartholmaeus Anglicus' *De Proprietatibus
Rerum*. Though in prose, all these works were issued with verse
prologues or epilogues. Caxton had used poetic prologues only
in exceptional circumstances, but for de Worde it seems to have
been the more natural medium to use. It is possible that some
of them were written by others, but we need not deprive him
of the credit of composing the rest. The syntax, it must be
admitted, is often clumsy and the sense difficult to disentangle,
but in their vocabulary and use of rhetorical features they show
a familiarity with the fashionable conventions of the day. His
L'envoye in his edition of *De Proprietatibus Rerum* is a good
example of his work:

> Ye that be nobly groundid in all grace,
> Experte in wysdom and phylosophy,
> To you this processe comyth a myghty pace
> Whyche I dyrect to you that perfytlye
> Ye may reforme to voyde all vylenye
> Of every thyng, yf ought be here amysse,
> Excusyng theym whiche ment ryght well in this.

However, in addition to using courtly or mercantile patrons,
he also made increasing use of clerics; by the time of his death
he was more frequently printing works for people in orders than
for anyone else. At the beginning of his career we cannot be
sure that the 'devout person' who asked for the *Treatise of Love*

was a cleric, though the 'devout student of the University of Cambridge' who requested the *Meditations of Saint Bernard* must have been in minor orders at least. Two of his other early patrons were Thomas, Prior of St Anne's Charterhouse, and Richard, Bishop of Durham. So even from his early days he had thrown in his lot with clerics, and clerics at that with standing and influence, for Durham was one of the richest and most powerful sees.

In 1500 de Worde made a clean break with the past and moved his shop from Westminster Abbey to the Sign of the Sun in Fleet Street. This move gave concrete expression to his change in publishing policy. It was an indication that he had now abandoned the court as the primary source of patronage and custom; he was to look to the whole country for his sales, and London at the centre of the distribution network was an obvious place to move to. It also indicates that his attention to religious books will become even more noticeable, for they are books that are read throughout the country rather than simply at court.

Two important new departures from Caxton's publishing practice can be detected in these later years. The first is his use of others to make translations for him. But these translators are not members of the aristocracy; they were his own apprentices like Robert Copland or freelance workers like Andrew Chertsey. Copland is known to have translated books for de Worde between 1508 and 1514. The way in which he worked is suggested by the translation of the *Calendar of Shepherds*. An English translation of this work had been printed by Verard in Paris in 1503. Copland read it and was so disgusted with it that he suggested to de Worde that a new translation should be made. This was done and it was printed in 1508. Whereas Caxton had kept all his translating activities to himself and discussed literary matters only with his courtly clients (or so he would have us believe), de Worde was forced to rely on his staff. But he accepted this state of affairs gracefully and was prepared to give them due recognition, whereas Caxton never mentions anyone who is not a noble or a merchant. His staff also looked for books to translate and brought them to de Worde for his approval; in this therefore he tends to be much closer to modern publishing practice.

The second is his method of recruiting contemporary writers to let him act as their publisher. Naturally there can hardly have been any legal commitment on either side, but both sides seem to have kept to each other loyally. As a system it meant that de Worde would have had less control over what he published, since he would seem to have published anything his writers produced, but this cannot have been a real problem. We can trace two authors whose work was consistently published by de Worde. One is Robert Whittinton, a master at Magdalen College, Oxford, who in 1513 was made a laureate of the University for his grammatical scholarship. From about 1513 de Worde started to print a large number of grammatical texts by Whittinton and by his former master, John Stanbridge. When Treveris, another printer, pirated editions of Whittinton's texts, de Worde countered with revised editions which contained a sharp attack on Treveris for his inaccurate printing. There seems little doubt that this attack was written by Whittinton and it provides us with an indication of his attachment to the de Worde publishing house; for we have signs here of their close cooperation and even indeed of the author's concern for the accuracy of his text. Nothing like this had happened in Caxton's time. The other writer with whom de Worde established a working relationship was Richard Whitford, a monk of Syon. The printer had established a relationship with this monastery from the beginning of the century and had printed editions of manuscripts in its library. He had also distributed some of his editions there and some of his books are recorded in the catalogue of the monastic library as his gifts. However, it was not till 1525 that he started to print Whitford; in that year he issued his translations of the *Rule of Saint Augustine*. There had been an old translation which Whitford thought was so old-fashioned that he had made a new one. That de Worde should have printed a rule of this sort, which could really be of interest only to monastic institutions, shows how closely connected with Syon he was. Over the next few years he was also to print several other of Whitford's writings. Whitford may also have suggested different titles to him, for de Worde's 1530 edition of the *Three Kings of Cologne* contains a request for the reader to pray for Whitford. By recruiting authors in this way de Worde was able to build up lists of religious and of grammatical texts. The former were presumably used in monasteries and parishes, the latter in schools. There was not so clear a homogeneity in the works published by de Worde as in those issued by Caxton; he was forced to seize whatever opportunities came his way. In doing so he showed how publishing would develop in the future. It is by considering de Worde's output that we can come to a juster appreciation of Caxton and his publishing policy and realise how far in advance of his time he was.

X
CAXTON'S EDITIONS

This chapter is meant simply as a guide to the dates of the editions issued by Caxton's press. Translations by him are noted with an asterisk.

Bruges (1473–76)

Six books were printed in Bruges, the only one with a date being the first edition of the *Game of Chess*, finished on 31 March 1474. The English translation of the *History of Troy* was the first book to be printed by Caxton. It is likely that the *Game of Chess* followed next, though as the French version of the *History of Troy* was printed in quinternions like the English version, the only two of his editions to have this feature, it is possible that this was the second book printed. If so, it would mean that the English version appeared earlier in 1473 than generally assumed. The six books are:

(1473) *History of Troy.*
31 March 1474 *Game of Chess*, first edition.
Four editions in French, all undated: *History of Troy, Jason, Cordial*, and *Penitential Psalms*.

Westminster (1476–91)

John Russell's *Propositio* may have been printed in Bruges, though it is now generally accepted that it appeared in Westminster; it need not have been the first text to appear.

The earliest fixed date we have of a work from Westminster is the *Indulgence* with the inserted date of 13 December 1476; the first dated book is the first edition of *Dicts or Sayings* translated by Earl Rivers, printed on 18 November 1477; the next dated book is the *Moral Proverbs*, also translated by Earl Rivers, which appeared on 20 February 1478. A host of undated books have to be placed between Caxton's arrival in 1476 and the end of 1478.

*Jason, his version of the French text printed in Bruges.

Canterbury Tales,
Anelida and Arcite, } poems by Chaucer.
Parliament of Fowls, }

Horse, Sheep and Goose, two editions,
Stans Puer,
Churl and Bird, two editions, } poems by Lydgate.
Temple of Glass,

Cato, two editions, a poem by Benedict Burgh.
Book of Courtesy, an English poem.
Horae, first edition.
Advertisement, in English advertising the *Ordinale* below.
Ordinale.
Infantia Salvatoris.
***Boethius**, Chaucer's translation.

As the *Boethius* uses two types, one for the text and the other for headings, it may be a late one in the above group.

The *Cordial* from 24 March 1479 is the first dated book to use type 2*; it is a translation by Earl Rivers. Undated books in type 2* are probably from about this time or later.

Nova Rhetorica.
Dicts or Sayings, second edition.
Indulgence, with inserted date of 31 March 1480.
The *Epitome*, which appeared after 24 January 1480 is an abridgement of the *Nova Rhetorica*, which may have been printed at the same time. Both are Latin rhetorical texts by Traversagni.

Other dated works from 1480 are:

22 April *Ovid's *Metamorphoses*; the date is for the completion of the translation; no printed copy survives.
10 June *Chronicles of England*, first edition.
18 August *Description of Britain*, based on Trevisa's translation of Higden's *Polychronicon*.

From 1481 and 1482 are the following dated texts:

6 June 1481 **Reynard the Fox*, translated from Dutch.
12 August 1481 The composite volume *Of Old Age*.
20 November 1481 **Siege of Jerusalem*.
**Mirror of the World* was translated on 8 March 1481 and so the first edition probably preceded *Reynard the Fox* in 1481.

2 July 1482 *Polychronicon*, Trevisa's translation with additions by Caxton.
8 October 1482 *Chronicles of England*, second edition.

Undated works from about this time include:

Horae, second edition.
Festum Visitationis, a service book in Latin.
Psalter.
Court of Sapience, English poem.
Vocabulary, a parallel text with French and English.
Three indulgences.
Cato, third edition and the first with woodcuts, to be dated with the first edition of *Mirror of the World* in the period March/April 1481.

Many texts can be dated to 1483:

Sex Epistolae, Latin letters prepared for the press by Pietro Carmeliano and published after 14 February.
6 June *Pilgrimage of the Soul*, Lydgate's translation.
30 June *Festial*, Mirk's text.
2 September *Confessio Amantis*, Gower's poem.
20 November *Golden Legend*.

To this year may probably be assigned:

Canterbury Tales, second edition, ⎫
Troilus and Criseyde,   ⎬ poems by Chaucer.
House of Fame,   ⎭
Game of Chess, second edition with woodcuts.
Quattuor Sermones, first edition.

In 1484 the following dated texts appeared:

31 January *Knight of the Tower* (translation completed 1 June 1483).
Caton, the translation of which was completed on 23 December 1483.
26 March *Aesop* (translation completed in '1483', i.e. from 25 March 1483 to 24 March 1484).
Royal Book (translation completed on 13 September 1484).

Other editions in this year include:

Curial, translated from French at request of Earl Rivers.
Deathbed Prayers.
Life of Our Lady, both editions, Lydgate's poem.
Order of Chivalry (completed in the reign of Richard III).
Quattuor Sermones, second edition.
Saint Winifred, translated from a Latin Life of the Saint.

Three dated texts are known from 1485:

31 July *King Arthur*, Caxton's adaptation of Malory's *Le Morte D'Arthur*.
1 December **Charles the Great*.
19 December **Paris and Vienne*.

Three undated texts are placed after this:

Speculum Vitae Christi, first edition.
Image of Pity, first edition.
Golden Legend, second edition.

The only dated text between 1485 and 1489 is **Book of Good Manners* from 11 May 1487.
Two undated texts, both religious works, may be from 1487:

Commemoratio.
Directorium Sacerdotum, first edition.

In 1489 the following texts have some date:

Indulgence, with inserted date 24 April.
*Doctrinal of Sapience, translation of which completed on 7 May.
*Feats of Arms, 14 July.

Undated texts probably to be placed in 1488 or 1489 are:

Governal of Health, formerly attributed to Lydgate.
*Four Sons of Aymon.
*Blanchardin and Eglantine.
Reynard the Fox, second edition.
Dicts or Sayings, third edition.
Directorium Sacerdotum, second edition.
Horae, third edition.
Statutes, of Henry VII.

Two texts are dated to 1490:

15 June **Art of Dieing*, translation completed at this date.
22 June **Eneydos*, translation completed at this date.

All other undated texts are allocated to the last years of Caxton's life; all are of a religious nature:
Horae, fourth edition.
Image of Pity, second edition.
Mirror of the World, second edition.
Speculum Vitae Christi, second edition.
Festial, second edition.

Quattuor Sermones, third edition.
Fifteen Oes.
Horologium Sapientiae.
Festum Transfigurationis.
Ars Moriendi.

NOTES ON THE PLATES

Frontispiece. The First English Printed Book
This plate shows a page of the first book printed in English, the *History of Troy* which appeared in 1473. The French original was written for Philip, Duke of Burgundy, by Raoul Lefèvre in 1464, so that when Caxton started to translate it in 1469 it was still a new work. The French text was popular, for several manuscripts of it are extant and it also was printed by Caxton about 1474–75. The type used is Caxton's type 1 which he acquired from Johan Veldener in Cologne during his visit there in 1471–72. This type was used only in books printed in Bruges. As an early book from Caxton's press it contains uneven line endings, no signatures and a paucity of punctuation. Apart from the ampersand the abbreviations include the abbreviated forms of *that* and *the*, the stroke through the descender of 'p' representing *par* in *departid*, and the macron over a vowel to indicate a nasal. Among letter forms may be noticed the two forms of 'd', one with and one without a flourish, and the 'h' with a stroke through it.

2 and *4. Death and the Printers* and *An Early French Printing Press*
Both these illustrations show what the inside of a printer's workshop looked like. The basic layout is the same except the press itself in the later picture looks more sophisticated. In each there is a seated compositor with his copytext on a stand in front of him.

In one hand he holds a composing stick, and with the other he picks up the type from his type case. A forme with type in it lies beside him on the bench in 'Death and the Printers'. The press is worked by the pressman and beside him stands his apprentice who inked the type; he holds the inking balls in his hands. The long lever forced the paper down on to the type with sufficient force to make an even impression. Bound books or manuscripts complete both scenes, though in 'Death and the Printers' we see a man behind a counter who may have been the owner who sold the books from there.

3. A German Printing Press
This illustration is from a book published in Zurich in 1548. There is little change from the earlier representation of a press except that there are now two compositors. But this picture shows the apprentice actually inking the type with his inking balls. It can be appreciated what a battering the type received in this process. The pressman is taking out a page of print. Two piles of paper, one unused and one printed, are in the foreground. In fact the finished sheets would have been allowed to dry before being stacked in this way.

5. Dürer's Printers
This unfinished drawing attributed to Dürer and dated to 1511 shows how useless official documents were produced in bulk by a blacksmith,

a printer and a baker instead of by a notary's clerk. It reveals that the printer had from an early date become such an accepted figure that his trade could be caricatured. See R. Nash, *Dürer's 1511 Drawing of a Press and Printer* (Cambridge, Mass., 1947).

6. Casting Type

This illustration from a German book illustrating various trades published in 1568 shows the typecaster at work. He sits in front of the oven beside which are the bellows and fuel. The metal to form the type is melted in a crucible on the top of the oven and then poured into the mould which the typecaster is holding in his left hand. The type was removed by opening the hinged side of the mould. The completed type can be seen in the basket at his side.

7, 15, 18 and 22. A Spurious Caxton Portrait, Edward IV at Caxton's Press, Caxton and the Abbot of Westminster, and The Caxton Window

These four plates reveal how Caxton was celebrated as his reputation grew in the eighteenth and nineteenth centuries. The spurious portrait is included in John Bagford's papers and was probably invented by him; it has no authenticity. The view of Edward IV at Caxton's press is a detail of an oil painting by Daniel Maclise. It is, however, extremely unlikely that Edward would have visited Caxton's workshop or even that he took the slightest interest in the mechanics of printing. His relations with Caxton would be on a purely formal and official level. Caxton did have dealings with the Abbot of Westminster. He mentions in *Eneydos* that the Abbot asked him to translate some old documents, and it is possible that some of the indulgences were printed through the Abbot's good offices. It is not likely that Caxton's workshop occupied such splendid Gothic premises. The Caxton window in St Margaret's

Church at Westminster, the parish church where Caxton's funeral took place, shows an imposing and dignified man, more like a scholar than a printer. Unfortunately we have absolutely no details about Caxton's size, physique or appearance.

8. Mercers' Hall, City of London

The so-called Agas map, of which this is a detail, is thought to have been made and published in the last quarter of the sixteenth century, but it survives only in two copies printed in the reign of James I. It is not thought that any major changes were made to it in this later edition. The site of Mercers' Hall can be seen on the corner of Ironmonger Lane and Cheapside. Blades has marked with a dagger what he considered the location of Large's house in Old Jewry where Caxton would have lived as an apprentice.

9, 16, 17, 25 and 26. Edward IV, Henry VII, Margaret Duchess of Somerset, Arthur Prince of Wales, and Elizabeth of York

These five plates are of other members of the royal family who patronised the printer. Among them only Margaret, Duchess of Somerset, took a particular interest in books. Margaret (1443–1509) married Edmund Tudor, Henry VI's half-brother, and a son (the future Henry VII) was born after his father's death; Margaret remarried twice. She lent Caxton her French manuscript copy of the romance *Blanchardin and Eglantine* so that he could translate and print it, which he did about 1489. Caxton states that he had himself sold this manuscript to Margaret 'longe tofore'. Margaret together with her daughter-in-law, Elizabeth of York, requested the printer to issue the *Fifteen Oes*, a series of prayers each beginning with the word O. Margaret later encouraged de Worde to publish books, and they included Hilton's *Scala Perfectionis* and some of John

Fisher's works. Indeed at one time de Worde adopted the style of 'printer to the Princess Margaret'. Margaret was a woman of strong religious conviction, as this painting suggests. Elizabeth of York, daughter of Edward IV and wife of Henry VII, shared the patronage of the *Fifteen Oes* with her mother-in-law, but seems to have taken no further interest in the press. Her father took little interest in the printer, who did dedicate his edition of *Jason* to the Prince of Wales through the good offices of the King and Queen. He did not dedicate it to the King, who he assumed already owned a copy of the French version. We may remember in this connexion that Caxton had printed the French text in Bruges. Henry VII was the patron of *Feats of Arms,* which was 'delyvered' to the printer by the King through the Earl of Oxford at the Palace of Westminster on 23 January 1489 with orders to translate and print it. Caxton makes it seem as though Henry's role in this business was less important than that of the Earl of Oxford. Prince Arthur, the son of Henry VII, died in 1502 before his father and he never came to the throne. His name shows the interest in chivalry and Arthurian story common at the end of the fifteenth century. Just as Caxton dedicated *Jason* to Edward IV's son, so he dedicated *Eneydos* to Henry VII's son.

10. The Hall of the English, Bruges
This illustration of the Hall of the English at Bruges was published first in *Flandria Illustrata* by A. Sanderus from 1641 and shows what the headquarters of the English nation looked like in the seventeenth century. There is no evidence that this building was in existence in the fifteenth century. It is, however, likely that the English nation would have had a building in which they could hold their meetings and celebrations, just as the various guilds did in London.

It is improbable that Caxton would have lived there as Blades suggested.

11. Margaret, Duchess of Burgundy
Margaret, the sister of Edward IV, married Charles of Burgundy in 1468. She was his third wife and there were no children. The marriage was intended to cement the alliance between the English and the Burgundians. Margaret was Caxton's first patron, though her work in establishing the work of the first English press has been exaggerated by previous scholars. However, as the patron of the first book to be printed in English she deserves to be remembered. A woman of considerable beauty and piety, she extended her patronage to many writers and artists, though she is not known to have taken any further interest in printing. This portrait is a detail from a painting by Hans Memling.

12. The Chessboard
This illustration shows a page from Caxton's second edition of the *Game of Chess* (*c.* 1483). There are sixteen woodcuts in this edition, but some were used a second time within the edition. In general each chapter begins with its title at the top of the page followed by a woodcut. The chapter then follows. The bottom of the page following the conclusion of the chapter is left blank so that this arrangement can be preserved. No doubt this procedure was adopted to ease the problems for the compositor in trying to accommodate the cuts. There were no illustrations in the first edition produced in Bruges. The woodcuts were made by Caxton's second and major artist, who also executed the cuts for the *Canterbury Tales*. Note his use of shading on the figure, which is also found on the pilgrims of the *Canterbury Tales* (plates 54 and 55). It seems probable that these woodcuts were based on Continental

models, but an exact source has not been found.

13. A Page of Caxton's 'Jason'

This book was printed soon after Caxton set up his press at Westminster. It has uneven line lengths and no signatures. The text is printed entirely in type 3. There is more punctuation in this text than in those printed earlier, and one may note how the fullstop appears at various heights in the line. The French version of *Jason* was printed by Caxton, possibly in association with Mansion, in Bruges. The English translation may have been started before he returned to England. This text forms a natural continuation of the *History of Troy*, Caxton's first translation and printed text. The capitals, which are two lines high, have been added by hand; the guide letters are clearly visible.

14. The Earliest Piece of Printing in England

This plate illustrates the earliest known piece of printing from the press at Westminster. It was discovered in the Record Office at London and published for the first time in 1928. Caxton is known to have paid rent for his house at Westminster from Michaelmas 1476 and this indulgence must have been issued not long afterwards, since this copy has the date 12 December 1476 written in by hand. The text is all in his type 2 except for the first seven letters, [I]Ohannes, which are in type 3. Indulgences were printed with spaces left for the name(s) of the recipient(s), the date and the year of the Pope to be added by hand later. In the third line the hames *benrico lanley et katerine vxori eius londoniencis diocesis* have been added. In the third line from the bottom we find the place and date inserted: *Westm(onasterium) xiii⁰ die mens(is) dece(m)bris.* The last two lines show that the year was 1476 (the six is added by hand), the sixth year

of the papacy of Sixtus IV. The Abbot of Abingdon got into trouble over the issue of this indulgence, for it had not been approved by his superiors. It was superseded on papal order by John de Gigliis on 15 December 1478; this John issued new indulgences to replace this one. Henry Langley and his wife lived in Essex. However, the main value of this document is to show that Caxton had started printing in 1476 and that even at this early date he was using two sets of type in the same document. See A. W. Pollard, 'The New Caxton Indulgence', *The Library* 4th Series 9 (1928–29), pp. 86–9.

19. Westminster Abbey Precincts

This map is based on the outline of the Abbey precincts as recorded by Keene in 1755. The Almonry is at the bottom, outside the ditch. It is thought that Caxton's house was the end one of those immediately after the ditch on the path leading from the Almonry to the main Abbey buildings. Tanner has suggested that Caxton's original shop was near the Chapter House, the venue of many important meetings both secular and religious, on the path which ran between the Chapter House and the South East end of the Abbey. This path led to Westminster Palace and so any shop on it was advantageously placed. Indeed Tanner suggests that his shop may have been more like a booth than a shop as we understand one today, perhaps on the lines of those often seen today clinging to the sides of the larger Continental churches. See L. E. Tanner, 'William Caxton's Houses at Westminster', *The Library* 5th Series 12 (1957), pp. 153–66.

20. The 'Advertisement'

The *Advertisement* is dated to about 1477 and was an early product of Caxton's workshop. It advertised the *Ordinale*, which appeared at this time in the same type 3, 'after the forme of this present lettre'. The *Ordinale* contained Latin directions for the Service Book after the Salisbury Use. Each church had to commemorate each week the Virgin Mary, its dedication saint and Thomas à Becket. When the dedication saint was the Virgin Mary it was necessary to have only two commemorations per week. Hence the *Advertisement* mentions this fact. The *pye* was the English name for the *Ordinale*. The *Advertisement* tells us that by 1477 Caxton was already settled in the Almonry at the sign of the Red Pale. It is interesting that although he should consider this information worth including here, it is never found in the colophons of his editions. Characteristic of his early work is the unevenness of the line-endings as here. One may also note that the compositor has made a little pattern with the fullstops at the end; this was one of the few kinds of typographical embellishment found in Caxton's prints. The *Advertisement* was printed on a small sheet of paper, which was presumably pinned up in and around the Abbey precincts. The Latin tag at the end, which may be translated 'Please leave the handbill alone', suggests a learned clientele; for indeed only clerics and those with Latin would be interested in buying the *Ordinale*.

21. The Almonry

This early nineteenth-century engraving is said to show the Almonry at Westminster at that time; the Abbey is in the background. While we cannot assume that the buildings in the fifteenth century were exactly like these, it does remind us that the home of Caxton's workshop was much less grand than nineteenth-century artists liked to imagine (cf. plate 15) and than most of us probably think.

23. George, Duke of Clarence

The Duke of Clarence was the brother of Edward IV and Margaret, Duchess of Burgundy. He was the dedicatee of Caxton's second English printed book, the *Game of Chess*, which was printed on 31 March 1474. He can hardly be called its patron, since Caxton never met him and probably never had any communication with him. It is likely that Margaret may have recommended to the printer that he use the duke's name, since George was her favourite brother. The choice was unfortunate, since he fell into disgrace and was imprisoned in the Tower where he met his death in 1478. His name was omitted from the second edition of the *Game of Chess*.

24. Elizabeth Woodville

The daughter of Sir Richard Woodville and his wife, the former Duchess of Bedford, Elizabeth was one of twelve children. One of her brothers was Anthony, who was also a patron of the printer. The family had Lancastrian leanings and Elizabeth was married first to Sir John Grey, who was killed at St Albans in 1461. In 1464 she married Edward IV. The marriage was not popular with the Yorkists and Elizabeth soon started to promote her family to provide a political counterweight to these Yorkists. Her father was made Earl Rivers, the title which Anthony inherited in 1469. It is thought that the 'noble lady' to whom the *Knight of the Tower* was dedicated is Elizabeth. She was then a close neighbour of Caxton's, for she had sought sanctuary in Westminster Abbey to escape from Richard III. After the accession of Henry VII, her daughter married the new king and so united the two houses.

27. Caxton's Ovid

This plate shows the end of book three of the manuscript of the Caxton Ovid. The last six books of this work were in a manuscript bequeathed by Pepys to Magdalene College, Cambridge. The first nine books were discovered recently among the papers of the late

Sir Thomas Phillips and have now been reunited with the other six in the Pepys Library. The manuscript is written in the Flemish *bâtarde* script so common at the end of the fifteenth century. A comparison of this plate with those illustrating Caxton's *bâtarde* type will show how closely the typecutters followed contemporary manuscript hands. Notice, for example, the ampersand and the flourish on the final 'd' in both cases. The major difference is that the typecutters could not imitate the scribal flourishes in the top and bottom margins and hence the printed page looks more sedate and less florid than the manuscript. As in Caxton's early prints the lines are not justified, though a flourish or a dot helps to fill the available space. It is not known whether the Ovid was printed, but it seems probable. In the colophon of the manuscript it says that the text was 'translated and finished' by Caxton on 22 April 1480. The manuscript may have been a presentation copy, which like the printed edition (if there was one) could have been produced from Caxton's rough draft. The manuscript was to have been illustrated, though some of the miniatures were never completed. This may mean that the manuscript was never given to the intended recipient.

29. Caxton's First Edition of 'Quattuor Sermones'

Caxton's first edition of *Quattuor Sermones*, which was printed about 1483, is in type 4*; and it will be noticed that the Latin quotation on lines 2 and 3 is not printed in a different type. As compared with the page from the *History of Troy* (frontispiece) there is plenty of punctuation, with the stroke as the principal feature. There are small gaps in the text which in some copies would be filled in with paragraph marks added by hand. Notice also that whereas the top two-thirds of the page is generously spaced out,

the last ten lines present a more bunched appearance as though the compositor was trying to fit in a fixed amount of text. In these last lines there are no gaps, but there are many abbreviations. And the words of the last line are much closer together than, say, those in the fifth line.

30. The Prologue to 'Eneydos'

Caxton completed his translation of *Eneydos* on 22 June 1490 and it was probably printed later that year. It is all in type 6. This page is from the prologue, a section which was added after the rest of the text was in print, for it contains its own set of signatures. In this prologue we find the well-known story of the mercer Sheffelde who was unable to make himself understood when he asked for eggs in a different part of the country because 'that comyn Englysshe that is spoken in one shyre varyeth from another'.

31. The Opening of 'Ars Moriendi'

This is the opening of a short tract on the art of dying. Such texts were popular in the fifteenth century and took different forms. This one was translated from a Latin original, possibly by Caxton himself, and it appeared about 1491. Another version, translated and abridged from French by Caxton, appeared in 1490 or thereabouts. This edition is in types 6 and 8, the larger type being used for the heading. There is no title-page, the only title being the heading which occurs at the top of this page. One may note the printed paragraph marks, the printed two-line initial, and the signature with its capital letter and Roman numeral.

32. Some Watermarks

This plate illustrates some of the watermarks found in the paper Caxton used: they are not exact copies, but have been redrawn by William Blades. Many other marks are found in his books and even those illustrated here occur in many different forms. The mark was formed from a wire reproduction of it forming the bottom of the tray in which the paper was made and sometimes it is possible to trace from the outline the mark where the wire is deteriorating, where it has been patched up or where it has been retied to the lines holding it in place. Most of the paper Caxton used came from Normandy or Northern France, though it may have been shipped through Flanders. Some of the marks also occur in the paper found in manuscripts, for no special paper was made for printing. While some of the marks may have significance, like the coats of arms, most were arbitrary signs like merchant marks.

33. Caxton's Second Edition of the 'Festial'

The second edition of the *Festial* appeared towards the end of Caxton's career. It differs in some important ways from the third edition of *Quattuor Sermones* (see plate 34). Whereas the latter is in type 6 only, this book is mainly in type 6, though the Latin quotations are in type 8, as can be noted in the left-hand column. The difference can easily be seen in the two forms of the ampersand. The half-lines in the *Festial* are slightly longer than those in *Quattuor Sermones* and this may have eased the problem of justifying the lines, since there are fewer broken words and hyphens in this plate. There are two examples of the printed paragraph mark on this page, though it was used regularly by Caxton after 1484. Among letter forms the two forms of 'r' may be noted in the word *Narracio* after the first paragraph mark. An example of lazy composing may be seen in the sixth line from the bottom of the right-hand column where the compositor has put the fullstop in the line below the one in which it should occur. This edition

of the *Festial* is textually different from the first and it may have been set up from the manuscript rather than from a printed book.

34. Caxton's Third Edition of 'Quattuor Sermones'

Caxton's third edition of *Quattuor Sermones*, issued about 1491, is in type 6. It is not known why this edition was in two columns, for the two preceding ones (see plates 29 and 39) are in single columns. It was difficult for the compositor to justify the shorter lines and a considerable number of them end with incomplete words and hyphens. Some broken words are not hyphenated. Although the stroke is still used, there is considerable employment of the fullstop, though the capitalisation is still erratic.

35. A Suggested Layout of a Compositor's Case

This layout of a type-case was suggested by Blades and is reproduced here so that the reader can see how many different sorts went to make up a particular fount of type. It gives a good impression of the many letter combinations used at that time as well as the various abbreviations. The size of the compositor's type-case can be appreciated from the plates which illustrate printing shops (plates 2–4).

36. Surigone's Epitaph to Chaucer

This plate illustrates the Latin epitaph for Chaucer written by the Italian poet Stefano Surigone. It is found following the epilogue Caxton wrote for his edition of Chaucer's translation of Boethius's *De consolatione philosophiae* (*c.* 1478). It is in type 3, which is used in this edition for headings and Latin quotations, the rest of the book being in type 2. There are no signatures in this work. The text of the epitaph was written on a tablet attached to a pillar by Chaucer's tomb in Westminster Abbey and Caxton no doubt copied it from there. There is no evidence that he knew or met Surigone. However, Caxton added four lines of Latin poetry (presumably written by himself) to this epitaph which emphasised his own contribution to the spreading of Chaucer's fame. See N. F. Blake, 'Caxton and Chaucer', *Leeds Studies in English* New Series 1 (1967), pp. 19–36.

37. De Worde's 'Life of Saint Katherine'

This is the opening page of one of the earliest books issued by de Worde. Originally the edition was attributed to Caxton, and it has points of similarity with the books appearing at the end of Caxton's life. Like the *Ars Moriendi* it is printed in two types (Caxton's 4* and 8 which correspond to de Worde's 1 and 2), the larger of which is used for the headings. There is no title-page, the only title being the heading at the top of the left-hand column. Like some of Caxton's later editions, notably the *Festial* and *Quattuor Sermones*, this book is also printed in double columns. No doubt it appeared about 1491–92, shortly after de Worde had taken charge of the business. A clearer representation of the woodcut initial is found on plate 45.

38. A Page of Copytext

This page from British Library MS Harley 3432 shows how a page of copytext could be treated by a compositor. Several corrections to the text have been made and written in the margin. At line 20 of the right-hand column can be seen the compositor's mark to indicate the end of a page of type.

39. The Conclusion of the Second Edition of 'Quattuor Sermones'

This is the final page of Caxton's second edition of *Quattuor Sermones* (c. 1484). Both Latin and English are in type 4*. The compositor has made some attempt to arrange his page agreeably in that there is a gap before and after the Latin prayer and the colophon has been centred within the line. No attempt, however, has been made to fit the available text within the page so that it is filled. One may note that abbreviations are used more frequently in the Latin prayer, as commonly in ecclesiastical texts, than in the English sections.

40. A Colophon

This plate of the last page of Caxton's *Fifteen Oes* shows how this one text was decorated with borders on each page. The borders are inexpertly assembled so that the overall effect is one of untidiness rather than of decorativeness; and the type itself seems to be cramped by the borders. The arrangement of the fatter borders at the bottom and outside edges of each page was standard. The colophon notes that the prayers were published for Queen Elizabeth and the Duchess of Somerset (see plates 26 and 17). Although printed towards the end of his life the Latin at the top of the page is printed in the same type as the English, which simply shows how erratic progress was at the press.

41. The Celestial Regions

This page is from Caxton's first edition of the *Mirror of the World* (1481), printed in type 2*. Of particular interest is the illustration on this page. The circles representing the heavenly regions were printed by woodblock, but the artist was evidently unable to produce small enough writing on his woodblock. So the words in the illustration have been added by hand—a tiresome business in a printed edition. Note how the 'a' in *planettes* and *ayer* has an open-top shape, whereas in the type it has a heavy top horizontal line with or without the thin middle one. The 'th' in *Erthe* is also very different from that found in the text itself. In the chapter heading one may also note how the compositor has spaced the *capitulo* and the xxxj° at opposite ends of the second line.

42. An Early Title-page: The 'Chastising of God's Children'

This book was among the first issued by de Worde and probably dates from 1491–92. It is his first step towards a title-page, though it has more the nature of a manuscript incipit than that of a book title. It is perhaps only with his edition of the *Canterbury Tales* in 1498 that we can say he had a definite title, which reads 'The boke of Chaucer named Caunterbury tales' with the last two words on a separate line. However, in the *Chastising of God's Children* this heading is the only printing to occur on the first page; the text begins on its verso. The heading stretches over the whole page whereas the text is divided into two columns. The heading is also in a different type from the rest of the edition.

43. Caxton's Device

This illustration of Caxton's device is from his third edition of *Dicts or Sayings* (*c.* 1489). The mark consists of the iritials 'WC' around a symbol which has been interpreted as '74', but which may have no particular meaning or significance. The rest of the device is purely decorative. The quality of the cut is poor and the design crude.

44. One of de Worde's Devices

This device is found in de Worde's edition of *Manipulus curatorum* by Guido de Monte Rocherii (1502). The book was issued from his house at the Sign of the Sun in Fleet Street, where he had moved in 1500, and so the sun surrounded by two large stars and countless smaller ones is included at the top of the device. The centre of the device is occupied by Caxton's old mark, except that the 'C' has been reversed. In the bottom section de Worde has included his name, a feature never found in Caxton's

devices, and some animals. This edition of *Manipulus curatorum* is noteworthy in that not all copies have the same device; at least two devices were used in this edition, though both have the same basic design. See R. B. McKerrow, *Printers' & Publishers' Devices in England & Scotland 1485–1640* (London 1913), Nos 10b and 12.

45. Some Woodcut Initials

Woodcut initials were used by Caxton from 1484 onwards. Before then initials were drawn in by hand following the guide letters provided by the compositor. These initials reproduced here are from books by Caxton and de Worde. The top two rows contain initials generally filling five lines of type; the first 'I' is found in de Worde's *Chastising of God's Children* and the second in Caxton's *Governal of Health*. The third row contains initials which normally filled three lines of type, a series found particularly in Caxton's edition of Malory. The fourth row contains those initials filling two lines of type. The last row contains the large initial 'H' of de Worde's *Life of Saint Katherine* (plate 37) and the large initial 'A' found only in Caxton's *Aesop* and *Order of Chivalry* (plate 46).

46. The Initial 'A'

This plate of a page from the *Order of Chivalry* is noteworthy for the large floriated initial 'A' which extends over eight lines. This woodcut initial was used otherwise only in *Aesop*, printed on 26 March 1484, and it may mean that the *Order of Chivalry*, which was printed in Richard III's reign (26 June 1483 to 22 August 1485), appeared shortly after *Aesop*. The signature 'aiii' may be noted at the foot of the page. The body of the text is in type 4*, but the heading and the first line of the text are in type 3, a *lettre de forme* type. Type 3 is bigger than type 4*, which would make it more suitable for ecclesiastical texts to be read from a lectern or desk at a service. The 'y' in type 3 has a dot above it in imitation of scribal usage in manuscripts where it was introduced to prevent confusion with other letters. Though not necessary in a printed book its use shows how early typecutters imitated scribal practice without considering the possibilities of the new invention. Type 4* still has the symbol ʒ representing 'gh'. Unlike the page from the first edition of *Quattuor Sermones* (plate 29) this page is more spread out at the bottom of the page, as though the compositor wanted to make his text go as far as possible.

47. The Presentation of a Book to Margaret, Duchess of Burgundy
This plate is described and discussed on pp. 132–5.

48. The Master and Scholars Woodcut
This woodcut illustration from Caxton's first edition of the *Mirror of the World* printed in 1481 was executed by the first artist to work for him. The whole touch is lighter and the lines of shading are shorter and more schematised in this plate than in those in the plates from the *Canterbury Tales* (cf. plates 54 and 55). There is also a noticeable difference in the representation of the faces. The woodcut is modelled on a miniature in MS Royal 19 A ix (see plate 49). The type used is 2*, and there is no separate type for headings or Latin quotations. Signatures are in lower-case letters and arabic numerals: this page has 'a4' at its foot. The top two lines conclude the table of contents with the relevant chapter number on the right. The paragraph marks have been added by hand as has the initial capital 'C' of the prologue, which in this case fills only two lines. The printed guide letter put in by the compositor is quite visible. The letter following the capital 'C' is upper case; lower case is used only from the third letter.

49. The Master and Scholars Manuscript Illustration
This is a page of British Library MS Royal 19 A ix which was made in Bruges in June 1464. The miniature of the master and four scholars is the model used by Caxton's artist for the woodcut in the previous plate. Though the design is the same, numerous minor changes have been made. The overall appearance of Caxton's book is not unlike that of the manuscript.

50. The Crucifixion
This woodcut is found as the frontispiece to Caxton's *Fifteen Oes*, printed c. 1491, though it is here reproduced without the borders used in that book. It was probably executed by a Continental artist, though Caxton used no other woodcuts by him. Christ is portrayed on a grained cross, flanked by the two thieves on much simpler crosses. Christ's side is being pierced by a spear held by a man on horseback, traditionally identified as the centurion Longinus. A spear with a sponge on it is held by another horseman. At the bottom left St John supports the Virgin; both have nimbuses. Christ carrying the cross to Golgotha is represented in a different scene on the right.

51. Two Woodcuts from 'Aesop'
These two woodcuts were made by Caxton's principal artist, who also made the cuts for the *Game of Chess* and the *Canterbury Tales*. Notice how similar the shading on the men is here as compared with that on plates 12 and 55. The first picture illustrates the fable of the man and the wood which has the moral that he who helps his enemy causes his own death. A man asked the trees for wood to make the handle of his axe. When he got it and made his axe, he proceeded to cut down the trees in the wood. The second picture illustrates the fable of the dog and the wolf. The dog is fat because he is fed by his master. The

thin wolf enquires about this and discovers that in order to be fed the dog has given up his liberty, which the wolf regards as his most prized possession. The bird has no relevance to the fable. The illustrations in Caxton's *Aesop* are modelled on the woodcuts found in the French edition of *Esope* that Caxton used, which were in their turn based on German originals. *Aesop* has running heads and is the first dated book with printed paragraph marks. It is printed in type 4*.

52. The Woodcut of a Different Artist in Aesop

The woodcuts in *Aesop* were executed by three different hands. The majority were made by Caxton's principal artist (see plate 51). But the one illustrated here is by an artist of greatly inferior talent who made only a couple of woodcuts. One may note the wedge-shaped nature of the shading on the animals and the general lack of clarity and design. The fable relates that the frog leapt up a mountain and pretended to be a doctor. Some of the animals believed him, but the fox poured scorn on his claims because his yellow colour showed he could not cure himself, let alone anyone else. One may also note the three-line printed initial 'N', for such initials occur in *Aesop* for the first time in Caxton's work.

53. The Transfiguration

This woodcut of the transfiguration occurs on the first page of a short text, *Festum Transfigurationis*, a service book for the Feast of the Transfiguration printed by Caxton at the end of his life. No other work by this artist is known. The poor quality of the drawing has led scholars to attribute it to an English hand. This makes this woodcut unusual in that Caxton did not otherwise commission any woodblocks from English artists after 1484. So it may be by a Continental hand, or if English it may have been acquired

by Caxton second-hand. In the middle Christ appears with a medallion inscribed 'IHC' on his chest. Rays from him illuminate the three disciples who witnessed the transfiguration, St Peter holding a book, St James lying down, and St John kneeling. At the top Moses holds the tables of the law and opposite him is Elijah. In the top centre God and a dove appear. The three top figures are partly hidden by their individual clouds. This woodblock was used again in several sixteenth-century books.

54. The Squire

The picture of the squire is from the beginning of the Squire's Tale (fol. n8^v) in the second edition of the *Canterbury Tales*. The same woodcut had been used earlier to illustrate the squire in the General Prologue (fol. a4^v). The cut was drawn by the artist who did the majority of Caxton's woodcuts. As with the yeoman, the squire exhibits some of the features found in Chaucer's description of him, such as his curly hair, but others are noticebly wrong. Similarly his clothes were embroidered with flowers; but the artist has compromised by portraying him holding a single flower. Other details of the edition are as listed in the following note, though it may be noted that while in this copy the initial capital has been drawn in, there are no painted paragraph marks.

55. The Yeoman

This illustration of Chaucer's yeoman by Caxton's principal woodcut artist is from his second edition of the *Canterbury Tales* (c. 1483), folio a5^r. Some attempt has been made to represent the yeoman's equipment accurately, though the horn hung from his arm may be a misunderstanding of *bracer*, a guard used to protect the arm or wrist from the bowstring. The body of the text is in type 4*, but the running heads are in type 2*. The paragraph mark before *Prologue* has been added by hand as there are no printed paragraph marks in this edition. A four-line gap for the initial to introduce the yeoman was left by the compositor, who included the guide letter 'a'. The capital 'A' was subsequently drawn in by hand.

56. Mary and Martha

This is a page of Caxton's edition of Nicholas Love's translation of the *Speculum Vitae Christi* attributed to Bonaventura. Four other woodcuts from this edition are on the following plate; this one illustrates the size of the woodcut in relation to the page of text and its disposition on the page. The text itself is printed in type 5, and the running head may be noted. This feature was probably taken over from the manuscript Caxton used. The woodcut illustrates Mary and Martha receiving Jesus at the gates of Bethany. Jesus is accompanied by his disciples, two of whose faces are visible, and the nimbuses of four others. The woodcuts are lighter and more delicate than those made in England; they were almost certainly imported from the Low Countries. This cut was used by Caxton in both his editions of the *Speculum* and in his edition of the *Royal Book*. It was used by de Worde in five of his printed books.

57. 'Horae' Woodcuts from 'Speculum Vitae Christi'

Although these four woodcuts are now found in use for the first time in Caxton's first edition of *Speculum Vitae Christi*, they are not by the same hand which executed the other woodcuts in that book (see plate 56). These belong to two separate series of woodcuts which were imported and which it is supposed were originally made for a Book of Hours. The top left-hand one and the two bottom ones belong to the so-called A series, the top right-hand one to the B series. The principal difference between the two series is

in the representation of hair, which in the B series contains small spiky protuberances as on the man kneeling under the cross. The woodcuts were already in a poor condition when Caxton received them, and they continued to deteriorate as they were used quite frequently by both him and de Worde. The four scenes are (i) Christ before Pilate; (ii) the Crucifixion; (iii) Joseph of Arimathea and Nicodemus taking Christ down from the cross; and (iv) Mary weeping over the body of the dead Christ.

58. The 'Image of Pity'

This illustration is of Caxton's second edition of the *Image of Pity* (c. 1490), which was produced on a single broadsheet; it is a type of indulgence. In the centre Christ is shown standing in the right side of a stone coffin. He exhibits bleeding hands and side, and he wears a nimbus with crown. Behind him is a grained cross, and a spear (used to pierce his side) and a reed with a sponge for the vinegar and gall flank him. In the panel beneath the picture of Christ there would originally have been the words of the indulgence, it now contains a modern note pasted on top. The image and its indulgence are surrounded by twenty-eight small boxes illustrating the instruments of the passion or symbols of the crucifixion. Thus in the top left-hand box we see the pelican tearing its breast to resuscitate its young with its blood—traditional image of Christ's own sacrifice.

59. An Indulgence

This indulgence was issued in the name of Pope Innocent VIII by John de Gigliis and Perseus de Malviciis. It was printed before 24 April 1489, since one of the other copies has that date written in. This copy is unused and the blanks left for the recipient's name and the date can be seen. It is in a poor condition because it was found in a binding. No doubt when further indulgences were printed, remaining copies of the previous one were treated as waste. The indulgence is printed in type 7.

60. Chaucer

This portrait of Chaucer forms a natural pendant to his epitaph by Surigone (plate 36). It is painted on an oak panel and is just under a foot high. It was probably painted in the time of Elizabeth and it is closely connected with portraits in British Library MS Additional 5141 and in the Bodleian Library, Oxford. That Chaucer was plump is something he mentions frequently in his own poetry, but it is unlikely that there are any other authentic touches in this portrait. He carries a pencase and a rosary, the latter being a feature of all early portraits of him. See M. H. Spielmann, *The Portraits of Geoffrey Chaucer* (London, 1900).

61 and 62. Philip the Good, Duke of Burgundy, and Charles the Bold, Duke of Burgundy

The two Dukes of Burgundy with whom Caxton may have come into contact were Philip (*ob.* 1467) and Charles (1467–77), for as a frequent English negotiator he came into contact with the Burgundians in an attempt to arrange favourable trading terms for English wool and other goods. Both dukes were lovers of books, and inventories of their libraries are extant. Both were regarded by many contemporaries as the true inheritors of the chivalric tradition. Several of the books Caxton translated, such as *History of Troy* and *Jason,* were written in French for their court. Both wear the insignia of the Golden Fleece, the order of chivalry founded by Philip, to which several English kings belonged. In *Jason* Caxton mentions how Philip's castle at Hesdin had scenes from the life of Jason on the walls.

63. De Worde's Tribute to Caxton

This plate of folio 005^r of de Worde's edition of *De proprietatibus rerum* (*c.* 1495) contains part of his epilogue to that work. This edition is the English translation of the well-known Latin text, a copy of which had been issued in Cologne. De Worde states here that Caxton was responsible for the edition. The epilogue consists of a series of verses about the book and its merits, its patron and various other people. In addition to Caxton, de Worde praises John Tate, the first English manufacturer of paper. Caxton and Tate are jointly mentioned in the third stanza on this page. A slightly modernised version of the first half of this stanza is found on p. 25.

FURTHER READING

Bibliographies of Caxton can be found in *The New Cambridge Bibliography of English Literature I. 600–1660*, ed. G. Watson (Cambridge: University Press, 1974), pp. 667–74; *A Manual of the Writings in Middle English 1050–1500*, vol. 3 ed. A. E. Hartung (New Haven: Connecticut Academy of Arts and Sciences, 1972), pp. 771–807, 924–51; and N. F. Blake, *Caxton and his World* (London: Deutsch, 1969), pp. 240–9.

The most recent life of Caxton is that by Blake above. Others include: N. S. Aurner, *Caxton: Mirrour of Fifteenth-Century Letters* (London: Allan, 1926); William Blades, *The Life and Typography of William Caxton*, 2 vols (London and Strasburg: Trübner, 1861–63); W. J. B. Crotch, *The Prologues and Epilogues of William Caxton*, EETS o.s. 176 (London: Oxford University Press 1928); E. G. Duff, *William Caxton* (Chicago: Caxton Club, 1905); and H. R. Plomer, *William Caxton 1424–1491* (London: Parsons, 1925).

On the general historical background see O. Cartellieri (trans. M. Letts), *The Court of Burgundy* (London: Kegan Paul, 1929); E. F. Jacob, *The Fifteenth Century 1399–1485* (Oxford: Clarendon, 1961); C. Ross, *Edward IV* (London: Eyre Methuen, 1974); G. von Schanz, *Englische Handelspolitik gegen Ende des Mittelalters* (Leipzig: Duncker and Humblot, 1881); M.-R Thielemans, *Bourgogne et Angleterre. Relations politiques et économiques entre les Pays-Bas bourguignons et l'Angleterre 1435–1467* (Brussels: Presses Universitaires, 1966); and R. Vaughan, *Charles the Bold* (London: Longman, 1974).

On the literary background of the late fifteenth century see H. S. Bennett, *Chaucer and the Fifteenth Century* (Oxford: Clarendon, 1947); G. Doutrepont, *La littérature française à la cour des ducs de Bourgogne* (Paris: Champion, 1909); D. Pearsall, *John Lydgate* (London: Routledge and Kegan Paul, 1970); R. Weiss, *Humanism in England during the Fifteenth Century*, 2nd edn (Oxford: Blackwell, 1957); S. K. Workman, *Fifteenth-century Translation as an Influence on English Prose* (Princeton: University Press, 1940).

For details of Caxton's editions see Blades, as above (still the most detailed work); E. G. Duff, *Fifteenth-century English Books* (London: Bibliographical Society, 1917); S. de Ricci, *A Census of Caxtons* (London: Bibliographical Society, 1909); and the catalogues of the major libraries.

For general background bibliographical studies see G. Bone, 'Extant Manuscripts printed from by W. de Worde with Notes on the Owner, Roger Thorney', *The Library* 4th Series 12 (1931–32), pp. 284–306; C. F. Bühler, *The Fifteenth-century Book: The Scribes, The Printers, The Decorators* (Philadelphia: University of Pennsylvania, 1960); L. Febvre and H.-J. Martin, *L'Apparition du livre* (Paris: Michel, 1958–59); E. Hodnett, *English Woodcuts 1480–1525*, 2nd edn (London: Oxford University Press, 1973); P. Simpson, *Proof-Reading in the Sixteenth, Seventeenth and Eighteenth Centuries* (London: Oxford University Press, 1935); and D. B. Updike, *Printing Types: Their History, Forms, and Use*, 2nd edn, 2 vols (Cambridge, Mass.: Harvard University Press, 1937).

For studies of Caxton as a literary critic see N. F. Blake, 'William Caxton: His Choice of Texts', *Anglia* 83 (1965), pp. 289–307; C. F. Bühler, *William Caxton and his Critics* (Syracuse: University Press, 1960); A. J. P. Byles, 'William Caxton as a Man of Letters', *The Library* 4th Series 15 (1934–35), pp. 1–25; H. B. Lathrop, 'The First English Printers and their Patrons', *The Library* 4th Series 3 (1922–23), pp. 69–96; and D. B. Sands, 'Caxton as a Literary Critic', *Papers of the Bibliographical Society of America* 51 (1957), pp. 312–18. A volume of selections of Caxton's works is edited by N. F. Blake (Oxford: Clarendon, 1973). His prologues and epilogues are edited by N. F. Blake (London: Deutsch, 1973) and W. J. B. Crotch, as above. The Early English Text Society has issued the following editions of Caxton's works: *Charles the Great* (ed. S. J. H. Herrtage, 1880–81); *Four Sons of Aymon* (ed. O. Richardson, 1884–85); *The Curial* (ed. P. Meyer and F. J. Furnivall, 1888); *Blanchardin and Eglantine* (ed. L. Kellner, 1890); *Eneydos* (ed. M. T. Culley and F. J. Furnivall, 1890); *Siege of Jerusalem* (ed. M. N. Colvin, 1893); *Mirror of the World,* (ed. O. H. Prior, 1913); *Jason* (ed. J. Munro, 1913); *Order of Chivalry* (ed. A. T. P.. Byles, 1926); *Feats of Arms* (ed. A. T. P. Byles, 1932); *Paris and Vienne* (ed. MacEdward Leach, 1957); *Reynard the Fox* (ed. N. F. Blake, 1970); *Knight of the Tower* (ed. M. Y. Offord, 1971); and several other works printed, but not translated, by him, Other editions of his translations or adaptations include *Game of Chess* (ed. W. E. A. Axon, London: Elliott Stock, 1883); *King Arthur* (ed. H. O. Sommer, London: Nutt, 1889–1900); *Golden Legend* (ed. F. S. Ellis, London: Kelmscott, 1892); and *Aesop's Fables* (ed. R. T. Lenaghan, Cambridge, Mass.: Harvard University Press, 1967).

Numerous facsimiles of Caxton's works have been issued. Among the recent important ones are: *Ovid's Metamorphoses* (2 vols, New York: Braziller, in association with Magdalene College, Cambridge, 1968); and the second edition of the *Canterbury Tales* (London: Paradine in association with Magdalene College, Cambridge, 1974).

For details of Wynkyn de Worde see N. F. Blake, 'Wynkyn de Worde: The Early Years', *Gutenberg-Jahrbuch* (1971), pp. 62–9, and 'Wynkyn de Worde: The Later Years', *ibid.* (1972), pp. 128–38; J. Moran, *Wynkyn de Worde* (London: Wynkyn de Worde Society, 1960); and H. R. Plomer, *Wynkyn de Worde and his Contemporaries from the Death of Caxton to 1535* (London: Grafton 1925).

INDEX